ROMAN ARCHAEOLOGY
AND ART

Sir Ian Richmond

Roman Archaeology and Art

essays and studies by

SIR IAN RICHMOND

edited by

PETER SALWAY

Fellow of All Souls College, Oxford

FABER AND FABER

London

First published in 1969
by Faber and Faber Limited
24 Russell Square London WC1
Printed in Great Britain by
R. MacLehose and Company Limited
The University Press Glasgow

SBN 571 08841 4

CONTENTS

[7]

Contents

ILLUSTRATIONS

PLATES

FIGURES

[9]

EDITOR'S PREFACE

When Sir Ian Richmond died in October 1965 his papers passed under his will to the Ashmolean Museum, Oxford. There were several uncompleted major works which various of his colleagues have undertaken to finish, but not least in interest were the type-scripts and manuscripts of a number of lectures given over the years at different places and for different purposes. For some of these proposals had been from time to time made for publication, but nothing had come of them. Charles Monteith, of Fabers, had already asked me to look into the possibility of collecting a volume of Richmond's scattered essays when this bulk of unpublished material came to light. It then seemed to us preferable to produce a collection of the more complete of the unpublished lectures and through the good offices of the Librarian of the Ashmolean per-mission to publish was obtained, with the consent of the Executors and of the various institutions to whom the lectures had been given and the presses who had originally hoped to publish some of them.

The problems facing me as editor were threefold. Firstly, the text of the lectures in many cases existed in several differing versions: in fact Richmond had sometimes corrected the latest version and sometimes an earlier one without obvious method, and there was considerable difficulty in establishing his latest thoughts or way of expressing a particular point. The second problem was that almost no footnotes existed, though in some instances Richmond had inserted numbers to indicate where foot-notes were required. Partly because it was often impossible to know what he would have written and partly because some of the references could easily be obtained by consulting standard works published since the writing of the particular paper, these numbers have been abandoned in the present volume. The third problem was that much of the discussion had been overtaken by more recent work. Re-writing of the text would clearly have been unacceptable: moreover it deserves to stand in its own right as an expression in his own words of Richmond's views at specific periods in his career. Instead it was decided to provide a completely new set of footnotes to include the essential references and to attempt to bring the matter in the text up-to-date by means of providing recent information and by commentary. All those footnotes which do not bear the name or initials of one of my many informants were written by me, and the responsibility for them is mine, not Richmond's. The very few footnotes which survive in Richmond's manuscripts are labelled with his initials. In one particular respect the notes have been reduced from the number Richmond intended. It seemed unnecessary, except where I knew of very recent material, to include references for the multitude of Romano-British sites mentioned in the text, since the bibliography down to the end of 1959 is now admirably available in W. Bonser's *A Romano-British Bibliography* (1964).

It is important to remember that the views stated by Richmond are those he held at the time the particular lectures were given, and that for the most part he did not have the chance to revise them. Where contrary opinions are expressed in the notes this is in no way intended as criticism of Richmond but an attempt to carry out that revision, though it cannot be claimed that the results are what he himself would have done. I have been only too well aware how impossible it is to match his erudition and perceptiveness over a remarkably wide range of Roman topics. It is impossible, too, to forget the remarkable personal characteristics of his lecturing style and if the present volume conveys to those who did not have the good fortune to hear him something of the felicity of his spoken word it will have served a good purpose.

Oxford, March 1969.   P.S.

ACKNOWLEDGEMENTS

I am glad to express my gratitude to the owners of the Richmond papers, the Visitors of the Ashmolean Museum, Oxford, for permission to publish, and to their Librarian for much assistance. I am also indebted to various institutions for waiving any claim on the material in this volume: the Clarendon Press, the Cambridge University Press, the Museums Association, the German Archaeological Institute, Madrid, the Royal Institution and the Warburg Institute. The names of the many people who helped in tracking down often obscure references appear in the footnotes and without their assistance the volume would not have appeared. It is also true that without the close proximity of the Codrington Library of All Souls I should have had much more difficulty and taken much longer in hunting down those references which I have supplied myself: the facilities of this splendid library deserve a note of appreciation from a grateful user. The ability to use the library of the Ashmolean and that Museum's photographic service has also proved of the utmost value and deserves to be recorded here.

The illustrations

All the plates except the frontispiece are from photographs by myself: for permission to reproduce the frontispiece I am grateful to Godfrey Argent.

The figures have been re-drawn by me from a variety of originals. For assistance and permission to make use of published and unpublished plans I am glad to acknowledge my debt to the following: Istituto di Topografia Antica, Rome (Professor F.

[13]

Acknowledgements

Castagnoli) and the University of Michigan Press (figure 1); Rheinisches Landesmuseum, Bonn (Professor H. von Petrikovits; Dr. I. Scollar; Dr. C. Rüger) (figures 2, 3); Dr. R. M. Swoboda (figure 4); Publishing House of the Hungarian Academy of Sciences (figure 5); Römisch-germanische Kommission (Professor H. Schönberger) (figures 6, 7); Dura-Europos Publications (Mr. C. Bradford Welles) (figure 8); Holle Verlag G.m.b.H. and Methuen and Co.Ltd. (figure 9); Rheinisches Landesmuseum, Trier (Dr.W. Reusch) (figures 10, 11).

P.S.

NOTE

In preparing the manuscripts for publication considerable difficulty has been experienced with inconsistencies in the spelling of place-names and erratic use of italics. As far as possible British place-names have been corrected in this edition to the most usual form in each case and italics have been used throughout as they are in some of the manuscripts for Latin place-names and for tribes, provinces and deities except where these have been anglicized – e.g. Vulcan – or are in common English use-e.g. Diana, Hercules.

ABBREVIATIONS

Titles of journals and books are normally only slightly abbreviated in the footnotes and will be readily recognizable. They are not listed here.

Books etc.

CIL	*Corpus Inscriptionum Latinarum,* Berlin, 1863–
EE	*Ephemeris Epigraphica,* Berlin, 1872–1913
ILS	H. Dessau, *Inscriptiones Latinae Selectae,* Berlin, 1892–1916
JRS	*Journal of Roman Studies*
NCH	*A History of Northumberland* (Northumberland County History), Newcastle upon Tyne, 1893–1940
RIB	R. G. Collingwood and R. P. Wright, *The Roman Inscriptions of Britain,* Vol. i, Oxford, 1965
SHA	*Scriptores Historiae Augustae*
VCH . . .	*Victoria County History of* . . . (The Victoria History of the Counties of England), London

Contributors etc.

E.B.	Professor Eric Birley
S.S.F.	Professor Sheppard Frere
M.G.J.	Dr. Michael Jarrett
J.C.M.	Dr. John Mann
I.A.R.	Sir Ian Richmond (surviving original footnotes or notes in or attached to text)
J.M.C.T.	Professor Jocelyn Toynbee
G.W.	Dr. Graham Webster

The names of other contributors to the footnotes are given in full in the appropriate footnote.

I

THE FORD LECTURES
(1951)

BRITAIN IN
THE THIRD AND FOURTH
CENTURIES

I

THE MILITARY AREA
FROM SEVERUS TO CARAUSIUS[1]

On the northern frontier of Roman Britain the second century had been a time of restless and expensive vacillation. Within a period of only seventy years Hadrian's vast frontier works between Tyne and Solway had been designed and built, soon to be half abandoned for a new Wall between Forth and Clyde, until in due time both lines were held in strength. In the hinterlands behind both Walls the distribution and posting of garrisons had at least twice been profoundly altered, first after a Brigantian revolt and secondly after a Roman revision of man-power.

So much emerges clearly from the inchoate mass of evidence which archaeology and literature combine to provide for the period. It is also undoubted that the struggle for the principate between Severus and Albinus in the winter of A.D. 196–7 denuded Britain of troops and that the defeat of Albinus overseas in February, 197, was followed by a disastrous invasion and wasting of the North.[2]

The Roman recovery and subsequent campaigns of Severus are the subject of a brilliant treatment by Mr. S. N. Miller.[3] Some amplification and revision of that account has of recent years

[1] The titles of these lectures vary slightly from those announced in the *Oxford University Gazette*, lxxxi, 274, but follow the typescripts.

[2] The re-dating of black-burnished ware by J. P. Gillam and work on samian stamp dies by B. R. Hartley make it almost certain that both Walls were never held together. It now seems almost certain that the second occupation of the Antonine Wall lasted till about 207, and the invasion was then and not in 197 (information from J. C. Mann and B. Dobson).

[3] *Cambridge Anc. Hist.*, xii, 36 ff.

[19]

become possible. The damage is now known to have been less widespread than was thought and not universal within those narrower limits. While the north-eastern legionary fortress at York fell into enemy hands,[1] the north-western sister fortress at Chester escaped the devastation. The third-century repairs to Chester's internal buildings, which belong to the time of Severus Alexander, did not follow upon destruction, and can be viewed as a routine operation. Again, the rebuilding of the north wall of the fortress, hitherto connected with Severus, has been shown to belong to the late third century. Nor was Chester the only base which escaped destruction. The fort at South Shields in County Durham, commanding a valuable harbour for sea-borne supplies, was found by the Severan builders still standing, with internal buildings containing cement floors and wooden partitions yet intact. No doubt the place had owed its safety to its isolated position, in an isolated corner of territory well to one side of Dere Street, the main line of penetration from the north: Corbridge, astride the direct approach, had by contrast shared in the general devastation. But the survival of the Durham coastal base explains why the earliest work of Virius Lupus, the first Severan governor, should have included, in A.D. 197–8, the forts at Bowes and Binchester in the hinterland of Hadrian's Wall, though work on the Wall itself did not commence for another eight years.[2] These and the forts at Ilkley and Brough-under-Stainmore, which he also restored, formed a defensive screen behind which the reconstruction of the legionary fortress at York could go forward.[3]

The restoration of Hadrian's Wall, which came later, in A.D. 205–7, under the governor Lucius Alfenus Senecio, has also begun to take more significant shape. If garrison duty on the Wall may be conceived as originally dividing its functions between patrolling and fighting, then it can be seen that a new kind

[1] There is now no evidence for this (J.C.M.).

[2] It is most improbable that so energetic an emperor as Severus would have left the Wall in ruins for eight years (J.C.M.).

[3] Destruction at York in 197 is no longer certain (J.C.M.).

of emphasis was placed upon these tasks. On the Wall as restored by Severus the patrols ceased to be regularly disposed, as of old, for many turrets were now disused. Again, the milecastles lost their wide gateways and received narrow service entries or exits. They became in fact mere guard-posts, no longer sally-ports for rounding-up movements[1] on a large scale by the fighting garrison. Patrols and local movements thus occupy a far less important place in the tactics of the frontier barrier than before. The new emphasis is upon the forts and operations based upon them only.

The reason for the change lies in the new importance attached to the forward zone to north of the Wall. In the later form of the Hadrianic design outpost-forts to north of the Wall had existed in Cumberland, where the relatively poor outlook from the Wall and a dense population of natives on the fringe of the forward area had made their provision necessary. Under Severus the Cumberland outposts were again occupied, but the system was now extended to the east, where two more were provided, on the site of Antonine forts at Risingham and High Rochester. At Risingham,[2] the magnificent defensive wall of ashlar and an imposing gateway with polygonal bastions attest the importance attached to the new step. But more valuable to the historian is the dedication-tablet of the gate, dated A.D. 205–8.[3] This reveals the work not as a consequence of the Scottish campaign, but as part of a plan initiated at least a year before that series of events had begun.[4]

When once the Scottish campaigns of Severus came, there is no evidence that their objective was the land between Tyne and Forth. The view that this area was by-passed, the Romans using their sea-power to establish advanced general headquarters at Cramond on the Forth, wins new and cogent support from the fact that recent excavations at three positions on the North road across the Cheviot, two of them important, have failed to

[1] It seems unlikely that they ever fulfilled this function (J.C.M.).
[2] For the character of the building see *NCH* xv, 82–84 (I.A.R.).
[3] *RIB* 1234 (where it is dated 205–7).
[4] The Scottish campaigning actually began in A.D. 209 (I.A.R.).

disclose the slightest sign of Severan occupation. But if the rearward operational base was Cramond and the route to the *Caledonii* lay through Fifeshire and so northward, then the *Maeatae* belong not to the Southern Lowlands but to the '*civitates trans Bodotriam sitas*', in a phrase from earlier Roman experience. The Wall 'near which they dwelt', mentioned by Cassius Dio,[1] is the Antonine Wall, not Hadrian's; and this harmonises with the evidence from place-names, which associates the Maeatae with Clackmannanshire and Angus.[2] In short, the double division is that described later in slightly different terms by Ammianus Marcellinus and continuing into the Dark Ages as Northern and Southern Picts. The object of Severus was to prevent a coalition between the two groups. But his first peace terms, following the campaign against the Caledonians, imposed an abandonment of territory. This no doubt affected the *Maeatae* rather than the *Caledonii* and it explains their revolt, chastised in a punitive campaign by Caracalla. Next followed a combined rising and at this moment Severus died, on 4 February, A.D. 211, while preparing what he intended to be a final punishment.

Caracalla had now to reach a settlement. The coinage, which reflects Imperial policy, attests an ultimate campaign in A.D. 211,[3] crowned by Victory and Peace. The surviving literary tradition, hostile to Caracalla, represents this return to permanent disposition as a rapid and undignified withdrawal. The northern posts, Cramond and the like, were indeed evacuated and the garrisoned frontier was withdrawn to south of the Cheviot. But this means no more than that the frontier based upon Hadrian's

---

[1] Dio, xxvii, 12. S. S. Frere, *Britannia*, 1967, 164, argues that the wall must be Hadrian's Wall. It does indeed seem possible that to Dio 'the Wall' could have been Hadrian's Wall, which would bring the *Maeatae* south to include at least the *Selgovae* and perhaps the *Votadini* as well (there is no reason to think the latter were *always* faithful to Rome). On the other hand recent re-dating of pottery in the North has suggested that the second occupation of the Antonine Wall continued into the third century, so that Dio, writing of events in 208, could have had the very recent situation in mind and have been referring to the Antonine Wall.

[2] Dumyat and Myot Hill are both in Stirlingshire (J.C.M.).

[3] This seems wrong (J.C.M.).

Wall, as planned by Severus before the campaign, came to take the strain for which it was designed. The situation had, in fact, been met. As summarized in a first report by Senecio the danger had consisted of frontier disorders so severe as to demand either a larger permanent garrison or an Imperial expedition. In terms of previous Roman policy, the only precedent available, there is no doubt that this meant either a garrison to re-occupy southern Scotland or a punitive expedition so formidable as to render such a step unnecessary.[1] Severus had chosen the second line of action. And while the meagre and hostile literary tradition represents his entire expedition as a costly and ignominious failure, an examination of the disposition of Caracalla's settled frontier tends to show that, whatever the cost of the campaign in man-power, its result was to create a new and fruitful political order north of the Wall.

The most striking manifestations of the new arrangement were the long-range frontier patrols. The forts at Risingham and High Rochester, into each of which a milliary part-mounted cohort[2] was tightly packed, became the administrative headquarters for irregular detachments of *exploratores*, who, as on the German frontier, took their name[3] from the fort upon which they were based. To *Bremenium* (High Rochester) were attached the *exploratores Bremenienses*; on *Habitancum* (Risingham) were based both *exploratores* and *Raeti gaesati*.[4] Netherby, in the west, whose main garrison[5] was the milliary part-mounted *cohors I Aelia Hispanorum*, must have been associated with at least one similar detachment, since the *Antonine Itinerary* names it as *Castra Exploratorum*. Nothing is known of the garrisons in this period at

---

[1] One may compare Agricola's policy of defeating the *Caledonii* in a pitched battle before establishing a frontier on their southern borders (I.A.R.).

[2] At Risingham *cohors I Vangionum milliaria equitata*, CIL vii, 1003 (*RIB* 1234), 1010 (1243), 987 (1216), 988 (1217), 986 (1215), 1002 (1235), 1009 (1231), (I.A.R.).

At High Rochester *cohors I fida Vardullorum C. R. milliaria equitata*, CIL vii, 1043 (1279), 1045 (1280), 1039 (1272), 1046 (1281), 1051 (1285), 1030 (1262), (I.A.R.).

[3] *Exploratores Bremenienses*, CIL vii, 1030 (1262), 1037 (1270), (I.A.R.).

[4] *vexillatio exploratorum* and *Raeti gaesati*, CIL vii, 1010 (1243) (*expl.*), 990 (1219) (*R.g.*), 988 (1217) (*R.g.*), 1002 (1235) (both), NCH xv, 143, no. 53 (1244) (*expl.*), (I.A.R.).

[5] *RIB* 968.

Bewcastle or Birrens, though the continued occupation of at least the former is beyond doubt; indeed, Bewcastle was completely re-planned as a polygonal fortress of the newest model. But the three known patrol-bases cover the principal northern approaches to the Wall. *Bremenium* watches Dere Street, *Habitancum* controls North Tynedale and central Northumberland; Netherby surveys Eskdale and Liddesdale, Bewcastle the central waste. All three forts could supervise with their main units the areas mentioned, which lie within range of a comfortable day's patrolling. The *exploratores* went further: and their duties are described in the fourth century, when they had been superseded by secret agents or *arcani: 'ut ultro citroque per longa spatia discurrentes, vicinarum gentium strepitus nostris ducibus intimarent'.*[1] The wording, it will be observed, fits patrol movements, not military intelligence.[2]

This arrangement, however, implies a very large forward zone in which the *exploratores* were free to move, as in a Roman sphere of influence. Much more is involved than the creation of a neutral strip, for such strips were not normally very wide. On the Danube frontier under Marcus five-mile zones were prescribed for the *Buri* and *Marcomanni*, a ten-mile zone for the *Iazyges*. The British arrangement corresponds to a stricter control of actual tribal territory, such as the regulation of public assemblies among the *Marcomanni*, *Quadi* and *Iazyges* to one a month, at one fixed point and under Roman military supervision. Indeed, a geographical record for Britain wherein just such regulations are implicit has come down through the *Ravenna Cosmography*, which contains a list of *loca*,[3] or places of assembly, confined to Britain north of the Wall and embracing a territory extending from the Solway to the Tay. The supervised area in fact corresponds as closely as may be to the older occupied territory of Antonine times.

The gains which can be attributed to the Imperial expedition of Severus and Caracalla were thus permanent and valuable. Quite

[1] Ammianus Marcellinus, xxviii, 3, 8.   [2] This is obscure.
[3] *Archaeologia*, xciii, 15 f.

[24]

clearly terms were imposed, and those severe ones, upon the northern tribes from the Cheviot to the Tay. But there was a further achievement of the highest importance. The tribes beyond the Tay were so cowed that they respected the Roman arrangements and acquiesced in a settlement which converted the old area of occupation into a protectorate. Equally significant was the reverse side of this picture. The war gained for Rome some valuable man-power, draining the barbarians of exuberant strength and furnishing the raw material of Imperial defence. The Walldürn inscription of A.D. 232,[1] from the Outer German *limes*, is obscure in details; but no one disputes that it mentions *Brittones dediticii Alexandriani*, and as an American scholar has observed,[2] these levies, whose title proclaims them to have been exacted from an enemy on surrender, must represent fruits of the Severan victory. As he further reminds us, those victories had involved a Caledonian *deditio* or unconditional surrender, as literature records,[3] and it well may be that the attached condition 'to abandon no small amount of territory' refers to a frontier arrangement foreshadowing that of Caracalla. The form of the subsequent relationships is shadowy. In what capacity, apart from friendship, the Caledonian chieftain Argentocoxus and his wife came to the Imperial Court of Severus and Iulia Domna in Britain is uncertain;[4] but under Alexander Severus yet another Caledonian notable, Lossio Veda, was dedicating at Colchester, the port for the Rhineland, a bronze tablet[5] to a native war-god and to the Victory of the Emperor. The gods chosen for this double dedication very strongly suggests a connexion with Caledonian levies, and its date, between A.D. 222 and 236, raises the question whether new drafts were forthcoming or whether old drafts were being kept up to strength.

Among the natives within the protectorate the effects of the new arrangements are less easy to gauge. Inside the strongly garrisoned

---

[1] *CIL* xiii, 6592: H. T. Rowell, *Yale Class. Stud.*, vi, 88 ff.

[2] See n. 1 (Rowell, esp. p. 96 ff.).   [3] Dio, lxxvi, 13, 4.

[4] Dio, lxxvi, 16, 5: where it is stated to have occurred 'after the treaty' – were they perhaps noble hostages?   [5] *RIB* 191.

zone south of the Cheviot exploitation of natural resources followed as a matter of course. The new weapon-workshops established at Corbridge used for their raw material blooms of iron brought in from native hearths and re-smelted: and the iron-field in question was the Redesdale deposit, which was already being worked by natives in the second century, if not before. An improvement in native dwellings due to better tools begins now to show, as at Edgerston (Roxburghshire). But the outstanding feature, common to all the native settlements, large and small, which are datable to this period is the lack of formidable defences. This is so strikingly different from conditions in the pre-Roman era on the one hand, or in the Dark Ages on the other, that its import is unmistakable. It becomes a reasonable inference that in the protectorate fortification on the grand scale was forbidden. Nothing is more impressive than the carefree manner in which, at many native sites, the huts of the *pax Romana* obliterate and straddle the demolished defences of earlier days. Frequently these open villages lack even an enclosure wall. Where such walls exist, as on Traprain Law, they are low and unimposing structures, suitable for repelling wild beasts or petty thieves bent upon pilfering but useless for stemming a sustained attack or harbouring rebellious elements.

There is good reason for thinking that a very similar policy was at this time applied to Wales, though it is in North Wales that the effects are clearest. As was long ago observed by Haverfield and confirmed by Professor Mortimer Wheeler, the Roman forts in Wales had in general certainly been evacuated by A.D. 140, most of them in direct connexion with the first Antonine occupation of Scotland.[1] During the rest of the second century, the land either lay empty of Roman troops or was held by a skeleton garrison, and the sole observable revival of military activity occurs at Forden Gaer about A.D. 160. The third century saw a change. Under Severus came a full re-occupation of the fort at Caernarvon

[1] The re-examination of the finds from Welsh forts (G. Simpson, *Britons and the Roman Army*, 1964, *passim*) makes this hypothesis now doubtful. Further excavation is very necessary to check all the theories in this paragraph.

and, it is thought, a rebuilding of the fort at Caersws. But the peculiarity of this third-century activity, which affects Forden Gaer also, lies in its sporadic distribution. In North Wales, it is true, the work included repairs to at least the western sector of the trunk coast road. Yet key-positions like the forts at Caerhun[1] and Tomen-y-Mur remained empty: and, if it has been stressed that the very isolation of Caernarvon forbids its re-occupation to be viewed as part of general measures against sea-raiders, it may be observed with equal cogency that the rehabilitation of a single fort can hardly connote general unrest in North Wales as a whole. Even in Caernarvonshire and Anglesey, over which *Segontium* presides, there is no indication of a restlessness calling for military measures, such as coin-hoards or destruction in the native settlements might signalize. It may therefore be observed that the reason for the renewed activity may well have been economic rather than political; and in this respect the treatment of the Peak District offers a useful pointer. In the heart of that region the fort of *Navio*, at Brough-on-Noe, which had been rebuilt in stone in A.D. 158, was substantially consolidated under Severus, while its neighbour forts remained empty. The quantity of lead ore found on the site indicates that it was a control-centre for the Derbyshire mining area: and the association of the re-occupation of the fort with the Brigantian revolt soon after the middle of the second century indicates the jealous watch kept by Rome upon the lucrative lead-deposits of the area. The parallel may now be further developed. Anglesey and Caernarvonshire are not rich in lead, but they contain valuable copper mines at Aberffraw, Parys Mountain and Bryn-du in the island and at Great Orme's Head on the mainland. Anglesey alone has yielded, largely by chance discovery, no less than 15 copper cakes or ingots, and such stamps[2] as exist suggest that the working was farmed out to private lessees in both areas. Further, the distribution of the cakes, of which over twenty five per cent have an attested

---

[1] Dr Simpson (*op. cit.*, 163) thinks Caerhun was probably repaired under Severus.
[2] *CIL* vii, 1200 etc.

[27]

association with villages, suggests that natives were taking an active part in the initial smelting, as in the iron-field of Redesdale in Northumberland. But in dealing with private lessees, big or small, the State insisted upon the maintenance and steady working of concessions and was directly concerned in assuring the necessary peace and quiet for the purpose. It may therefore be suggested that, as in Derbyshire, the Severan military occupation was directly related in north-west Wales to State mining concessions. And it may be added that this explanation may well turn out true also of the activity at Caersws and Forden Gaer, which lie in much the same relation to the lead deposits of Plynlimmon and Stiperstones as Caernarvon does to Anglesey. Disturbances in the mining districts during the fifties, while Brigantian revolt was in progress, would very suitably explain the re-occupation of Forden Gaer at a time when most other districts in Wales were devoid of garrisons.

On the mainland at large, and in certain Anglesey centres, there was already beginning a fresh concentration of native population in many of the old hill-fort sites. Din Silwy and Caer-y-Twr in Anglesey, Tre'r Ceiri, and Penmaenmawr in Caernarvonshire are well-known examples of this interesting social phenomenon. At Caer-y-Twr and Tre'r Ceiri the defensive walls still exist, parapet and all, with rampart-walk three to four feet high, on which stands a three-foot breast-work.

Such defences, as has been remarked of those in Scotland, are good enough against wild beasts and chance raiders: to the Roman they would be mere *aestivalia*, valueless against sustained attack. These neo-British *oppida* do not compare, any more than in Scotland, with the massive structures which preceded them. Further, they go side by side with extensive open settlements, as at Ty-mawr and Porth Dafarch, which are both near Caer-y-Twr, or as at Llangoed and Penmon, which are adjacent to Din Silwy. In addition there appear in Anglesey also the small enclosed forest-dwellings, as at Caer Leb, Rhuddgaer, Hen Drefor and Bryn-Eryr. These indicate a first attempt to open up and exploit the forest-land, an operation made possible by iron tools, and

[28]

promoted by an expanding population, not to mention the demand for charcoal as fuel for smelting. The picture is thus of new demands upon the industry or productive capacity of a populace living in largely native fashion and expanding under the Roman peace.

On the military side this implies an increased amount of economic control in the fort districts. A remarkable indication of the elaboration involved is afforded by the extensive deposit of lead sealings from the fort at Brough-under-Stainmore (*Verterae*), which served as a collecting station for the economic produce of Cumbria.[1] Not less than seven separate auxiliary units, mostly known from other evidence to have formed part of the third-century garrison of the area, were sending to *Verterae* a variety of sealed consignments. Some of the sealings are simple. Others are highly complicated and bear departmental marks, closer to the elaborate system of marking by issues and workshops used in the Imperial mints than to any other known series. A third class, associated with the Second Cohort of Nervians at Whitley Castle, bears the legend *Metal*, for *Metal(lum)* or *Metal(la)*. Yet another series, upon which private seals accompany the name of the cohort, is most readily explained as securing official packets from commandants or other responsible officers. The whole group attests a development in district administration which is of real value as demonstrating the detailed application of military control. Only two of the raw products exploited are known, namely, the Alston lead and silver, but the intensity of exploitation is in itself amply illustrated.

The Severan Age thus emerges as the time in which on the British frontiers the fruits of a century's experience were being garnered. The occupied area was reduced, an extra-Mural protectorate in the North was in process of development, the mineral resources of the island in particular were being attacked with a

[1] Richmond, *Trans. Cumb. & Westm. A. & A. Soc.*, 2nd ser., xxxvi, 104 ff.: in this article Richmond suggests that an agent of the provincial procurator was stationed at Brough, for whom the military units collected and sent the consignments.

new thoroughness. No doubt this combined policy of retrench-
ment and development was intended to offset the rising cost of
government, but it probably also reflects a deliberate intention
to convert the debit balance of the second century, upon which
Mommsen rightly laid stress,[1] into a credit balance; in other
words, the intention was to turn Britain into a province which at
least paid its own way, if not helping to pay the way of others.
The panegyrists who recount its potentialities at the close of the
third century do so in terms so glowing as to suggest that the
result was by then achieved.[2]

It is natural that an arrangement so carefully fostered and so
elaborately planned should be regarded as a permanent institution.
Its whole value depended upon a continuing stability, since only
so could the extra-Mural protectorate develop. Thus, the successors of Severus are seen to be reinforcing the new system
rather than revising it and this consolidation takes two forms.
Defences are improved and amenities are introduced. At High
Rochester the years A.D. 219–220 saw the introduction of torsion-
propelled artillery on a large scale for a systematic covering of the
approaches to the fort.[3] Massive and resilient platforms were
fitted in between the towers along the north and west ramparts
and the machines which they held were handling stone balls
weighing from 100 to 175 pounds, as surviving missiles show.
The value of such curtain-fire in breaking up massed attacks
must have been great, both in actual damage and in its effect
upon morale. Similar missiles from Risingham attest the same
kind of provision there. It is thus clear that the outpost forts were
equipped to deal with sudden risings or raids like that of the
Corionototae,[4] though these must be conceived as rare incidents
rather than part of the regular pattern of frontier control. Everyday routine in the forward zone is better typified by the *beneficiarius consularis* at Risingham, who, on completion of his first

[1] Appian, *Bell. Civ.*, introd. 5 (I.A.R.).
[2] *Paneg. Constantino Aug.*, 9 (R. A. B. Mynors, *XII Panegyrici Latini*, vi (vii), 9)?
Paneg. Constant. Caes., 21, 2 (Mynors, viii (v), 21, 2).
[3] *NCH* xv, 97 ff.   [4] *RIB* 1142.

turn of duty, dedicated an altar for himself and his staff.[1] His business there is not stated, but such soldiers detached for special duty were normally military police concerned either with taxation, road control or mine administration. All three possibilities may have been actualities at Risingham, where frontier dues and traffic were in question, as well as the adjacent iron ore.

The work of consolidation, designed to give stability to the new deal and contentment to the troops who operated it, is represented far and wide over the northern districts. At Chester-le-Street in A.D. 216 there was a wholesale reorganization, involving not merely the water-supply but the *territorium* of the fort;[2] Chesters on the Wall has produced two important and elaborate building inscriptions of A.D. 221 and a little later, which do not, however, categorize the work done, though it was accompanied by an outburst of loyal sentiments from the *ala* in garrison;[3] Netherby was furnished with a cavalry drill-hall or riding-school (*basilica equestris exercitatoria*) in A.D. 222;[4] in A.D. 223 South Shields received an aqueduct;[5] at Chesterholm a monumental gateway was built in A.D. 224;[6] at Greatchesters a granary in A.D. 225.[7] At some of the forts in the hinterland the work is even later. Lanchester, in County Durham, was wholly reconstructed under Gordian III, and two notable inscriptions record the restoration of its headquarters and armouries and the building of a bath and drill-hall.[8] At Lancaster, in the other Palatinate, a bath and drill-hall were rebuilt under Postumus, the Gallic seceder-Emperor.[9] Side by side with material consolidation there came also a consolidation of man-power. During the second century the epigraphy of Roman Britain is curiously silent about the presence of the irregular formations known as *numeri*. From Hadrian's time onwards these had been an increasingly common feature of the Roman army: their use upon the German frontier is

[1] *RIB* 1225.   [2] *RIB* 1049.   [3] *RIB* 1465, 1467.   [4] *RIB* 978.
[5] *RIB* 1060, where this stone is dated to A.D. 222.
[6] *RIB* 1706, where this stone is dated to A.D. 223.
[7] *RIB* 1738.   [8] *RIB* 1092, 1091.   [9] *RIB* 605.

amply attested in the second century, and it is clear that they undertook a major part in frontier-patrol duties, such as in Britain fell to the occupants of the milecastles upon Hadrian's Wall or of the numerous convoy-posts in the hinterland of the Antonine Wall. But sources for Britain do not mention the subject and only in the third century is the *numerus* actually vouched as an outstanding factor in the composition of the Roman army of Britain.

The *numeri* in Britain are not all of one kind: they are normally infantry but can also be *numeri equitum*. On the other hand, cavalry formations are frequently distinguished by the special title of *cuneus* or *vexillatio*, both words gaining now a specialized use, different from their former military sense. The best attested of these formations are the *cunei Frisiorum* or *Frisionum*, of which three are known, each distinguished by the name of their head-quarters base. The *Vinovienses*[1] belong to *Vinovium*, now Binchester in County Durham; the *cuneus* at Housesteads carries the name of that fort in abbreviated form;[2] the *Aballavenses*[3] lie at Papcastle in Cumberland, but derive their name from the Wall-fort of Burgh-by-Sands, upon which a second irregular unit, the *numerus Maurorum Aballavensium*,[4] was also based. It seems certain that in each case these units supplemented a regular garrison. The *ala Vettonum* is well known at Binchester,[5] the second[6] cohort of Tungrians still better at Housesteads, and the *cohors I Nervana Germanorum* for Burgh-by-Sands.[7] At Housesteads there was in addition a second irregular unit named after the chief or princeling who commanded it, the *numerus Hnaudifridi*[8] or 'Notfried's unit'. It may be that the latter irregulars were posted to milecastle-duty. But it may also be recalled that the entire operational range of patrols based upon the Wall was now,

---

[1] *RIB* 1036.   [2] *RIB* 1594.   [3] *RIB* 883, cf. 882.

[4] *RIB* 2042: in fact the title of this unit as given on this stone was *numerus Maurorum Aurelianorum*.

[5] *RIB* 1028, 1032, 1035.

[6] This should read 'first' (J.C.M.): *RIB* 1578, 1579, 1580, 1584, 1585, 1586, 1591, 1598, 1618, 1619.

[7] *RIB* 2041.   [8] *RIB* 1576.

as already observed, vastly increased and that patrolling and interception north of the line of the Wall may have formed an additional task, certainly more suited to the cavalry of the *cuneus*. In the outpost forts beyond the line of the Wall a very similar state of affairs existed, as has already been observed. At *Bremenium* the milliary part-mounted cohort in regular garrison was supplemented by the *numerus exploratorum Bremeniensium*.[1] At *Habitancum* there were in addition to the main garrison both *exploratores*[2] and *Raeti gaesati*,[3] Tyrolese irregulars from within the Empire. And at both these advance posts there occurs in acute form a problem which is present, though less immediately obvious, at Housesteads, namely, the problem of accommodation. The headquarters forts are barely big enough for the main unit and there is no room whatever inside their walls for the irregulars. The irregulars must, then, have been housed elsewhere, either in outstations or in special forts close at hand. On the Wall the difficulty can be in part met by assuming that the irregulars were quartered in the milecastles, but this can hardly be the whole answer in the third century and perhaps the large barrack-like buildings, visible but unexplored, immediately west of Housesteads in reality provide the solution there. Certain it is that the forts of regular units were the official headquarters of the irregulars. Epigraphy attests not merely their share in official cults but the establishment outside the forts of their unofficial extramural worship. The *Antonine Itinerary*, in according the name *Castra Exploratorum* to Netherby, gives the sanction of literature to the same relationship; for the essential meaning of the term *castra* is the home fortress or headquarters-base of the unit to which it applies.

Much the same kind of arrangement seems to obtain in the hinterland. Reference has already been made to the *cuneus Frisiorum* at Binchester, in County Durham. The neighbouring fort of Lanchester served as the base not only for the part-mounted

---

[1] *RIB* 1262.
[2] *RIB* 1235, 1243, 1244.
[3] *RIB* 1216, 1217, 1235.

First Cohort of *Lingones*[1] but for a *vexillatio Sueborum Longovicanorum*.[2] Here again, as at Housesteads, the *vicus*[3] of the main fort was the scene of an exotic German cult which these irregulars brought with them. Evidence concerning other units is not quite so complete. But at Lancaster there is an interesting body of irregulars specially selected for a task peculiar to the district. The *Barcarii Tigrisienses*,[4] who were there brigaded with the *ala Sebosiana*,[5] doubtless represent some of the fruits in man-power of the Eastern campaigns of Severus. But it was a happy stroke to post them where their skill in negotiating shoals and blind channels would be of particular service, amid the shifting sands of Morecambe Bay. At Old Penrith (*Voreda*) a *vexillatio Germanorum*[6] provided some particularly uncouth personal names and German deities. The *numerus equitum Stratonicianorum*[7] represents an exploitation of the restless highlanders of Caria, equivalent to that which produced in the West units of *Raeti gaesati*. It was based upon Brougham (*Brocavum*), near Penrith, but the regiment to which it was subordinated remains as yet unrevealed. Similarly, the *numerus Concangiensium*, based upon the fort at Chester-le-Street (*Concangium*) and attested by a Binchester tile-stamp,[8] remains without a named senior companion unit, though the *equites* mentioned in the inscription of A.D. 216 seem to attest that it was an *ala*.[9]

There is, it seems clear, enough evidence to make the principle of this increase of forces plain. Forts which had previously held single units now became the headquarters of *numeri* as well. The immediate purpose of installing these irregulars is sometimes

---

[1] *RIB* 1075, 1092.   [2] *RIB* 1704.

[3] But see P. Salway, *The Frontier People of Roman Britain*, 1965, 150 f., for some reservations on the existence of a *vicus*.

[4] *RIB* 601.

[5] *RIB* 605 (*ala Sebussiana* on the stone).

[6] *RIB* 919: *vexil]latio M[a]r[sacorum* . . . (a tribe from the mouth of the Rhine); *RIB* 920: *vex(illatio) Germa[no]r(um)V[o]r[e]d(ensium)*; cf. *e.g. RIB* 926.

[7] *RIB* 780.

[8] *CIL* vii, 1234: *cf. Archaeologia*, xciii, 29; *RIB* p. 347, correcting misprint in *Archaeologia*; (not necessarily earlier than the fourth century – J.C.M.).

[9] *RIB* 1049.

[34]

clear and sometimes dark.[1] North of the Wall it is evident that they formed *explorationes* or groups of frontier scouts, whose purpose has already been discussed. South of the Wall patrol-work can hardly have been their principal duty, but escorts for convoys and guards for signalling-posts or police-duties were urgently needed. The doubled garrison meets the increased routine duties rather than new pressure on the frontier, where relations were tending to improve. A wider motive can, however, be deduced from the composition of these units. It will be observed that they are mostly drawn from outside the Empire and some-times from depressed areas within it, and that for the most part no homeward return will have been looked for by their men. The general intention of those who posted them is to plant them, like the Burgundians and Vandals settled in the island in 277,[2] and thereby to create a static frontier *militia* which, according to contemporary Imperial theory, would fight the better for owning the land which it was to defend.[3] A developed instance of even-tualities in such cases is afforded by the *numerus equitum Sarma-tarum*[4] at Ribchester (*Bremetennacum*). All are agreed that this unit began its existence as part of the Sarmatian cavalry transplanted by Marcus Aurelius to Britain in A.D. 175. Their connexion with Ribchester is dated to the third century, and at the same time the fort, the unit and the district are placed under a legionary centurion who bore the title *praepositus numeri et regionis*. The organization of *Bremetennacum* as a special *regio* won for it in provincial geography the name *Bremetennacum Veteranorum*, a title which discloses the political status of the *regio* as a veterans' allotted district with special privileges. An echo of the conferment

---

[1] J.C.M. suggests that the *numeri* etc. were brought in to replace large drafts removed to fight on the Continent.

[2] Zosimus, i, 68.

[3] But see Salway, *Frontier People of Roman Britain*, 33 f., for a contrary view. In particular a third century source in the *Digest* (xlix, 16, 13) states that serving soldiers were not permitted to own land in the province in which they were on active service, lest in farming they should lose their military preparedness.

[4] *RIB* 583: it may have later become a regular *ala* (*RIB* 594, of unknown provenance).

or amplification of those privileges is depicted upon an altar of A.D. 238–44, where a gift is passing between a senior and a junior territorial personification, as if the province of *Britannia Inferior* were conferring upon the *regio* a privilege.

An important change was thus coming over the garrisons of both the frontier and its hinterland. The cohorts or *alae* which had formerly proved sufficient for their district as single units are now supplemented by *numeri*. Those who so increased the strength were planting for the future, by converting the frontier stations into the nurseries of a hereditary militia. This was in turn related to land tenure; for tenure of government-leased land was conditional upon the existence of serving sons. It was, then, the long service-men and their families who got the benefits, and it is no doubt the growth of the system that accounts for the very large village-settlements which now tended to grow up round the forts, both on Hadrian's Wall and in the hinterland. If the size of these *vici* is a criterion of success, a successful policy, this half-political, half-military experiment was crowned by success indeed.[1]

In the legionary fortresses there is also a story of change, but of a different kind. The evidence is clearest at Caerleon, the base-fortress of the Second Legion, where some twenty-three out of the total of sixty barrack-blocks have been excavated, completely or in part. Ten out of the twelve barracks which filled the north-west half of the *retentura* are known to have been intensively occupied throughout the second century and the latest coins from their floors show that this occupation certainly continued into the early years of the third century. Thereafter relics become scanty and even the sparse use of the buildings seems hardly to have continued beyond the middle of the century, to judge from the meagre finds in Barrack 3 and Barrack 10. It seems clear that this group of barracks as a whole was evacuated not very long

---

[1] It is possible to explain these settlements by the presence of the families of serving soldiers (now allowed to marry) and traders alone. There is no need to involve a farming militia. There are very few veterans recorded in the frontier region: presumably most preferred to move to a more comfortable area (or simply did not live long enough to secure honourable discharge).

after A.D. 200 and that in this part of the fortress a body of troops representing some two cohorts was despatched for duties away from base. On the *intervallum*, however, a substantial store for small arms, including legionary javelins, bows and arrows and calthrops, was built about A.D. 200 and remained in service throughout the century. In the south-east half of the *praetentura* conditions were altogether different. Here there is the clearest evidence from nine barracks for a thorough-going restoration in the years preceding A.D. 222. This activity must have followed close upon restorations in the area of the headquarters building dated to the period A.D. 197–211, and the occupation thus begun lasted till late in the century. These, then, were not the barracks of the Seventh Cohort, presumably six in number, which were rebuilt from ground-level in A.D. 254–9, under Valerian and Gallienus,[1] and which must thus be sought in a different part of the fortress from any of the barracks so far mentioned. Continuous third-century activity is also proved for the central area, on either side of the headquarters building, in official buildings, tribunes' houses and four barracks. The story is thus one of reduced numbers, reflected in the deserted barrack-blocks of the *retentura* and the inscription of Gallienus: while in the *praetentura* and in the central area the evidence, so far as it goes, is for continuous occupation, even if some room has to be allowed for the restoration of the later fifties. Outside the fortress, the *ludus* or training-ground, also used as an amphitheatre, was brought back into commission, after a long period of decay, in the years A.D. 212–22, and was thenceforward kept in order throughout the century.

At Chester, the base of the Twentieth Legion, the case is less clear. In the east half of the *retentura* there is good evidence for an intensive second-century occupation, but hardly a hint of later use. In the *praetentura* abundant third-century finds suggest that this part of the fortress was the scene of busy and continuous activity though little information is forthcoming from the barrack area. Recent excavations, on the other hand, have afforded

[1] *RIB* 334.

evidence of a drastic reconstruction of the central area, including the headquarters and a barrack to west of it, soon after A.D. 222.

York, the home of the Sixth Legion, has yielded even less information than Chester. The fortress-wall was restored under Severus to include the full area and even the reduced fourth-century fortress still covered fifty acres. But while there seems clear evidence in the fourth century for a garrison either greatly reduced or living outside its fortress, the third-century position is uncertain and evidence non-existent. Only in the *retentura*, once more, is there a suggestion of a barrack unoccupied during the third century and finally demolished in the fourth.

The impression at Caerleon and Chester is thus one of fortresses only partly manned, as if the legions of *Britannia Superior* were either notably below strength or widely dispersed. There is no reason to think that numbers were much reduced. Not only could these legions furnish drafts to reinforce the Pannonian armies in the early or middle sixties, but they could spare detachments for duty in Lower Britain.

The military arsenal or weapon-factory at Corbridge was staffed by a vexillation of the Second Legion and it has been suspected that this special connexion with iron-working was somehow connected with the proximity of the Second Legion's base to the larger and famous deposits of the Forest of Dean. At all events the detachment stationed at Corbridge during the third century has left notable monuments of its sojourn in the form of inscribed and sculptured stones from both official extra-mural shrines. There is good reason also for thinking that, at some time during the third century, vexillations of both the Twentieth and Sixth were on duty at Corbridge, either supplementing or substituting the detachment from the Second. It is thus possible to outline at least one striking illustration of the manner in which the strength of the legions was dissipated in special tasks or special appointments.

But among the troops who remained at the base fortresses there is no sign that the enactment of Severus, which legalized their marriages and perhaps allowed them an extramural domicile, meant that they lived out of barracks when on duty. On the contrary, such evidence as exists for *Britannia Superior* suggests that, while the number of barracks in use had dropped, those which continued in service were regularly occupied. The reduction in accommodation is, in short, due to the posting of men to outstations rather than to the fact that they now lived in their own private homes. It is impossible as yet to say how the policy applied to the Sixth Legion in *Britannia Inferior*, but if detachments from the Second and Twentieth had to be borrowed from the Upper Province, the inference will be that its resources were already heavily stretched. It should be noted, too, that both Upper and Lower Provinces also had their sprinkling of *stationes* or military-police posts under the care of senior legionaries, allocated by the consular governor of Upper Britain. Three are known in the Lower province,[1] two in the Upper,[2] and the collection of the *annona* may have demanded many more.

To the steady consolidation of the Severan plan for Britain which is represented by the military history of the province in the third century the usurpation of Carausius comes as an epilogue. It was not the first British episode of the kind in the century: a governor had rebelled in A.D. 276, following the fashion of the times. But the revolt of Carausius, after suspected collusion with Rome's enemies, arose out of the measures taken to meet a new danger, the pirate raids from overseas by Frankish and Saxon bands. The facts about the previous career of Carausius, as admiral in charge of Channel defence, make it clear that the method adopted had been to meet the pirates at sea with a strong Channel fleet, and such complementary measures as may have been taken ashore to meet the danger find as yet small reflection in archaeology At Richborough the central area of the site, which contained a

---

[1] *Beneficiarii* are known from Greta Bridge (*RIB* 745), Chesterholm (1696), Risingham (1225), Lancaster (602), Binchester (1030, 1031), Lanchester (1085) and Housesteads (1599). A further example, from Catterick (725) is definitely too early, being dated to A.D. 191.

[2] A *beneficiarius* is known from Dorchester, Oxon. (*RIB* 235). One further example, from Wroxeter (293), is probably not third-century, while another, from Winchester (88) was dated by Hübner to the late first or early second.

large and lofty triumphal monument, perhaps a tetrapylon, was enclosed by triple ditches not long after A.D. 250,[1] as if the monument itself were now being used as a fortified look-out post or signal-station. This implies a tactical scheme of intercepting action by the fleet, following observation of the enemy from appropriately high points ashore: and similar tactics are ascribed to Allectus in 296 with 'a fleet based upon the Isle of Wight in watch-towers and ambushes'.[2] There is, however, good reason for thinking that Carausius had already reinforced the coast-line, partly against raiders but no less against an attempt to recapture the island, by the first of the Saxon Shore forts.[3] It seems certain that Richborough belongs to this period; Pevensey has yielded Carausian coins in its earliest occupation layer; Lympne has produced a coin-series very strongly Carausian in flavour; Bradwell also exhibits a markedly high proportion of Carausian coinage, while Brancaster tells the same story. Excavation has not in fact supported the suggestion that these forts of widely divergent design belong to different dates: the variation seems rather to reflect the employment of two schools of architects, some familiar with the progressive Continental designs, others devoted to the static tradition of the British backwater. Fourth-century military architecture in Britain was to continue to manifest precisely the same illogical combination of archaism and novelty.

Another feature of the usurpation reflects strongly the tendency of the age. The panegyrists who celebrate the recovery of the

---

[1] These ditches appear unfinished, possibly due to Carausian fort-construction: date should perhaps be 260-70 (B. W. Cunliffe). For Richborough see now *Fifth Report on the Excavations of the Roman Fort at Richborough, Kent* (*Soc. Ant. Res. Rep.* xxiii), ed. B. W. Cunliffe, 1968.

[2] *Paneg. Constant. Caes.*, 15 (Mynors, viii (v), 15).

[3] B. W. Cunliffe writes 'The only forts which I think are reasonably Carausian are Portchester, Lympne, Richborough and ?? Dover; i.e. he was fortifying channel coast as opposed to North Sea Coast. Brancaster and Reculver must surely be mid-third century, whilst Pevensey coins demand a *circa* 340 date of origin. Bradwell is very odd. The fort looks earlier but the coins suggest a similar date to Pevensey. I would not like to be dogmatic on this one.' Cf. Cunliffe (ed.), *op. cit.*, 255 ff.

province for Rome lay much stress upon the Frankish mercenaries[1] employed by Carausius and Allectus. Such troops may have been new to Britain, but they were not new in the Empire at large. If Carausius and Allectus had formed out of them an Imperial guard, they were only doing what had been common practice since the time of Caracalla and had been extended to other divisions of the army by his successors, notably Gallienus. Doubtless the need to support these extra concomitants of resident Imperial Power was reckoned a serious burden by the British provincials unused to such extras, and this may be one reason for the stress laid upon it. But it is to be emphasized also that Britain was a province which had on the whole escaped such burdens during the third century because it had been outside the main stream of Imperial events. A nursery of soldiers rather than a battlefield, a province whose army was engaged in economic exploitation rather than military exploits, this island province had escaped the notice of the political historian. The *rationes imperii*, which might have supplied an illuminating economic picture, had for long been unpublished secrets.

[1] *e.g. Paneg. Constant. Caes.*, 17.

2

BRITANNIA SUPERIOR

According to Cassius Dio, *Britannia Superior*, the more important of the two provinces into which Severus divided Britain, contained the legionary fortresses of Caerleon and Chester, while *Britannia Inferior* contained that of York.[1] In addition, it is known that the *colonia* of Lincoln lay in *Britannia Inferior*, indicating that the division was not altogether dictated by military considerations but actuated also by a desire to accord to the Lower Province a substantial slice of civilian territory. London, however, by now manifestly the principal administrative centre of the province, must have remained the headquarters of the consular governor of *Britannia Superior*. It will thus be observed that while present evidence seems to allot to *Britannia Inferior* the rich and fertile canton of the *Coritani*, in which the Lincoln *colonia* was an enclave, there is no compelling reason to bring the boundary of the Lower province further south. Indeed, if the point were put in the form of a question whether the *Iceni* of Norfolk and the Eastern Fens were included in *Britannia Inferior* or not, it may be observed that at the very period of partition the canal system which once linked this rich corn-growing district with the military district to north was allowed to fall into decay, as if the connexion no longer operated.[2] It can further be asserted with

[1] J.C.M. argues that from 197 to the Caracallan reforms *Britannia Inferior* was consular and included Chester. For the moving of the frontier from south to north of Chester he cites as parallel Caracalla's shifting of the Pannonian frontier from east to west of *Brigetio*. (See also now J. C. Mann and M. G. Jarrett, *JRS* lvii, 61 ff.)

[2] All the links in this canal system have not been proven. Re-examination of the pottery from the Cambridgeshire Car Dyke at Bullock's Haste (on which Richmond's statement is based) by B. R. Hartley makes it certain that the canal

some confidence that, whatever the nature of previous arrangements, the northward sphere of auxiliary garrisons allotted to the
legionary fortress at Chester did not extend in the third century
as far as the river Ribble. The fort at Ribchester and its territory
were by then regularly subject to a centurion-commander detached from the Sixth Legion at York and presumably thus lay
within *Britannia Inferior*. Again, the close commercial connexion
between the Derbyshire lead mines and the Humber water-way
would suggest that the Peak District should be related to *Britannia
Inferior*, rather than to *Britannia Superior*. Reasons are thus accumulating which tend to support the view that the dividing-line
between the two provinces ran from the Mersey to the Wash,
leaving the Trent basin within *Britannia Inferior*. It is sufficiently
curious to be worth note how closely such a division corresponds
with the known distribution of Brigantian[1] coinage two centuries earlier; as if an ethnic distinction may also have entered
into considerations of partition.

The first object of inquiry must necessarily be the towns. In the
history of Imperial town-life, the third century is a dark period;
and in Roman Britain, as in the Empire at large (and Roman
Britain is in many ways no exception); it is, however, at least clear
that the century cannot be reckoned an age of expansion. The
generous encouragement of civic ambition which had marked
the first consolidation of the province had been associated with
Hadrian and Antoninus Pius. The major towns, such as London,
St. Albans and Wroxeter, had then been equipped not only
with good public and private buildings but with imposing town-
walls,[2] attesting both the Imperial enhancement of their status

did not fall out of use until much later. It is moreover not at all clear that the
post-Boudiccan *Iceni* held much of the Fens, the greater part of which was
probably an Imperial estate. Their territory may have included the group of
villas on the eastern and south-eastern margin, though there is some evidence for
confiscation by the Severan house in the third century (*Ant. J.*, xxxviii, 91 f.).

[1] Coritanian? (J.C.M.).

[2] It now seems (Frere, *Britannia*, 251 ff.) that the stone town walls are mostly of
mid to late third-century date, with a few in the fourth century, though monumental stone gateways associated with earth ramparts of second-century date are

and their own local pride. Even smaller townships, probably the administrative centres of *pagi*, such as 13½-acre Dorchester and 27-acre Alchester, both in Oxfordshire, had already been walled. But it is notable in one town of large size recession had already begun in the second century. Silchester (*Calleva Atrebatum*) had received about A.D. 150 an earthen bank and ditch[1] which had reduced the area of the town by nearly one half, cutting it down to about 100 acres. This operation had scrapped a still earlier bank and ditch enclosing a larger area, which had also been at least partly furnished with regularly planned streets. The seal was now set upon the decision. Early in the third century, the Antonine rampart of earth was fronted by a fine stone wall and furnished with imposing recessed gateways.[2] A more precise date for the change is not provided by the evidence, and it would therefore be inappropriate to connect it specifically with the name of Severus, though there is no room for doubt that the Silchester town-wall is the immediate outcome of Severan policy.[3] In defining that policy, however, a distinction should be made. The act of reducing the area of the town and defending what remained with new defences was not new, but had in fact already been undertaken two generations earlier. The decision now made was to consolidate firmly and finally the town's defences and so to perpetuate the second-century reduction.

In other towns of the Upper Province there are traces of a comparable and contemporary act of consolidation. At Caistor-by-Norwich, *Venta Icenorum*, the town wall has been shown by Professor Donald Atkinson to belong to about A.D. 200.[4] Here,

occasionally found (e.g. Cirencester and St. Albans), up to which third-century stone walls have been brought. There is now no reason to think of the third century as a depressed period in the towns (see Frere, 254).

[1] They cannot be earlier than about 160 and may be as late as the end of the century (G. C. Boon, *Roman Silchester*, 1957, 75).

[2] According to Frere (p. 252) the pottery used to date the walls has been put too early: the style of the gates seems to be mid third-century (cf. St. Albans, S.W. Gate – not later than 250).

[3] This remains to be proven (see n. 1).

[4] The main gates seem to fit stylistically with the gates mentioned in n. 2.

however, the bank behind the wall is not of earlier date, but wall and bank are contemporary. As at Silchester, they cut off outer squares of a chess-board street-plan, although at Caistor the precise previous limits are not as yet defined. The reduced area is much smaller than 100-acre Silchester, comprising only 35 acres. In two ways, then, the third-century action was here more drastic. The reduction was an exclusively Severan decision: secondly, the resulting walled town was so small as to be comparable with a *pagus*-centre rather than a cantonal capital of standing.[1] This point is considered later in another connexion.

At Canterbury, *Durovernum Cantiacorum*, the town-wall and bank also belong to the opening of the third century. The area enclosed is about 130 acres and seems now to have been walled for the first time. Further, there is reason for thinking that at *Durovernum* the building of defences was accompanied by some civic development within them. The fine set of public baths discovered in St. George's Street belongs to this period. On the other hand the large and imposing theatre recently discovered appears to belong to earlier, more expansive days.

At Chichester, *Noviomagus Reg(n)entium*, the ancient capital of the *Regnenses*, or folk of the *regnum* of Cogidumnus, there is evidence tending towards a rather similar conclusion. The town wall again encloses an area of about 100 acres. A section cut through the bank behind it reveals that the wall and bank are certainly contemporary. The bank produced abundant pottery up to the close of the second century but none of later date, showing that both bank and wall belong to the beginning of the third century. But there is a further interesting circumstance. The amphitheatre of the town, identified in 1934, lay outside the circuit of the town-walls and it seems clear that it hardly outlasted their construction; indeed, it has been considered possible that the stones of the amphitheatre had actually been used for the wall itself. Whether this was so or not is at present without proof, but the fact remains that the amphitheatre was certainly

[1] The western region of the *civitas* territory may have been partially confiscated as Imperial estate under Severus.

demolished. Here then, as at Canterbury, the town was now walled for the first time and there is suggestive evidence for concentration within the walled area.

Further west still lies Exeter, *Isca Dumnoniorum*.[1] The tale of events here seems closely to match that at Silchester. The line of the town-wall is dictated by an earlier earthwork, which, upon the latest evidence, is assignable to the Antonine period. This earthen bank was in due course fronted by a well-built wall of local stone, dated by associated pottery to about A.D. 200. It is doubtful, however, whether at Exeter the earthen rampart had much reduced the area of the original town. Topographical records suggest that the place had never been very much bigger than the area of about 80 acres enclosed by the defences, though its abundant Greek coins tell us that it counted for much among mariners as the town served by one of the first ports of call in Britain for ships coming up Channel from Spain or the Mediterranean.

Finally, at Caerwent, *Venta Silurum*, there is evidence much like that from Chichester. The bank behind the town-wall is contemporary with it and contains nothing later than the second century, though late second-century pottery is certainly present.[2] Further, the bastions are mid-fourth-century additions. But the design of the wall itself has nothing in common with fourth-century walls. It very closely resembles that of Silchester, particularly in the provision of widely-spaced rearward expansions or counterforts. The area contained, however, is much smaller, only some 44 acres. Nor was Caerwent ever a large place; although prosperous, it remained one of the small towns of Roman Britain.

This accumulated evidence from the towns affords an interesting and suggestive picture. It becomes clear that the régime of the Severi was marked by a systematic provision of defences in such towns as did not previously possess them and by a thorough

[1] See now J. S. Wacher (ed.), *The Civitas Capitals of Roman Britain*, 1966, 48, fig. 8.

[2] The pottery seems to have been dated too early (Frere, *op. cit.*, 252).

overhauling of any ramparts whose design fell below the standards of the age. Architecturally, moreover, the new walls emerge as a class with interesting and distinctive characteristics. They lie between the second-century town-wall of St. Albans, *Verulamium*, which followed the imposing and costly standards of the Augustan age in its monumental gateways and widely-spaced impressive towers, and the defences of the late third century in Gaul, which bristle with external bastions. The Severan town-walls of Britain are of severely practical design.[1] Their gateways are frankly utilitarian in plan and they exhibit no external bastions. Where such bastions exist, as on the wall of Caistor-by-Norwich, Chichester and Caerwent, they are proved to be later additions. In short, these Severan defences are designed with the maximum economy compatible with efficiency; and the homogeneity of their design can best be understood as the result of a common policy, very probably implemented by Government architects, such as Cleodamus and Athenaeus, who operated in Thrace under Gallienus. But in respect of size these rationalized cantonal capitals of Britain stand alone. In no other western province outside Britain does this intermediate class of town-wall appear. In Gaul or Spain, as those lands were in the third century to learn to their sorrow, there was seldom found a half-way stage between the wide circuit which was too large to hold against barbarian attack and the minute *cité administrative*[2] which so often took its place. So on the Continent town-life too grandiose for the canton mostly perished, to leave only an administrative framework behind it;[3] while in Britain, on the other hand, a compromise seems to have been reached which remodelled the towns or kept them small, producing the kind of town-life which was not an artificial growth but did in reality meet the governmental, social and economic requirements of the Romanized tribal unit. In this respect these Romano-British towns represent a modified

---

[1] There is some evidence that the earlier examples among the third-century walls (*e.g.* Colchester) could have monumental gateways (Frere, *op. cit.*, 253 f.).

[2] More properly a citadel (J.C.M.).

[3] In fact life continued outside the later-Roman citadels (J.C.M.).

[47]

type of city-state, which was a real compromise between the tribal and the urban ways of life and is unique in the firmly consolidated form which third-century political theory[1] gave it.

The normal size favoured is about 100 acres. From such towns as Silchester and Caerwent it may be seen what this area was intended to contain. In many respects these cantonal capitals resemble a small country town of the eighteenth century. They contain an impressive town-hall, which served also as a law-court and exchange, a limited number of temples, plenty of small shops, often combined with workshops, a considerable number of large town-houses for the county[2] families and a fair sprinkling of small houses representative of the professional or administrative classes or of the successful merchant. So far the correspondence is striking: but the amenities differ much. Public baths were not an eighteenth-century feature:[3] they would then have seemed as strange as would eighteenth-century public houses in the Roman world. The one hotel approaching an eighteenth-century hostelry in amenity was maintained at public expense, as are sometimes Judge's lodgings, for travelling government officials using the Imperial Post. Plainly, the Romano-British town of third-century standard is intended to contain very much what was necessary to the continued existence of the canton as an organized social unit. There is liberal accommodation for the machinery of local government and for the seasonal presence of the local aristocracy who were to work it; there is ample provision for market-days and shopping; there are limited public amenities, suited to the rather small circle of cultivated folk in permanent residence. Only the amphitheatre can be reckoned as designed for crowds drawn from the centre at large. It has often been said, though perhaps not always with a sufficiently close analysis of the facts, that Romano-British town-life was an imposition upon Celtic

[1] J.C.M. thinks this did not exist: that the towns are simply the result of normal Roman urbanization.

[2] J.C.M. thinks this should be amended to 'city': I believe there is no clear distinction between the villa-owners and the upper-class city dwellers; in many cases they must have been the same people.

[3] Bath, Hotwells?

tribal structure with the implication such an institution was unnatural. But granted the *pax Romana*, the situation disclosed in these towns is rather the consolidation of the true and natural requirements of the tribe as an organized social unit. It may well be considered that the smaller Romano-British towns were in themselves a more natural and less artificial growth than the bigger examples, and that for the average British canton, the hundred-acre capital, to take a convenient round figure, was about the right size. Just as over a century of past experience enabled the Severan government to make a correct decision with lasting effect in the military area, so in *Britannia Superior* the credit for the appropriate estimate of urban needs goes to the House of Severus also.[1]

The military decision was the outcome of a crisis. Was there any relation between this striking programme of civil defence and the Maeatian invasion of A.D. 197?[2] It has been clearly demonstrated both by epigraphy and excavation that when the barbarians broke the Northern frontier their raids extended deep into the military hinterland. But there is, however, no suggestion from the towns which border that area of destruction reaching the urban communities. Neither Wroxeter nor Lincoln nor Brough-on-Humber produce destruction-layers of this date, and the inference will be that their walls provided sufficient deterrent or protection against raiders. But for the open countryside the coin-hoards tell in general a rather different story, of widespread nervousness, insecurity and hidden wealth unretrieved. It is noteworthy that this wave of uneasiness hit Icenian territory particularly hard and while it is impossible to be sure whether the cause was civil commotion or raiding from overseas, it is evident that this isolated corner of Britain was one of the most likely to feel the impact of sea-raiders first. Pictish raids had become chronic by the end of the century. It would not be surprising if the temporary collapse of Roman power in Britain in A.D. 197 gave them a start, and Norfolk would be a handy

[1] It no longer seems necessary to attribute such a policy to the Severi.
[2] See p. 19, n. 2, above.

land-fall for pirates. The fortification of cantonal capitals from the Wash to the Bristol Channel could then be seen as a first stage in the measures which culminated in the establishment of the Saxon Shore defences.

No reference to the Norfolk area of Roman Britain can fail to take into account one of the most important discoveries in recent decades, that the exploitation of the Fenlands goes back to Roman times. A consideration of the system may be the starting-point for a review of the third-century countryside. By this time an ordered system of dykes, drains and canals had long existed[1] and had made the Fens one of the most productive agricultural areas in Roman Britain. Geologically, the ancient water-courses can now be recognized as banks of alluvial gravel,[2] left high and dry by the shrinking of the peat due to modern drainage. Archaeologically, the whole Fenland from Cambridge to Wisbech and beyond has been shown, partly by air photography and partly by field reconnaissance, to have been extensively developed under Roman rule for agriculture. The hamlets or homesteads, the lanes or accommodation roads and the field-boundaries are all presented in a vivid picture of shadow-sites and crop-marks of which the crisp impression must be seen to be believed. Here and there are the Roman canals, broad and shallow cuts, comparable with railway works, by which the barges laden with the produce of the region moved in seasonal procession northwestwards[3] towards the military zone. What has not emerged, and post-Roman coastal erosion may well have removed the significant traces, is the system of dykes by which the low-lying land was protected from inroads of the sea.[4] But that such incursions happened there is good evidence; and a particularly severe inundation,

[1] The evidence to be published in the forthcoming Royal Geographical Society Memoir on the Roman Fenland indicates that the provision of 'straight-line' artificial water courses started about A.D. 120, but it is still not certain which were *primarily* drains and which canals.

[2] Actually silt.

[3] Waterways on the same pattern also exist from the southern Fens to the Wash and as branches north-eastwards from the northbound system.

[4] These are still unknown: lower sea level may have made them unnecessary.

whether due to earth movement, to neglect of man or to superabundant natural flooding is unknown, came at the close of the second century.[1] It was, however, repaired and the outstanding feature of all the homestead sites which have been identified by fieldwork is the rich yield of both third-century[2] and fourth-century pottery and coins. As to the character of the farmsteads and associated field-systems, there is an important comment to make. They are not expressly Roman in character: neither the symmetry nor the system of Rome marks their wayward outline. On the contrary, they can be matched, detail for detail, by almost any group of native fields[3] and farms from Salisbury Plain, the Somersetshire downlands or the Yorkshire dales. It was, then, native labour which was employed and settled upon these rich alluvial lands, stamping them with an indelible and characteristic hall-mark.

It has more than once been suggested, notably by Professor Hawkes, that this rich and profitable area was Imperial domain-land. Certain it is that until Roman engineering and expenditure opened it up, the Fenland saw no large-scale development. It is equally clear that at least its eastern half once belonged to the territory of the *Iceni*. But if this potentially rich territory had belonged in its exploited and developed form to the canton, whether as *ager publicus* or as the estates of private individuals, the possession of such wealth would naturally reflect itself in the cantonal capital, which might properly be expected by the standards of the contemporary world to be of exceptional size or splendour or both. It has been seen, however, that, contrariwise, third-century *Venta Icenorum* was exceptionally small, only about one third the size of the normal smaller tribal capital; as has already been remarked, it is more like the *chef-lieu* of a *pagus*

[1] The trouble now seems to have been largely inland flooding, not a marine transgression, probably in the early third century.

[2] There is now a significant third-century gap in occupation on most of the lower-lying southern Fen sites.

[3] In fact very few fields, as opposed to house and farm enclosures or gardens, are known. The alleged area of 'Celtic fields' at Hockwold was proved by excavation in 1961-2 to be a large settlement (*Proc. Camb. Ant. Soc.*, lx, 39 ff.).

than the centre of a canton. This late and stunted growth of town-life among the *Iceni* cannot be wholly due to that time-lag in Romanization, which has been detected in their cultural products and connected, no doubt correctly, with their punishment for the rebellion of A.D. 61. It is rather to be connected with the point that the punishment involved the ground-work of the Fenland draining[1] and, if this can be viewed as the subtraction for Roman benefit not only of territory but of the labour for its development, then the shrinkage in importance of the Icenian canton is explained and there is a permanent and standing reason for its comparative depression. Not that the canton was so afflicted that no wealth existed: the known Icenian villas, as at Gayton Thorpe, compare well enough with the medium-sized country-houses of other cantons, just as what there is of the capital itself compares not badly with others. It is, in fact, not a lack of Romanization but rather a low pitch and reduced scale which furnishes the indication of resources curtailed and transferred to the credit of the central Government.

The site nearest to the Fenland, and one which compares very closely in size with Caistor-by-Norwich, is Chesterton on the Nene, the Roman *Durobrivae*, a 33-acre walled town, which lies on the western fringe of the area in the Nene valley. This was the administrative centre of the district engaged in the production of the famous Castor ware, elegant pottery with glazed finish,[2] which flooded the markets of Roman Britain throughout the third century and later. The date of the defences of the little town is as yet unknown. But a milestone measured from it belongs to the year A.D. 276, and has been invoked with persuasive learning by Mr. C. E. Stevens as proof of its status as a *civitas*.[3] It may be remarked that, if such was its status, the territory which it governed could be well explained as a detached enclave

---

[1] See p. 50, n. 1: large-scale development was from *c*. 120 and there was practically no pre-Flavian occupation and little in the Flavian period. Forced labour immediately after the Boudiccan rebellion can therefore be ruled out.

[2] Properly, 'colour-coated finish'.

[3] *RIB* 2235; Stevens, *Eng. Hist. Rev.*, lii, 199.

of native territory cut off by the domain-lands or even as a centre of the domain-land administration itself.[1] Further, that *Durobrivae* was fortified not later than the third century is rendered extremely probable by the treatment accorded to the next posting-station to the north on Ermine Street, at Great Casterton, where the main road crossed the river Gwash. Here recent excavations have demonstrated that the 18-acre station received a massive rampart and wall at the opening of the third century. When a minor posting-station was thus treated, a neighbouring administrative centre is not likely to have lagged behind. It is, however, manifest that, like the folk of Caistor-by-Norwich, the citizens of Chesterton were not reaping the fruits of the rich lands which lay at their doors. The case for assuming that the produce of those lands was reserved for the Government becomes overwhelming.

Reference has already been made to the canals by which the Fenland produce was carried northwards in bulk to Lincoln and York. It is important to observe that in the third century parts of the system were falling out of use. At Cottenham, as Dr. Grahame Clark has shown, an important link in the series was blocked by a road-causeway in the third century,[2] while the granaries[3] on its bank were allowed to fall into disuse (plate 1). This implies a new economy in which barge-traffic no longer played a part and it is tempting to connect this drastic revision of the original design with a new orientation of the economy connected with the new partition of the province. If the area now fell to *Britannia Superior*, the northward link would no longer operate.

The identification of a second and highly important example of domain-land is due to the late Professor Collingwood, and a valuable preliminary study of its economy has been made by Professors Hawkes and Piggott.[4] There is now no reason to doubt

[1] The Fenland remains without a certain administrative centre, though the large Castor villa is a possible residence for a *procurator saltus*.

[2] See p. 42, n. 2 above.

[3] There is no evidence that the earthworks generally referred to as 'asparagus-beds' were granaries. Slight traces of woodwork, perhaps sluices, suggest some sort of fish-raising. (See pl. I.)

[4] *Arch. J.*, civ, 27 ff.

that Cranborne Chase and the vast area of Salisbury Plain was an enclave which received special treatment from the moment of Roman conquest onwards. This will help to explain the highly exceptional provision of a Claudio-Neronian legionary garrison in the native hill fort of Hod Hill, which commands what seems geographically the back door of the area, yet may politically have been a front entrance. It is clear that not very long afterwards no garrison of this size was needed: the natives had learnt their lesson, and a grim one at that.[1] The storage-pit statistics worked out by Professor Hawkes suggest that rather over half of the annual harvest was seized as the share of the Roman government. This was what was asked in Sparta from Helots, very different from the fifth, seventh or tenth which the ancient world reckoned as a fair taxable rate. The folk who produced it were peasants and the uniformly squalid character of their dwellings shows that they were kept at poverty level. Further, this squalor was not, as may happen in peasant communities, a matter of choice. If the poor personal trappings of these folk are compared with those of the contemporary peasantry in the Yorkshire or Derbyshire dales a difference in economic status at once becomes clear. The Brigantian peasant could afford to put money into solid silver jewellery, as is evident from the contents of his cave-dwellings and associated villages: and this represents the authentic instinct of the prosperous peasant-farmer, the wide world over. But no such innocent capitalistic delights came the way of Cranborne Chase: there tinned brooches stood for silver, and those neither many nor costly. The one known exception to the wholly native type of homestead is the basilican house or barn-dwelling at Iwerne, rescued from oblivion in the valuable study which forms the basis of these comments and put in its place among house types by Sir Cyril Fox. This building is dated to the first half of the third century. It belongs to a well-known type which in the larger estates frequently forms the servants' quarters. A second-century example may be quoted from Llantwit Major: third-century

[1] It now seems that garrisons were kept in this part of the country till at least A.D. 60.

examples from Clanville and from Castlefield in Hampshire may be added. But the house at Iwerne had no embellishments. It succeeded a dwelling of purely native type and it remained undecorated, almost devoid of separate rooms and unprovided with the bath-building which so generally characterizes even the least pretentious of Romano-British farm-houses. The stamp of poverty and official restriction marks this building also: so mean a dwelling can hardly have accommodated even a bailiff, and is much more likely to have housed the *vernae* of an Imperial domain.[1]

What the occupants of the Iwerne establishment were at this period engaged in doing is not clear. But it is evident that an important change came over the district as a whole in the later third century. This was the transition from agriculture to stock-breeding, represented by the abandonment of villages and the obliteration of field-systems by stock-enclosures or ranches. The change was not confined to domain-land. It is clear that it affected downlands elsewhere, as, for example, at Lowbury on the eastern end of the Berkshire downs, where intensive occupation begins in the middle of the century. The consequences of the measure are well known. By the close of the third century Britain had taken a place among the wool-producing areas of the Empire: *'tanto laeta munere pastionum'*[2] cries one panegyrist; *'pecorum mitium innumerabilis multitudo, lacte distenta et onusta velleribus'*[3] exclaims another. By the close of the century it is evident that wool had become one of the principal assets of *Britannia Superior*, and that while the Fens were under intensive exploitation for corn[4] the Cranborne Chase area had been largely converted from cornland to sheep-walks. It would be wrong, however, to conclude that the two changes were connected. In the inflationary economy of the third century both of these raw materials were

---

[1] Or of a large private estate (J.C.M.).

[2] *Paneg. Constant. Caes.*, 11, 1 (Mynors, viii (v), 11, 1).

[3] *Paneg. Constantino Aug.*, 9, 2 (Mynors, vi (vii), 9, 2). I owe this reference to A. L. F. Rivet.

[4] It seems certain that the Fens were chiefly a pastoral area.

valued in a world of rising prices. The same process is implied in Salisbury Plain by the earthworks on Wilsford Down and Stapleford Down, but how widely it extends is unknown.

A third enclave which is specifically identifiable as an Imperial domain upon the basis of an inscription[1] is that of Combe Down, south of Bath. Here a procurator's assistant restored the administrative headquarters in A.D. 212–22. The kind of production which was thus being administered is not stated, but it is surely significant that the quarries of the famous Bath stone, very widely and early exploited in Roman times, fill this particular nook of the Downs, between the Fosse Way and the Avon. Quarries were properly an Imperial monopoly, and these had evidently now become so, though they may previously have been worked by *conductores*, under lease-hold.[2]

In *Britannia Superior* it thus proves possible to detect in relation to civilian production the operation of the same kind of policy on the part of the Imperial Government as in the military area. This can be described as consolidation combined with maximum economic development. It is a development very closely related to basic commodities or raw materials, which now became more important than ever, as the depreciation of the Imperial coinage during the third century divorced the ordinary money of exchange from real values to such an extent as in the end to render it almost worthless. In Britain this economic storm is reflected in the highly conservative attitude to the coinage perceptible throughout the century, as Dr. Sutherland has demonstrated. During the first four decades the old-fashioned but intrinsically valuable *denarius* was hoarded and held in such general esteem as to become worth both forging and uttering in local issues. Then follows a half-hearted adoption into favour of the *antoninianus*, nearly always with backward looks of regret; and when the Gallic Empire came into being, between A.D. 259 and 273, Britain joined with it – *sub principe Gallieno . . . harum provinciarum*

[1] *CIL* vii, 62 (*RIB* 179) (I.A.R.).
[2] There is no reason why, even under a procurator, the quarries should not have been worked by *conductores*, rather the reverse.

a Romana luce discidium[1] – and welcomed the coinage of the
Emperor Postumus, who attempted to restore standards. Thereafter chaos reigned. When possible the worst coinage was avoided
in hoards; but it was of necessity circulating in immense quantities
as small change and was much imitated, probably to make up for
lack of regular supplies. Money of this sort, of the lowest worth
in relation to real commodities, could be hoarded, as was certain
inflated paper money in recent times, in the hope of recovery and
redemption at better value later. But it must have been to meet the
British longing for stabilization, that Carausius set about restoring
as soon as possible a good standard coinage. Significantly enough,
this coinage was at first conservatively based upon a *denarius* of
fine silver, and only later came into line with the reformed
antoniniani of Diocletian. At first this monetary stabilization of
Carausius looks like a triumph for conservatism. But there are
other considerations which might suggest that it may after all
have been dictated by opportunism. Rare though gold was, it
still remained the ultimate standard within the orbit of the
Central government. But in an isolated Britain gold could hardly
have performed this function, for British sources of the metal
were too few and too exiguous in output. The sole alternative
was fine silver in which the province was mineralogically rich,
apart from the much greater potential of bullion resources. Thus,
local conditions tended to impose a silver rather than a gold
standard. Secondly, the power of Carausius was from the beginning upheld by Frankish mercenaries; and for these wild and
unsophisticated men pay, of the old-fashioned silver coinage
which they understood and esteemed,[2] would be needed in
quantity. The immediate needs then supply sufficient reason for
the measure without looking further afield.

The coin-hoards of the period of Carausius have, however, a
political as well as an economic story to tell. They occur with
marked incidence in Wales, where a state of alarm is reflected by

[1] *Paneg. Constant. Caes.*, 10, 1 (Mynors, viii (v), 10, 1). I owe this reference
to S.S.F.
[2] J.C.M. comments that they would probably have preferred gold.

heavy deposits in both north-west and south-west. This significant form of reaction is continued in South Wales under Allectus. The same conditions are also evident in Somerset, with a tell-tale extension into Gloucestershire and Oxfordshire. It seems clear that the Bristol Channel was now becoming infested with Irish pirates, and excavation has on this point a confirmation to contribute.

At Ely, near Cardiff, a small farm, which had been established in the latter half of the second century, was drastically curtailed and surrounded by an earthwork at a date after A.D. 270 and well before A.D. 320. Similarly, at Llantwit Major, in Glamorganshire, the farming establishment recently[1] examined by Dr. Nash-Williams exhibits throughout the third century a static tenacity on the part of its owners of second-century conditions. But at the close of the century occupation of the main house came to an end and continued use of the establishment was confined to the quarters of slaves and bailiff, a state of affairs which occurs on other country estates at a later date (see p. 103), and of which this is an early example. At Woolaston Pill, many miles further up Channel, an early house of considerable size and wealth was destroyed and reconstructed in much less pretentious style. One of the most eloquent proofs of the fall in standards involved is the use of two excellent and little-worn power-driven millstones as paving-slabs instead of units in the machine of which they should form part. Still further inland, on the Fosse Way at Bourton-on-the-Water, a house was destroyed by fire at this time, though whether a destruction so far from the Severn waterway is to be attributed to raiders must remain doubtful. The doubtful case throws the certainties into sharper relief. This picture is, however, in the sharpest contrast with that afforded by south-eastern Britain, where the coast was protected by the Saxon Shore forts; that area remains astonishingly free from signs of alarm, as if the measures taken for its protection had been almost wholly successful. Only the conflict between Allectus and the invasion forces of the central government finds a very exact distributional

[1] 1938 and 1949: *Arch. Camb.*, cii, pt. 2, 89 ff.

confirmation in a little trail of hoards extending from Hampshire
to the London area.

These archaeological data tell mostly of Government provisions
or of their lack. What of the prosperity of the province as a
whole? For it is after all possible to conceive conditions in which
Government concerns may be booming amid the languishing of
private enterprise. It is evident that many of the factors tending to
restrict private enterprise were now present. The collapse of the
coinage had certainly induced hoarding of the older and valuable
issues and cautious spending. The increasing preference and need
for taxation in kind instead of cash must have enhanced the value
of real property while at the same time notably increasing the
costs of initial building or repairs. Here a pith of negative evidence
is of considerable significance. It can be no accident that many
of the country houses that have been carefully excavated during
the last twenty five years within the area of *Britannia Superior*
reveal remarkably little change between the second century
and the fourth, showing that their owners may have been holding
their own economically but were not enjoying such prosperity
which might have induced them to pull down barns and build
greater. The same rise on economic pressure explains why in the
bigger towns there was no room for upkeep of amenities.
Verulamium, situated upon a great trunk road and wide open to
official exactions, presents a picture of decay, not merely in its
public buildings but in the town-houses of the wealthy.[1] This
neglect of amenity, which has been interpreted as antipathy to
town-dwelling upon the part of the cantonal aristocracy, is
perhaps more directly explicable as a natural first concession to
the need for economy imposed by the times. Further, it must be
realized that, unless the numbers of Romano-British *decuriones*
were exceptionally small, they can never at any time all have been
living in the canonal capital. A large number must always have

---

[1] Frere (*Britannia*, 254) points out that the stone houses of the second century
might be expected to last at least a century with ordinary maintenance, so that
there was probably little call in the third century for extensive building of town
houses.

lived upon their estates; and their town-houses thus represent either a personal luxury, or dwellings rented by those who, in rotation or by election, were most intimately concerned with cantonal government. Nor is it sure that the picture presented by *Verulamium* is typical. The whole scale and incidence of urban economies was plainly different at Silchester and different again at Caerwent. The excavation of both sites came too early to supply detailed information but a comparison of the incidence of larger houses alone is sufficient to show what a different scale of wealth was involved and how radically the number of wealthy inhabitants might vary as between one town and another.

It would, moreover, be erroneous to conclude that development in the countryside was at a standstill. There were some estates on which the introduction of Romanized houses and servants' quarters, actually began in the third century. Such was Atworth in Wiltshire, where a substantial small farm came into being. Castlefield, near Andover, is another, and Clanville, with its unusual inscribed statue-base of the Emperor Carinus.[1] A bath-house at Farnham, accompanying a house yet to be identified, has the same history. A substantial reconstruction of a medium-sized villa at Farningham, in the Kentish valley of the Darenth, belongs to the close of the second century, and the same is true at Walton-on-the-Hill. It seems certain that these are only examples of many cases which suggesting that, whatever was happening in the towns, development of the countryside was not static, as indeed might be expected during a period of rising prices for basic commodities. The movement extended even to west Cornwall, where at Magor Farm, near Camborne, a modest villa came into being in the later second century, and is comparable with second-century Ditchley and larger than second-century Lockleys. But this venture did not last long, in contrast with the others cited above. In the forties of the third century Magor had already ceased to be occupied by civilized folk, and for some thirty years longer continued to be used in squalid state by rough and primitive occupants. This second phase of occupation has

[1] *RIB* 98.

been assigned to squatters or to slaves, most probably the latter. The social implications seem to lie between two possibilities. The economic blizzard of the times may have forced the owner to part with his property, which was then united to another estate and run by slaves.[1] Alternatively, the first sea-raids may have begun and driven the owner of this vulnerable coastal estate to the shelter of a fortified community, while bailiff and slaves were left to face a storm whose precise incidence no one could predict. In either case this Cornish site represents the darker side of the picture.

All these cases are symptomatic of an economic situation which demanded and encouraged concentration upon the countryside and its raw products. If comment may be passed upon the individual establishments, it must be observed that they display a noteworthy simplicity. They are not merely devoid of luxury but often attain only the barest level of comfort. Many may undoubtedly be recognized as the quarters of slave and bailiff, *villae rusticae* in the true Catonian sense. In other words they stand for a policy of maximum profit and minimum expenditure, which is entirely in harmony with the exigencies of the age. To call the third century in *Britannia Superior* the age of rationalization might suggest too rigid an application of political theory. But if the rationalization is conceived as measures imposed by stringent economic needs, then it may be suggested that the word summarizes the outcome of the age as well as any single term is likely to do.

[1] Surely the unification of estates, whether by purchase or marriage, can be envisaged in good times as well as bad?

3

BRITANNIA INFERIOR

The northern boundary of *Britannia Inferior* lay at the Wall and it was no doubt in order to define it that the rearward boundary dyke, known to us though not to the Romans as the Vallum, was rehabilitated, after desuetude during the last sixty years of the second century.[1] There is fair reason for thinking that the southern boundary, marching with *Britannia Superior*, ran from Mersey to Wash, leaving Derbyshire and most of the Trent valley to the Lower Province (see p. 42 f.).

The capital of the province was York, headquarters of the Sixth Legion: and the style *ad legionem sextam* was at least once used to describe the praetorian who was the provincial governor. Adjacent to the fortress there grew up a capital and it is known that before A.D. 237 this town had become a *colonia*. An immense fillip must have been given to the town not only by the selection of it for a capital of a province but by the residence there of the Imperial Court during the British campaigns of Severus and Caracalla. An Imperial rescript of 5 May, 210, is dated from *Eboracum*,[2] and it was there that the old Emperor died on 4 February, 211. The life of Severus mentions, in that incidental fashion which inspires belief,[3] a *domus palatina* to which he had returned shortly before.

The *canabae* or extra-mural settlement of the fortress extended for some distance outside its north-west and south-east gates, the *portae principales*, and occupied the eastern bank of the Ouse. The

[1] The original boundary may have been the Antonine Wall. The rehabilitation of the Vallum was perhaps *c.* 158 and its final obliteration near the forts by civil settlements certainly Severan.

[2] *Cod. Just.*, iii, 32, 1.   [3] SHA *Severus*, 22, 7.

western bank, reached by a bridge just outside the *porta praetoria*, was in the first and second centuries occupied by a small but growing bridgehead settlement, yet it had been predominantly an area of cemeteries, lining the southwestward main road. In this area, was created the new town of the third century obliterating the bridgehead village and the tombs and leaving the legionary fortress and its shadier suburbs in undisputed possession of the east bank. It has not as yet been proved by systematic excavation that the new town was walled,[1] but it is extremely likely, for there is a credible local tradition of an ancient wall buried inside the great bank which enclosed the 100-acre pre-Norman town and carries the surviving Plantagenet wall.[2] Further, the rich and tightly-packed cemeteries of the third and fourth centuries crowd round this area without anywhere penetrating it, in such a manner as strongly to suggest both that defences existed and that they occupied this very position. Within the inhabited area little is known about buildings in detail. But in 1939 portions of a large and imposing set of third-century baths were discovered: while a massive double colonnade, nearer the river, indicates yet another important monumental building on the grand scale. The medieval Ouse Bridge has yielded some interesting architectural decorative details re-used in its foundations. If, in addition, account is taken of the trade connexions by river and sea of the wealthy freedmen, of the sumptuous grave furnishings of the dead, and of fragments of monuments indicating expensive and richly adorned tombs, then the total impression conveyed by the civilian side of Roman York is that of a vigorous and well-equipped town, not unworthy to be the provincial capital. Constitutionally, little can be said about its status. One decurion of the *colonia Eboracensis* is known, a young and delicate man, to judge by his skull;[3] while his name, Flavius Bellator, suggests a

---

[1] A rather rough wall was seen in 1939 – see R.C.H.M., *Eboracum*, 49.

[2] See R.C.H.M., *loc. cit.*, for other details of the *colonia*.

[3] R.C.H.M., 85 f. points out that the skull is that of an adolescent, whilst Flavius Bellator died at the age of 29 (*RIB* 674). The burial may have been secondary or the skull in the Yorkshire Museum may be wrongly attributed.

native provincial, and the gold ring buried with him attests his rank as an equestrian. But nothing is known of an allotted *territorium* attached to the town and there is no compelling reason to suppose that in the third century the grant of colonial status was accompanied by land-allotments of the old style.[1] Even of grants in the new style, by which soldiers might become lessees (*conductores*) of land in the legionary *prata*, have as yet left at York no trace.[2]

After York came Lincoln, a *colonia* of older standing, founded under Domitian for men of the Ninth Legion[3] who had moved their base from Lincoln to York in or soon after A.D. 71. There must have existed from the time of foundation a '*vetus consuetudo*' between the two places and the trade connexions in common which are represented by the freedman who was a *sevir Augustalis* in both *coloniae* had no doubt obtained long before A.D. 237, the date of the inscription in question.[4] As first founded the town of Lincoln lay on the hill-top north of the Witham, and it was the shell of the original walled *colonia* of 41 acres that the Normans chose with purposeful imagination to contain their Castle and Cathedral. There had lain a compact regular town, planned *more Romano* with good chessboard sewered streets and containing some stately public buildings and comfortable private houses. But on the hill-top itself the Roman town did not expand: as in medieval and industrial Lincoln, the tendency was to extend downhill, towards the river-port and the long narrow tongue of land by which the Roman road from the south and its modern successor approaches the city. It is clear that there was ribbon development along this line in the earliest days of the colony and that on the outskirts, as at York, cemeteries were in time levelled to make way for buildings.

In later Roman times, however, the lower town had so grown

---

[1] The colony may have taken over part of the Brigantian territory, perhaps the part confiscated in the mid second century (Pausanias, viii, 43, 3).

[2] There is no satisfactory evidence for such grants.

[3] J.C.M. points out that after Augustus colonies were not founded for specific legions.

[4] *JRS* xi, 101 ff.

in importance as to receive a defensive wall. This ran almost straight southward from the two southern angles of the upper town as far as the north bank of the Witham, where it turned and formed a south front along the river-bank. The effect of the extension was to raise the area of the walled town from 41 to 97 acres, more than doubling its size, but the date of the operation was until recently unknown. It can now be assigned to Severus, for recent excavation of these defences on the west side of the city has shown the wall to have been backed by a contemporary bank which contains much rubbish of the late second century and nothing of later date.[1] The measure can thus be seen as in step with contemporary action in *Britannia Superior*. The result was to bring the reorganized *colonia Lindensium* into line with the rationalized cantonal capitals (see p. 46ff.) although it was not itself a capital but in origin a veterans' town, whose *territorium* of allotted lands was carved out of the canton of the *Coritani*. It is also plain that the two towns of highest status in the new province were much alike in size, though York had all the additional prestige and commercial advantage attaching to the presence of the legion and the provincial governor. None the less, a clear sense is conveyed of the parallel efforts being made to advance standards in the new province and to ensure the safety and welfare of its principal towns.

It is clear that the plan of the new lower town at Lincoln was to a very considerable extent systematized. In lesser degree what now happened is reminiscent of the Augustan replanning of the lower town in the colony of *Tarraco*. Like Tarragona, Lincoln stands upon a steep hillside, and the street system was related to massive terraces, in the manner of Priene. In Lincoln at least two such terraces have been observed. The first lies high up the hill, and its

[1] F. T. Baker, *Ten Seasons' Digging, 1945–1954*, 1955, 20 ff., reports a rampart containing pottery with a terminal date of *c.* 180: this bank was increased in height with tipped material which contained pottery extending a little way into the third century. The relationship between wall and bank could not be examined, but the evidence would be consistent with a late second-century earthwork to which a wall had been added in the third century, possibly towards the middle of the century.

great retaining-wall fronted an artificial platform measuring 180 feet from back to front, the back coinciding with the south wall of the upper town. No date within the Roman period, to which the work can be assigned without doubt, is given to this major engineering operation on present evidence, though its connexion with a drastic late revision of the town-plan is self-evident. But the lower terrace, discovered a little way above the foot of the steep slope in Flaxengate, is securely dated by excavation to the third century, and obliterated two sets of earlier stone buildings. Structures of the later fourth century had in turn blotted out such buildings as the terraces had carried: but fragments of mouldings and veneers cut from at least four different kinds of imported Mediterranean marble suggest that expensive and important structures were involved.

The Romanization of the new town is further expressed in its inscribed architectural mouldings connected with the cults of *vici* or town-wards whose guilds or associations were named after their Roman patron deities, Mercury and Apollo.[1] The place has also yielded some interesting sculpture, not now in good condition, which has so strong an affinity with third-century sculpture of the Rhineland and the Moselle that its date can hardly be in doubt and its connexion with the reconstructed *colonia* becomes certain.

But in both York and Lincoln one of the most important factors in everyday life was the river-port. In York the link with the sea, as later in Alcuin's day, was direct by way of Ouse and Humber, and portions of the Roman wharves on the east bank of the river are known. In Lincoln the connexion was with the Trent by means of the canal now called the Fossdyke, as continued into medieval times, so that the shipping of both towns met in the Humber estuary. It is not certain, indeed, it is highly doubtful, whether sea-going ships reached the Lincoln river-port. Barge-traffic, as on the river-ways of Roman Gaul, is much more likely. But there is no doubt that the connexion between the markets of the two towns was close. The wealthy freedman, M. Aurelius

[1] *RIB* 270, 271.

Lunaris,[1] who was a *sevir Augustalis* of both towns, was himself shipping direct from York to Bordeaux in A.D. 237. His ship will not have gone to *Aquitania* empty, but what it carried is uncertain; the return cargo, on the other hand, will almost certainly have been wine, with oil as a remoter possibility. Rough wine for military rations and finer vintages for retail to richer customers were both highly profitable commodities in which to deal.

In addition to York and Lincoln, *Britannia Inferior* was furnished with three cantonal capitals, at Leicester (*Ratae Coritanorum*),[2] Aldborough (*Isurium Brigantum*) and Brough-on-Humber (*Petuaria*). Of Roman Leicester, following Haverfield's brilliant study and the detailed excavation of the town baths and the attached great hall by Miss Kenyon, there is little new to say,[3] especially about the state of the town in the third century. The one observable fact seems to be that there was an abortive effort to feed the Baths with an effective supply of running water; a fact which in itself reflects ill upon the choice of site for the building and the management of the town's resources. It would be interesting to know how far the presence in the canton[4] of a prosperous centre like Lincoln detracted from the full development of Leicester as the cantonal capital. Nevertheless, as far as size goes the 100-acre area ascribed to *Ratae* comes up to the standards of the rationalized cantonal capitals of *Britannia Superior*.

Aldborough (*Isurium Brigantum*) is not quite so large, but it is considerably larger than Caerwent and a little behind Exeter (*Isca Dumnoniorum*) in size, its area being calculated at some 65 acres. There is no doubt that by the opening of the third century it had been walled: but it is not certain, pending the appropriate report, whether this protection had been afforded after the Brigantian troubles at the opening of the later half of the second

---

[1] *JRS* xi, 101 ff

[2] See J. M. Reynolds, in *The Civitas Capitals of Roman Britain* (ed. Wacher), 1966, 73, for evidence that Leicester was promoted to chartered status (citing *CIL* xvi, 160).

[3] For a presumed *forum* see *JRS* liii, 134; liv, 162; lv, 207; lvi, 203.

[4] Lincoln cannot have been 'in the canton' of the *Coritani* (J.C.M.).

century, or whether the provision belongs to the Severan age.[1] Inside the walls there is good evidence for the existence of comfortable houses and the age of their foundation is clearly older than the third century, when some at least had been reconstructed. The important fourth-century features are considered elsewhere (pp. 121, 131).

Brough-on-Humber (*Petuaria*) is totally different in character. It had been provided during the Antonine period[2] with a wall which reduced it to $13\frac{1}{2}$ acres in size only, and at an unknown later date[3] external bastions were added. But this very small fortified area does not represent the curtailment of a large town. *Petuaria* was never a big place and its constitutional title is known to have been *vicus*. The *Parisi*, whose administrative centre it was, thus lived, like the Gallic *Allobroges* in Caesar's time, 'by villages' (κωμηδόν): and it might have been said of *Petuaria*, as Strabo said of *Vienna*, the Allobrogic capital, that it was 'a village, but at the same time called the metropolis of the tribe'. (κώμην . . οὖσαν, μητρόπολιν δ᾽ὅμως τοῦ ἔθνους λεγομένην).[4] The name *Petuaria*, which is a place-name based upon the ordinal form of the Celtic number four, suggests a relationship to a numbered series of *pagi* and thus hints at a decentralization of tribal government greater in degree than that usual in Roman Britain at large and perhaps owing its perpetuation, as among the *Allobroges*, to the allied status of the community. *Vici* of the same kind certainly existed in other parts of the Parisian territory.[5] Evidence is steadily accumulating for the existence of a township at least as large as *Petuaria* at Norton, on the south side of the Derwent, opposite the fort of Malton, the sole garrison known among the *Parisi*.

[1] Probably rather later in the third century (Frere, *Britannia*, 252).

[2] Not before *c.* 180 (Wacher, *Ant. J.*, xl, 62, citing Corder and Richmond, *Journ. Brit. Arch. Ass.*, 3rd ser., vii, 15) for the stone wall: a rampart of *c.* 125-145 enclosed a larger area.

[3] Perhaps mid fourth-century (Corder, *Arch. J.*, cxii, 31).

[4] Strabo, *Geog.*, iv, 1, 11. But J.C.M. points out that this was the pre-Roman situation and that Strabo goes on to say that *Vienna* was 'now a city'.

[5] J.C.M. points out that there is no evidence that the *Parisi* ever became a *civitas*, though it is a little difficult to see what else they could have been – imperial estates?

At Millington, half-way between the two places, records imprecise yet wholly credible point to another extensive Roman settlement. The long-eroded site at Bridlington, where the foreshore has produced a very large quantity of coins covering the entire Roman period, is another. The arrangement, in short, represents the territory of a tribe where a predominant cantonal capital was lacking because the several constituent communities had local or regional feelings too strong or permit such ascendancy. The Gallic *Vocontii*, with twin capitals,[1] are in rather similar case, and the Aquitanian *Novempopulana*[2] is another example. Thrace was full of such village communities of an even more primitive kind.

In the neighbouring canton of the Brigantes there certainly existed, in addition to the tribal capital, minor centres comparable with those of the *Parisi*. Such a place was undoubtedly Catterick (*Cataractonium*), where air-photography has recently confirmed the nineteenth-century observations of Maclachlan. Here exists a walled township some 18 acres in size, with a street-system and many of the shop-like buildings typical of such a market-centre. But excavations carried out just before the second World War were not successful in revealing the date of the wall and further work is obviously required.[3] There was a wide extension of buildings in the adjacent area; they have been observed up to a mile and a half away from the walled centre.

In the catalogue of towns and townships a spa may have a place. On the assumption that Derbyshire is to be included within the bounds of *Britannia Inferior* the Roman curative baths at Buxton call for mention. Their name, *Aquae Arnemetiae*, is preserved in the Ravenna list and shows that like the springs of *Aquae Sulis* at Bath they were sacred to a native goddess: but in

---

[1] This is inaccurate in the view of J.C.M.

[2] This is a whole province, not just a *civitas*, and the villages were all in the territories of cities (J.C.M.).

[3] See *JRS* xlix, 108; l, 218. The town wall seemed to date from not earlier than the middle of the third century. The broad ditch (52 ft.) suggests that that feature in that form dated from the fourth.

this case her name, which means 'over against the sacred grove', very specifically links the deity with a British sanctuary. The baths themselves are little known, but Haverfield was able to collect enough evidence to show that spacious lead-lined bathing-pools had existed. No doubt the scale was smaller than at Bath, where the establishment was exceptionally large. The Upper German Badenweiler or Wiesbaden might afford a readier parallel.

Further north the area of towns and townships comes to an end. So far as organized civilian communities of Roman pattern appear at all, they are represented by the *vici* or villages outside the forts.[1] These places now tend to grow large: not uncommonly they cover an area three or four times as big as the fort itself, so that a settlement covering nine or ten acres is normal enough. The typical buildings within them are the long and narrow shops or taverns with living quarters at the back of the building or on an upper floor. The organization of such communities as legally constituted groups of *vicani* is well attested, and so far as they express themselves in inscriptions[2] they do it in Latin, and with tributes of regard for the Imperial House. No less significant are the unofficial religious cults.[3] Whether the dedicators are from regular auxiliary units, or from outlandish *numeri* worshipping non-Roman deities, the medium of expression is always Latin and the form of representation the *interpretatio Romana*. The highest standards are set in the dedications by the commandants. Their notable excellence and interesting iconography must have made them a strongly educative force, the starting-points for an infinite variety of inquiries and instruction concerned with Roman thoughts and Roman outlook. In the same way the official religious calendar of the regiment, strictly observed and punctuated with the great festivals and holidays, had a highly important

---

[1] See Salway, *Frontier People of Roman Britain*, *passim*. Corbridge and Carlisle seem to be left out of account (but see below) and now the territory of the *Carvetii* has to be included.

[2] *RIB* 1700; 899; 1616; *JRS* xlvii, 229 f. no. 18.

[3] It ought to be emphasized that the existence of dedications by soldiers or the commandant's household does not prove a *vicus*.

part to play in promoting appreciation and understanding of Roman traditions, which by precept and by unofficial contacts became the heritage of the *vicani* as well as of the troops. Normally, the *vici* are unwalled and in planning tend towards haphazard ribbon development, along the roads approaching the fort. The single certain example in Britain of a walled third-century *vicus*[1] is at Brough-by-Bainbridge (*Virosidum*) in Wensleydale, an outlying fort on the edge of some of the wildest hill-country in the Pennines, where extra precautions against robber-bands seem appropriate enough.

The *vici* of the military stations must thus form part of any estimate of the civilian resources of *Britannia Inferior*. It must further be recognized that the military area contains at least two small townships less immediately tied to the normal class of garrison. Carlisle (*Luguvallium*) had been in the first century a fort, but its military existence ceased when Hadrian's Wall was built and presently equipped with a new fort north of the river Eden. This fort held a cavalry regiment one thousand strong, earning more pay than auxiliary infantry and therefore providing a more attractive market. The effect of this attraction was to create a trading settlement at Carlisle, and abundant civilian and religious objects proclaim that by the third century the place had grown into a flourishing civilian community. Its well-to-do trading populace comes to life in a small but eloquent series of sculptured funeral reliefs, of which the quality compares with that of the best civilian tombstones from outside the legionary fortresses. Such tombs lined the southward road for at least a mile. In extent the settlement approximately coincides with medieval Carlisle, reckoned at 74 acres, but there is today no trace of the ancient walls which St. Cuthbert inspected in A.D. 685 nor is it known at what moment in the Roman period they were supplied. Another factor promoting the growth of Carlisle is the existence in the neighbouring Cumberland sea-plain of a

[1] The *vicus* at Brough-by-Bainbridge apparently started much earlier. Kirkby Thore, which has been proven by Miss Charlesworth to have walls, extended over at least 30 acres and may perhaps have advanced beyond the status of *vicus*.

dense native population. Air photography reveals an intensive occupation of the area. It has, indeed, been suggested by Mr. C. E. Stevens[1] that *Luguvallium* was a *civitas*, on the basis of a milestone measured from it: and the hypothesis has a great deal to commend it, upon geographical and topographical grounds.[2]

The second township, at Corbridge, is of a different kind. In the third century this Tyne bridgehead became a stores-base and the seat of military workshops, which attracted to themselves a large number of *vicani*, the more so because the outstationed legionaries who ran the depot were still better paid than an auxiliary cavalry regiment and so offered a yet more lucrative market to traders. The site seems yet to exhibit traces of an ir-regular later-Roman circuit, but it appears unlikely that this belongs to the third century,[3] when the workshops, for example, had enclosures of their own. For this period may be visualized rather an open settlement covering about 40 acres. Another flourishing *vicus* connected with a supply-base is at South Shields, where two notable tombstones again introduce the trading populace. One commemorates Victor the Moorish freedman,[4] whose master was a serving cavalryman. The other is a British freedwoman,[5] who became the wife of the Palmyrene banner-maker, Barates:[6] with her workbasket at her feet she is perhaps the first British needle-woman to earn a place in history. But like Antigonus Papias the Greek,[7] at Carlisle, or Diodora the high priestess of the Tyrian Hercules, at Corbridge,[8] she and her husband illustrate the cosmopolitan nature of these communities.

[1] *Eng. Hist. Rev.*, lii, 200.

[2] *RIB* 933 and *JRS* lv, 224, no. 11 (dated A.D. 258–268) prove the existence of a *civitas Carvetiorum* in the North-West in the third century. Carlisle is the most probable centre and this is supported by Stevens' interpretation of *RIB* 2283.

[3] In 1959 Mr. Robin Birley exposed part of the northern defences: the *terminus post quem* was a *mortarium* of *c.* A.D. 130. The phases in these defences are not yet clear. There are now signs that Corbridge had ceased to be a normal fort in the second century.

[4] *RIB* 1064.   [5] *RIB* 1065.

[6] *RIB* 1171. J.C.M. suggests that he was *vexillarius* of a merchant guild, not a banner-maker.

[7] *RIB* 955.   [8] *RIB* 1129.

All about the towns and settlements lay the open countryside. In this sphere much remains unknown, but this need not obscure the fact that interesting items of knowledge exist. The turn which events were now taking in the southern region of the province is illustrated by two villas in the Trent Basin, at Norton Disney and Mansfield Woodhouse. At Norton Disney a small stone-built house with front corridor and a single wing had been erected at the close of the second century, on the site of an earlier primitive farm almost entirely built in timber. This little house was associated with a much larger barn-like building entered from a court-yard at one end. In the early third century both buildings were reconstructed after a fire; at least one mosaic was introduced in the house and the barn was largely floored in concrete. Between house and barn was laid down a new and very substantial threshing-floor. The third-century picture here is thus not one of initial development but the rebuilding and improvement of an existing establishment.

Mansfield Woodhouse is a much older discovery of the late 18th century and the assignment of its buildings to their chrono-logical place was achieved by selective excavation in 1938.[1] The earliest buildings, which go back to late-Flavian times, were of timber, and were superseded in the second century by a small house of stone, closely comparable with the very simple earliest stone houses at Lockleys and Park Street. In the third century this house was improved by the addition of a front corridor running between large projecting rooms. The result is a small farm-house of the distinctive plan common throughout North-Western Europe, and classified by Swoboda as the *Eckrisaliten-Villa*. At the same time a large barn-like building was erected, which was later equipped with a bath-house and a single heated room, the bath-house being inserted into one end of the south aisle and south-west corner of the building. The establishment thus became an up-to-date owner's house, accompanied by the barn-like building for accommodation of slaves and stock.

---

[1] *Trans. Thoroton Soc.*, liii, 1 ff.

When the two estates are compared it can be seen that at Norton Disney the third-century changes comprised finishing touches to a farming establishment already fully conforming to the pattern of the smaller Romano-British estate. At Mansfield Woodhouse the change from simple main house and scattered farm-buildings to an improved house and accompanying *villa rustica* belongs itself to the early third century and marks the growing prosperity of the countryside in the new province.

This suggestion of an expanding prosperity is powerfully and suggestively reinforced by the evidence from the canton of the *Parisi*. At Langton, south of Malton, the first of the Roman farms in East Yorkshire to be systematically studied, there had existed since the late first century a native farmstead, of which the most distinctive feature is the irregular ditch-system, reminiscent of the villages on Salisbury Plain. In the early third century simple stone buildings of Roman structure and pattern took the place of what had gone before. The contrast, however, between the Langton establishment and those of the Trent basin is noteworthy. While Mansfield Woodhouse and Norton Disney manifestly represent the farms of resident owners with bailiff and slaves, Langton denotes with equal clarity only the first strivings after comfort and convenience on the part of an owner who had formerly lived in much more primitive conditions. The great barn-like building typical of the systematic *villa rustica* is absent. The farm remains an incoherent medley of small and scattered units, in the manner of a native homestead, but the buildings are now structurally sound and efficient. The scene is the same but the dress is new. Not enough is known of the establishment at Rudston to be sure whether its history was the same. But it is at least certain that it began as a native farmstead which had a long life before the erection of Roman buildings. Again at Harpham and North Newbald[1] the Roman buildings are associated initially with third-century pottery and coins. This general evidence of growing prosperity must be connected with the rise in real values, and in relation to this factor the new importance of York

[1] *Leeds Phil. Soc.*, v, part iv, 231 f. (I.A.R.).

and its expansion as a trading and administrative centre must have created very quickly an improved market for local agriculturalists. If, as there is good reason to think, *Britannia Inferior* was now divorced from the Fenland by the new subdivision of provinces, the rich corn-lands of the Wolds would begin to come into their own.[1]

In the Brigantian area also there are signs of an upward movement in prosperity. The bath-house of a farming establishment at Stancil, near Tickhill, engaged, like the villa at Styrrup, in developing the marsh-land south of Doncaster, belongs to this period, while at Castledykes or North Stainley, near Ripon, a very large villa, far from completely revealed, certainly underwent substantial reconstruction at this time. At Well, in a district where two other villa-sites are known, the house and bathing-pool, reminiscent of Wittlich, held their own during the period without alteration. No less interesting is the development of the outlying districts. It seems clear that this was a selective process, specifically concerned with land of exceptionally productive value. At Gargrave, in the Aire gap, the occurrence of a substantial farming establishment seems wholly unexpected and appears to be entirely isolated. Both its presence and its isolation are explained when it is realized that it stands upon the shore of an ancient glacial lake where rich alluvial soil is present. Similarly, the isolated farmstead at Old Durham, on a terrace of the river Wear, backs onto the magnesian limestone ridge which carries today some of the best agricultural land in the county.

Limestone, indeed, had no small part to play in determining the rural economy of the Brigantes. The great belt of Carboniferous Limestone which forms the Peak District and dictates the outlines of Upper Wharfedale, Wensleydale and Ribblehead is thick with the fields and farmsteads of Romano-British peasantry. Economically it is the northern equivalent of the chalk of the Downs or the oolite of the Jurassic Ridge. There is a remarkable unity in this Pennine cultural area, divided though it is by the

[1] See p.51 n.3; p. 55 n.4 above for the view that the Fenland was *not* a major corngrowing area.

millstone grits that run from Kinderscout to the Craven Fault. The two types of third-century pottery characteristic of the Derbyshire area and the Dales are common throughout the northern Pennine limestone district, and both districts produce the same kind of cave-dwellings, as Haverfield pointed out when he studied all as a single group.[1] But whereas the caves are frequently considered as refuges, as indeed they may well from time to time have been, there is much evidence to show that they are often an integral part of villages which lie at their very mouths and that the villages in turn are closely related to field-systems which extend far and wide over the limestone shelves. In short, the cave-dwellers and the villagers are one and the same folk, the caves affording a shelter from the weather during the bleak Pennine winter rather than a bolt-hole for outlaws, robbers or refugees. The cave-deposits have thus preserved, far better than the hut-floors, a representative sample of the Pennine village culture. Fine brooches of solid silver or with elaborately enamelled surface attest a prosperous peasant culture. The sufficiency of everyday things is shown by the substantial amount of small coinage in circulation, bone objects in quantity and coarse pottery in abundance. But of everyday luxury there was none: for example, if these villagers ever drank wine as a habit, it was at market and not at home.

As the limestone thins out to north-west, the economy changes. Farms are more isolated in Westmorland, fields are always fewer and often non-existent, and it becomes plain that the district as a whole was given over to pasture. In such a valley as the Lyvennet, where the late Professor Collingwood and others[2] were able to map a settlement group in its entirety, there can be seen the whole development of a little clan, in which small settlements split off from the large until the area would support no more. This was not happening early. The pottery from the main settlement at Ewe Close includes pieces of the late third century. The suggestion conveyed is that it was the *pax Romana* which

[1] *VCH Derbs.*, i, 238 ff.
[2] *Trans. Cumb. & Westm. A. & A. Soc.*, 2nd ser., xxxiii, 201 ff.

pinned these shepherds down and promoted a rise in population.

In the middle Pennines, where the limestone is absent, the middle grits provide on the intermediate contours shelves and rolling ridges which lie clear of the boulder clay and are susceptible of habitation. The upper Calder basin and the Spen valley are tolerably well sprinkled with such settlements, and in the Spen valley at Bierley there is evidence for considerable iron-working associated with mid-third-century coins. In lower Calderdale, near Wakefield, the area of Romanized farms is again reached and on the magnesian limestone ridge between Aire and Calder they abound. The southward continuation of the same limestone to southwest of Doncaster again carries prosperous native villages which have produced some notable hoards of third-century silver coins, while the farming-estates push out into the marsh-land, as at Stancil and Styrrup. An interesting outlying district is Cleveland, where the Lias formations support a substantial native population and where at least one villa-site is suspected but not conclusively proved. The field-work of the late Frank Elgee here recorded much, but an application of the spade to this area is now overdue.

An interesting side-light upon the third-century development of the Brigantian area of *Britannia Inferior* is shed by an official[1] attempt to give it a tutelary cult.[2] The goddess *Brigantia* may previously have existed as a tribal deity, but she makes no appearance in inscriptions or sculpture until the Severan age. She is then figured in stone with attributes corresponding to the verbal titles on inscriptions, the wings of Victory and the aniconic stone and globe of *Caelestis*, the African tutelary goddess, surely out of compliment to Iulia Domna: and she wears also a native type of helmet encircled by a turretted crown which proclaims her status as a British territorial personification. Her dedications are divided sharply into two groups. The first is closely associated with the northern frontier Wall and its outposts, where *Brigantia* may be

---

[1] Not necessarily official (J.C.M.).
[2] *Arch. J.*, xcvii, 36 ff.

appropriately thought of as a *genius loci*. The second group belongs to southwest Yorkshire, to lower Airedale and upper Calder basin, where all the dedications are made by *Aurelii*. One stone is dated to A.D. 205,[1] seven years before the *constitutio Antoniniana* created the spate of newly enfranchized provincials, who in monotonous accord so widely adopted the Aurelian name. The suspicion is thus created that the newly popularized tutelary deity was here worshipped by provincials who had won the citizenship not by block-grant but by the older channel of army service, and that the dedications are to be connected with army veterans[2] returning to their native villages and acquiring lands by grant, purchase or hereditary right. It is notable how regularly the dedication is coupled with the *numen Augusti*, attesting the grateful loyalty of the dedicators.[3] If this interpretation is correct it affords a glimpse of men who must certainly have given impetus to the Romanization of the hill-districts, namely, the returned soldiers with a sense of civic responsibility.

This excursion into the realms of politico-religious art concludes our survey of *Britannia Inferior*. The observation made in a previous lecture that this province was designed as an entity in which the military element was balanced by a substantial civilian background is fully borne out by a survey of the area. There are, indeed, many gaps in the information. In particular, the rich and prosperous canton of the *Coritani* must have a wealth of information to disclose, and it seems certain that both Yoredale and the Cleveland area have yet to make a substantial contribution to knowledge. But the picture now attainable has this in contrast with *Britannia Superior*. In the southern area the *Pax Romana* was already fostering civilized life by the second century, and it is possible to make a tolerably accurate estimate of those earlier effects. In the northern area no such estimate is possible. It seems evident that unsettled conditions throughout the second century prevented or retarded development, and that only the settlement of

---

[1] *RIB* 627: now dated to A.D. 208.
[2] If so they would certainly state their status as veterans (J.C.M.).
[3] *e.g. RIB* 623.

Caracalla created the peaceful conditions in which the North could begin to thrive and become archaeologically vocal. No doubt the beginnings of many features are older. The farming estates have clearly begun in the second century: the first economic expansion of the native villages almost certainly began then too.[1] But in these as in other spheres the third-century organizers in Britain reaped the first harvest where others had sowed and tilled.

[1] On the Cumberland Plain the expansion of the native settlements certainly started in the second century and may have been extensive in that period.

4

THE FOURTH CENTURY

The fourth century in Britain, like the third, opened with a recovery from disaster. In 296 the island had been regained for the central government from the usurper Allectus by Constantius Caesar and the praetorian prefect Asclepiodotus. It seems clear that Allectus had drawn upon the northern garrisons for support and that their removal, followed by defeat and at least temporary disorganization, had brought about disastrous barbarian inroads. This time the blow was more severe than in the previous century, since it involved not merely the Wall and forts in the hinterland but both of the northern legionary fortresses, at Chester and at York.

At each fortress drastic repairs are in evidence. The new north wall at Chester, of which notable portions still stand to rampart-walk height, is built in large blocks of masonry, so well finished on the face as to disguise that many of them once formed part of early tombstones and funerary monuments outside the fortress. The line and pattern followed by the work was the old one, with a conservatism which is the more interesting because it contrasts sharply with the new practice at York. At Chester it was the back wall of the fortress which is known to have been reconstructed. At York, the main front on the river-bank and the whole of one side were rebuilt upon different lines from before, which slightly reduced the fortified area. The new side was well-equipped with internal towers and artillery platforms, but the river front was reconstructed in truly monumental style with an immense external polygonal tower at each of the two angles and an interval tower of the same style in between these angles and the massive new gateway. This splendid architectural scheme confronted the town across the river. It was the dramatic setting for the military headquarters of Constantius, who died there in 306, after completing a punitive action against the Picts. The proclamation of Constantine, which followed, has left its mark in the shape of a finely-carved head of the young Emperor, in stone, found within the fortress.[1] Contemplating these splendid manifestations of architecture and art, who would guess that behind such façades the new Emperor owed his promotion in part to the timely intervention of an Alamannic king, who had accompanied Constantius with troops?

Further north, the reconstruction, as at Chester, is marked by general adherence to older plans and older fashions. On the Wall the forts, milecastles and turrets were restored upon very much the same lines as before, with changes of a minor kind which do not affect the main scheme: the most drastic small change was in the Wall-fort at Halton, where an internal bath-house was placed in the *praetentura* while a compensating addition[2] was made to the west side of the *retentura*, screened by the Wall. Beyond the Wall, the outpost-forts of High Rochester, Risingham and Bewcastle and, inferentially, Netherby, were substantially rebuilt, and at High Rochester the Constantian fort-wall and gates are as remarkable as the work at Chester for their massive and careful build. But the application of the latest fashions in fortification discernible at York does not appear: the restored works present the spectacle of a new age working with old materials. This is true even where wholly new work is in question. A $10\frac{1}{2}$-acre fort now built at Piercebridge on the north bank of the river Tees, where the Roman North Road crosses it, was designed in the older style with rounded angles and without external bastions. At Chesterholm the new projecting gateway-towers of the contemporary fort make a clumsy concession to the tendency of the age, but the general plan is fundamentally old-fashioned. The same is true of the new $5\frac{1}{2}$-acre fort at Elslack in the Aire Gap.

---

[1] *Ant. J.*, xxiv, 1 ff.

[2] Now shown by M. G. Jarrett to date to the early third century (J.C.M.).

An impression is created that in certain circumstances the practice of the Constantian restorers was to make do with obsolete patterns.

This impression is strongly reinforced by the contrasting state of affairs upon the west coast. Here, as already noted, the fortress at Chester was restored in the old style. But in Wales important changes of a more up-to-date kind are discernible. The Glamorganshire plain, where devastations under Carausius and Allectus had already left a trail of ruin and alarm, was now protected by a new fort of Saxon-Shore type at Cardiff. The defensive wall and splendid polygonal bastions of this 8½-acre fort form as today restored one of the most remarkable sights in Britain. They can hardly, however, have stood alone. There must be a system of forts and signal-stations awaiting discovery further west, where milestones of the period provide explicit proof of interest taken in this sector of the frontier.[1] Not, however, until the north-west corner of Wales is reached do other elements of coastal defence appear. The Roman fort at Caernarvon was not re-occupied,[2] though the threat to this important economic area had become sufficiently acute to have caused an alarm reflected in coin-finds (p. 57f.). But a small fort[3] of the new style was built on the river-bank somewhat below the older fort site, with perhaps a fortlet[4] to hold the opposite bridgehead. Another garrison housed in a very similar fort was installed at Holyhead to watch that important Anglesey harbour. At Holyhead the import of the provision is clear. The garrison was not connected with patrols: for this would have called for a fort on the mainland. Its purpose was clearly to administer and protect a harbour-base and that must be the function of the Caernarvon fort also, for the mouth of the river

[1] *RIB* 2253, 2254, 2256, 2257.

[2] M. G. Jarrett writes that he can find no definite evidence that the fort was abandoned: indeed Wheeler's coin lists perhaps indicate the opposite (*Arch. Camb.*, lxxvi, 203; lxxvii, 313 ff.).

[3] Hen Waliau: this appears to be early third-century, and I.A.R. later suggested that it was a walled stores-compound (in I.Ll. Foster and G. Daniel, *Prehistoric and Early Wales*, 1965, 68).

[4] I.A.R. (in Foster & Daniel, *op. cit.*, 170 f.) later suggested a fortified beaching-point. I owe this reference and the preceding one to M.G.J.

Seiont forms a good haven. The Roman navy comes clearly into the picture; and it must be remarked that, small though these forts are if related to land patrols, they are not so small when connected with ships' crews as shore bases. But the story does not end at Anglesey. Recent excavations at Lancaster have disclosed that the ancient ruin known as the Wery Wall belongs to the fourth century and is part of a defensive wall equipped with external bastions, obliterating the buildings of a third-century fort. The size of the newly discovered fort is unknown, but if the new remains are related to older topographical evidence and the configuration of the ground its north wall was over 400 feet long and not much longer. If it is supposed that the Norman castle was planted in the other corner of the Roman fort, as at Cardiff and Porchester, there was room for a 5-acre fort, about 450 feet square. In any case, as the length of its north front shows, the Lancaster fort is in a different category from that of the North-Welsh fortlets. It matches Richborough much more closely, and is in fact the furthest north of the 'new model' type of forts to have been discovered. Manifestly, more attention was now being paid to the West Coast defences than has hitherto been detected, and it takes the new form, not the old.

The Lancaster fort might indeed seem to herald the discovery of a new series of coastal defences extending from the Bristol Channel to Morecambe Bay. But the existence of a continuous system is not so sure a likelihood. On the south side of the Bristol Channel two signal-stations, at Old Burrow[1] and Martinhoe,[2] seem to demand garrisons of the Saxon Shore type in connexion with them: and the century of prosperity which now followed in Somersetshire certainly implies that effective steps had been taken. Again, as already noted, the Glamorganshire plain will have needed more protection than Cardiff could by itself afford. But Wales as a whole was left to itself. The movement of the

[1] Old Burrow seems to have had only a short occupation in the first century (*JRS* liv, 171).
[2] Martinhoe, when excavated, produced finds only of the period A.D. 60–70 (*JRS* lii, 184).

native population back to the hill-forts, which had already begun in the third century, now became general.[1] There is no trace of new garrisons in the old forts: *Segontium*, for example, now lay empty. The only new elements are the riverside fortlet at Caernarvon and the harbour fortlet at Holyhead, and these might be taken as special protection for the mines, for it must be recalled that a garrison was still maintained, presumably for this task, in the Upper Severn mining district at the fort of Forden Gaer. A small detachment of the fleet patrolling the approaches to the Anglesey mining area: forts of large size to house patrols in more civilized districts: the Welsh *civitates* left to themselves and even now beginning to be subjected to infiltration by Irish immigrants: this might be a truer picture than a continuous system of defences. On the other hand, it would seem logical to expect forts of the new type on the Wirral and in the Fylde, if not elsewhere on the Lancashire coast, where Lancaster, like Cardiff, cannot have stood in isolation. Whether any provision was made for Cornwall and the tin-mines is unknown. But the milestones of the early fourth century indicate a quite new interest in that area and raise the question without solving it[2]

The particular import of this general picture of the restoration is best appreciated by a consideration of the garrison. The Wall-garrison is described in detail in the *Notitia* and in a roughly geographical order, which breaks down only at the western end, where some three forts and their garrisons are missing. The units are substantially those of the third century, but a few changes have undoubtedly taken place. The most striking is the up-grading of the *numerus Maurorum* as the garrison of Burgh-by-Sands, instead of the milliary cohort which had previously been brigaded with it as senior unit. In addition, there are perhaps three other forts in which different units of the old type replace the known third-century garrisons, though the caution must be entered that

---

[1] See Simpson, *Britons and the Roman Army*, 150 ff.: at only 3 excavated hill-forts are there signs of substantial fourth-century occupation. In general the evidence is against prolonged occupation of Welsh hill-forts in the Roman period.

[2] In fact three of the milestones recorded in *RIB* are of the mid third century (*RIB* 2230, 2232, 2234) and only two of the early fourth (*RIB* 2231, 2233).

textual criticism might reduce even this small number. In general, it is quite certain that the third-century garrison returned to its stations and was retained without substantial change. The explanation of this fact is probably to be found in the strategy of Allectus, who did not employ against Asclepiodotus all the troops which he had collected but preferred to trust the issue to a nucleus of old and trusted companions in mutiny and the Frankish mercenaries. Like Agricola in earlier days, Constantius had only then to let 'impunity recall to loyalty those conscious of their fault', to quote the panegyrist. If the Wall-troops were for the most part never engaged, they could return to their posts, where the ruin and devastation which awaited them was in itself a severe punishment. But with the exception of the *numerus* at Burgh-by-Sands, the attendant *numeri* or *cunei* seem to disappear. The inference would seem to be that they were left behind on the frontier and were largely wiped out, always supposing that they did not make common cause with the invaders.

The same suggestion of units now returning to the frontier area unscathed is to all appearance afforded by the legions. The Sixth and Twentieth seem to have come back to York and Chester intact, and there is no sign that they were now subjected to the new process of subdivision. The only British legion in which there is any evidence for division is the Second, which was ultimately divided into two if not three units. It looks, then, as if in strategy Allectus had relied too much upon his Franks and coastal garrisons and had failed to use the frontier troops in a pitched engagement. The political reason behind this decision may well be that there was bitter jealousy between these hired or newer contingents and the old-established frontier troops and that Allectus could not trust the northern regiments.

In the hinterland of the Wall the troops enumerated are those of the Cumberland and North Lancashire coast, the Stainmore Road, County Durham and Yorkshire. These contain some interesting survivals of *numeri* and it may be suspected[1] that in

[1] *Arch. J.*, xcvii, 125 ff. There is no positive evidence for this suggestion (a point I owe to J.C.M.).

these cases the *vigiles, defensores* and the like are third-century *numeri* up-graded to main garrisons, the senior troops having been withdrawn for the new coast defences.

But while the disposition of the northern section of these garrisons reflects the old arrangement, the southern group in Yorkshire does not. Among old-established sites Malton remains one of the most important. Templeborough is another. Among the new names not all can be given their geographical position. It is, however, certain that Doncaster was one of the places now to receive a garrison. Its position, upon an important main road and at a river-crossing, is admirably suited both for local control and for rapid movement of troops in all directions. Archaeologically, the re-occupation of other inland sites after a period of disuse is well attested. Piercebridge on the Tees: Elslack in the Aire Gap: and very probably Newton Kyme, at the Wharfe crossing of the North Road, all belong to the new arrangement. The advantages appertaining to Doncaster apply to them all. Here, then, may be recognized the stations of the more mobile troops of the *dux Britanniarum*,[1] available for wide deployment. The large size of the forts suggests that they were intended to house cavalry, and this is the class of garrison assigned to two out of the five unidentified names. There is no exact correspondence, however, between names and the known remains; and this is another proof that the *Notitia* for Britain, as Mr. Stevens has acutely demonstrated,[2] contains more than one stratum in its speciously complete lists.

In one area it is possible to trace the process of change in action, namely, in the outpost zone north of the Wall. Here it is established by excavation that after 297 High Rochester, Risingham and Bewcastle were re-occupied. The same can be inferred of Netherby and although the case of Birrens is less conclusively authenticated, it is inherently probable enough. There is, however, no evidence that the forts were now the headquarters of *exploratores*: on the contrary, it may well be that these patrol formations were by

[1] The control of the forces was probably taken from the *praeses* (governor) of the province and transferred to a *dux* during the reign of Constantine (J.C.M.).

[2] *Arch. J.*, xcvii, 125 ff. J.C.M. does not agree.

now abolished or transferred elsewhere. Long before A.D. 367 their place had been taken by *arcani*[1] or an intelligence service. This could not have been done, after the severe Pictish inroads of A.D. 297,[2] without a punitive campaign of the kind undertaken by Caracalla and Severus: and the need to enforce a settlement by such a campaign explains the Pictish expedition of Constantius, following the restoration of the Wall. But on the restoration of the protectorate without patrols, the problem of markets at least would have to be met, and the way in which this question was solved is revealed at Housesteads. Here a well established traffic route[3] from the north reached the line of the Wall and could be used as a feeder for trade. In immediate view of the fort the Wall was pierced by a special gateway, equipped with two sets of doors and two large guard-chambers for the perusing and surveillance of those who passed through it. A periodic fair or market could thus be held upon Roman territory for the benefit of those who lived beyond the Wall, in place of the regulated markets once held in the forward territory. It may be presumed that at Carlisle and north of Corbridge, where the western and eastern traffic-lines from the North reached the Wall, similar opportunities for trade were provided.

The relaxation of Roman control implies improved relations with the protectorate. Probably this was generally true, but two occasions are known when troubles occurred of the very kind that the *exploratores* had been intended to prevent. In 343 there was a crisis on the northern *limes* sufficiently serious to induce the Emperor Constans to intervene during the winter; and the outcome was commemorated by a medallion of the Emperor as *triumfator gentium barbararum*. Whatever its nature it involved the *arcani*, for that was the occasion upon which Ammianus

[1] Alternatively read as *areani* (Ammianus, xxviii, 3, 8).

[2] *Sic* (Richmond probably meant 296, but there is some question whether the campaign of Constantius was not in reaction to trouble in the period *c.* 296–300).

[3] J.C.M. points out, with reason, that there is no sign of such a route on the ground. For doubts about the dating and alleged purport of the Knag Burn gate see Salway, *Frontier People*, 89, n. 1.

Marcellinus, in a lost book, described the northern frontier arrangements. In 360 the trouble was slighter. Ammianus suggests that the matter was settled by negotiation, following a display of force.[1] But on one occasion or the other, and more probably the first, the outpost forts at High Rochester and Bewcastle were abandoned. Only the fort at Risingham is known to have been still in commission, and it may be surmised that this was retained because it controlled the Redesdale iron-field, while the purpose of the other posts had been strategic only.

The Saxon Shore, as already observed, was a defence area of more modern type than the northern frontier. Many of its forts seem to go back to Carausius and to the Channel patrols which he had commanded and as usurper-Emperor developed. These early forts include Pevensey,[2] and it might be suggested that the Continental *milites Anderetiani* and the *classis Anderetianorum* represented a transference overseas of its earliest garrison of sailors and soldiers used to combined operations, in a reorganization which thus disposed of the disaffected troops of Carausius and Allectus. At that time also the title *litus Saxonicum* was originally applied to both shores of the Channel, then united in single command of which Carausius was not perhaps the last holder.[3] The later organization under a *comes* is reproduced in the *Notitia*, but, as Mr. Stevens has shown, not until many changes in its garrison had taken place: and the final picture does not correspond with the earlier archaeological evidence. The coin-series at Porchester goes down only to A.D. 367, while the *Notitia* garrisons include elements transferred from the *tractus Nervicanus* at this time, when it was abolished. On the other hand, the system of paired forts which the document discloses, might well go back to an original arrangement of coastal patrols. Sea-patrols in particular would need a double base; and, if the units

[1] Ammianus, xx, 1, 2.

[2] B. W. Cunliffe thinks that Pevensey must date from *c.* 340 (see p. 40, n. 3 above).

[3] Eutropius, ix, 21–22 suggests that Carausius' official command was restricted to the Continental shore, and its extension to Britain an act of usurpation.

[88]

originating in *Anderetia* are any guide, the original type of garrison had comprised both soldiers and sailors, taking their name from the fort which they held.

The over-all picture of the British military command is thus one of new-style forts and garrisons on the Saxon Shore and in the Bristol Channel, and perhaps on the Lancashire and Cheshire coast. Outlying fleet stations shield the copper-mines of Anglesey. The Yorkshire area, centred about the modernized headquarters of the *dux Britanniarum* at York, is equipped with large mobile garrisons. But for the rest the arrangements are old-fashioned and carry forward into the new age both units and fortifications which were already obsolete before it began. For this improvization the province was presently to pay a terrible price.

The danger was already evident on the northern frontier in 360, when the Picts and Scots broke their standing agreements and began to raid the territory beyond the *limes*. Four years later it is noted that raids were becoming frequent and vexatious, and the *Attacotti* and Saxons are coupled with the Picts and Scots.[1] In yet another four years the storm broke. All four *gentes* made a concerted attack upon the province, having previously bribed the *arcani* or agents of the northern army intelligence.[2] The Count of the Saxon Shore was killed and the *dux Britanniarum* immobilized. The south was quickly recovered by Count Theodosius and in a year's time the situation was being restored in the north. It is particularly noted that the forts were very badly damaged.[3]

It does not appear that York was taken at this time. Neither town nor fortress show reconstruction of the period and it is very possible that the *dux Britanniarum* had been shut up here, out of touch with the mobile units which he might have rallied. But at Chester the coin-series drops so sharply, as Mr. Stevens has observed, as to suggest that the Twentieth Legion may now have

[1] Ammianus, xxvi, 4, 5.
[2] Ammianus, xxviii, 3, 8, says that these men had betrayed the Romans to the barbarians on several occasions (*aliquotiens*).
[3] Ammianus, xxviii, 3, 2.

disappeared. Thus, though for quite different reasons, neither of the northern legionary fortresses exhibits a restoration by Count Theodosius. But on the Yorkshire coast an immediate provision was a chain of signal-stations. These little works, comprising a high and massive keep-like tower set centrally within a little fort, closely resemble the Alderney signal-station, and are an improvement on those of the Devonshire coast. They are very well built, and an inscription from one of them attests that they were the work of military builders.[1] As for their situation, it is well known that they are perched upon high vantage points along the cliffs from Flamborough northwards, and there is good reason to suppose that north of the Tees the cliffs of the Durham coast were similarly equipped.[2] In a later age the Venerable Bede could describe such towers as '*phari*' or lighthouses,[3] no doubt thinking of them as beacon-posts. They were clearly intended to act as a chain, and their position relates them most naturally to a fleet based upon the main harbours if their signals were intended to invoke rapid action. In the event of a landing, the field forces could be invoked: but the known stations are situated so far inland, at Malton and Piercebridge, that they cannot have represented a first line of defence.

The look-out towers were in fact not the only means of keeping in touch with a raiders' fleet. The curious passage concerning Roman Britain in Vegetius on naval activities is entirely devoted to a description of the scout-ships employed to watch and to report movements of Pictish raiders.[4] They were light twenty-oared craft, of which the hulls, rigging and crew were entirely camouflaged in sea-green colour. The Pictish vessels, *curucae* or coracles, were not themselves large and the fact that the scoutships were intended not to engage the enemy but to observe them, implies that the Pictish habit was to raid in mass,

---

[1] *RIB* 721 (Ravenscar).

[2] No sign of these has yet appeared, either on the ground or from the air.

[3] Bede, *Hist. Eccles.* i, 11: only one *pharus* is mentioned, and it seems to be in the south. As A.L.F. Rivet points out it is more likely to be, say, Dover lighthouse than a Yorkshire signal station.

[4] Vegetius, *De Re Militari*, iv, 37.

swarming', as Gildas later remarks.[1] The business of the Roman scout ships was to keep in touch with their movements and to inform the destroyers.

In the Bristol Channel it is not clear what followed upon the Theodosian reconstruction. The occupation of the fort at Cardiff seems to have come to an end. On the other hand, there is no reason to think that protection was lacking. The wealthy pilgrim shrine at Lydney belongs wholly to this age and its existence assumes a Channel free from raiders. Here the significant point must be that the dedicator of one of the principal pavements in the shrine was a *praefectus reliquationis* or 'chief of a naval repair-yard' and with him is associated an interpreter, presumably used to interrogate Irish captives.[2] An active western fleet was thus still in being.

In North Wales the position seems to have been reversed. A garrison is now thrown into Caernarvon again, from which, according to Welsh legend, was to spring the usurper Magnus Maximus. There is no evidence as to whether the fleet-stations on the Seiont and at Holyhead were still occupied, but if the legion at Chester had disappeared, an extra garrison in the most profitable territory in North Wales would be appropriate enough.

On the Wall, and on the main road from Corbridge to Carlisle behind it, the restoration of Count Theodosius is remarkable. It is clear that it concerned forts only. The very large *vici* or external settlements lay waste and empty, never to be inhabited again. The forts, as to which archaeology strikingly confirms the literary statement on their severely damaged condition, were rebuilt, but with great clumsiness, using large ill-dressed masonry badly coursed and bedded. The contrast with the East-Coast signal-stations is as marked as can be. Inside the forts there is a tight fit, for within the walls now dwell not only the *limitanei*

---

[1] Gildas, *De Excidio*, 19 (i, 15). I owe the reference to S.S.F.

[2] W. H. Bathurst and C. W. King, *Roman Antiquities at Lydney Park, Gloucestershire*, 1879, pl. viii; R. G. Collingwood, in Wheeler, *Lydney Park* (Soc. Ant. Res. Rep., ix), 1932, 102 ff., reads *pr(aepositus) rel(iquationi classis)* – see Wheeler, *op. cit.*, pl. xix, A.

but their families.¹ Thus, in such a fort as Chesterholm the storage-space of the headquarters building is converted into granaries, no doubt in order that the large granaries themselves may be used for extra accommodation. At South Shields the same treatment was accorded to the cross-hall of the headquarters. Something like this seems to have happened also at Corbridge, where it is natural to suppose that the late-Roman defensive wall was now built,² to enclose some 22 acres. What kind of garrison now held the forts is uncertain. It seems clear that they were *limitanei* of the lowest class, whether native Britons, as the tradition of Gildas might induce us to believe, or barbarians from another frontier who were the fourth century equivalent of *numeri*. The practice of such moves was not yet dead. In or soon after A.D. 371, an obstreperous Alamannic king could still be transferred to Britain with a *numerus* and the rank of *tribunus*.³

The protectorate beyond the frontier now became of new importance. There seems no doubt that by this time, and probably now rather than earlier, as Mr. Hunter Blair seems satisfactorily to have shown, the ancestors of the fifth-century British kings of Strathclyde and Manau come into the picture. They bear Roman names;⁴ Clemens and Quintillus for Strathclyde, Tacitus, Paternus and Aeternus for Manau; and Paternus bears the title 'Pesrut' or 'scarlet cloak', which in the Roman world of the fourth century signifies a Roman official⁵ investiture. In other

---

¹ The presence of *limitanei* in the sense of a peasant militia is unproven, nor is it certain that families now lived within the forts: the alterations may have been due to purely military reorganization.

² Some of the modifications to the defences may have been late-Roman, but not their origin (see p. 72, n. 3 above and Salway, *Frontier People*, 56 ff.).

³ Ammianus, xxix, 4, 7: the wording of the text perhaps suggests that the *numerus Alamannorum* was already in Britain. J.C.M. queries rightly the word 'obstreperous' – he was in fact unfortunate rather than awkward.

⁴ J.C.M. points out that adoption of Roman names often an adjunct of the adoption of Christianity in the West and not necessarily of political significance. Indeed finds of dateable Roman material seem to stop abruptly after 367 as if trading had ceased and the lands north of the Wall were now hostile. The idea of a protectorate in this period was based on very flimsy evidence.

⁵ Not necessarily an official investiture (J.C.M.).

words, the frontier kingdoms over against the Picts became *foederati*, with Roman nominees for their kings.

But the presence of *foederati* so far north as Strathclyde and Manau implies that the country between these and the Wall was securely under Roman control, since such kingdoms normally occupy outlands co-terminous with the Roman province. This raises the question so often discussed, as to the whereabouts of *Valentia*.[1] This province was formed in A.D. 369, after its territory had been for a while relinquished to the enemy. In all the discussions of this question, two proposals alone are worth serious consideration, that *Valentia* might be Wales or that it was the country between Hadrian's Wall and the Forth. The suggestion of Wales may now be seen as the more difficult. It is true that the fort at Caernarvon was re-occupied under Valentinian, but this is only the reinforcement of an occupation of a limited area which had not in fact been intermitted. Elsewhere in Wales there is retrogression. Forden Gaer is no longer held and the occupation of the fort at Cardiff, as we have seen, comes to a close. The policy now adopted for Wales does not, in fact, seem to have been the vigorous action which might be expected as a prelude to the new restoration. If, on the other hand, the establishment of the federate kingdoms of Strathclyde and Manau belongs to this period, as Mr. Hunter Blair suggests,[2] this must have been accompanied by a display of force and a new control of the area between them and Hadrian's Wall. That control was not military, since at this very moment the military intelligence service for the area was abolished. Nor is the *consularis* for *Valentia* a military official. It might, therefore, be suggested that this new civil governor had his headquarters behind the shelter of Hadrian's Wall at Corbridge or Carlisle, and that the civil affairs of the district were administered from there. Since *Valentia* would, on this view, comprise principally the *Votadini* and the *Selgovae*, perhaps Corbridge is the more suitable centre and the presence of

[1] Ammianus, xxviii, 3, 7.

[2] *Cf.* P. Hunter Blair, *Roman Britain and Early England, 55 B.C.–A.D. 871*, 1963, 153 f.

an important official at Corbridge in late-Roman times is attested by the famous piece of late fourth-century silver plate known as the *lanx* and the hoard of gold coins of Magnus Maximus.[1]

As to Magnus Maximus, the consequences of his Continental adventure have been shown by Mr. Stevens to be directly traceable in the pages of the *Notitia*. It is certain that they involved stripping away the remaining garrison at Caernarvon and the archaeological evidence strongly suggests[2] that the western garrisons and troops of the Wall disappeared at this time too. In other words about half of the standing army of Britain was borrowed and there is no evidence of a return. The question of what took its place is in reality the question of what was the restoration of Stilicho.

It must first be asked, what was still intact? In the command of the *dux Britanniarum*, the headquarters at York, the eastern Pennine plain from Tyne to Don and the main route across Stainmore to the northwest were still under direct military control. No other moment will suit the archaeological evidence combined with the *Notitia Dignitatum*. It is the only time at which the western forts can be shown to have been evacuated and eastern forts still in commission. It is true that evidence of continuing activity from the eastern area is not as complete as could be wished. But, as it happens, such evidence as exists comes from the fringe of the area, from Corbridge, South Shields, Brough-by-Bainbridge and Malton. On the other hand, it looks as if the Yorkshire coast signal-stations did not survive the reforms of Stilicho. Here is something subtracted; it is not clear that anything was added.

On the Saxon Shore also the position is doubtful. If Mr. Stevens is right[3] and the garrisons from these forts become *comi-*

---

[1] *Valentia*, under its *rector*, is perhaps more likely the northern frontier region, possibly from the Tees to Hadrian's Wall, which must have still contained a substantial civil population even if the *vici* were now abandoned. Carlisle is perhaps the most likely seat of civil government. J.C.M. remarks that the find-spots of the *lanx* and the hoard do not prove anyone special stationed at Corbridge.

[2] No longer necessarily so (J.C.M.).   [3] J.C.M. thinks this unlikely.

tatenses on the Continent early in the fifth century, there seems to have been an intermediate stage, when they were already a field-army in Britain. That would imply new garrisons found for the coastal patrol-work. The question whence these new garrisons were drawn may be answered by the wide distribution of late Romano-British pottery with Saxon decoration in the Saxon Shore area. This pottery, as Dr. Philip Corder has shown, is now dated as early as the period soon after 375 by its discovery in the Roman villa at Great Casterton, and its production in large quantity can only have been intended to supply Saxon customers.[1] The implication is that by the time of Maximus Saxons were already stationed in large numbers in the Saxon Shore area, where garrison duty might well have become one of their tasks. In that case they could have furnished the garrison which was needed, freeing the older garrisons for service as a field-army. The process would be a repetition of what had already taken place on Hadrian's Wall and these irregular formations would find no place in the Roman army list. But there is no clue whether such a change happened before Stilicho's time or not.[2]

On the western front, however, it looks as if Stilicho's work can be traced in a policy of reducing pressure by drawing off the enemy. The *Attacotti*, who had been one of the four principal groups of raiders in 367, were under Honorius supplying contingents to the field-army of the Continent. This implies that Roman diplomacy had by now reached an understanding with these wild people, whom St. Jerome had seen in the 70's in Gaul feeding upon steaks of human flesh. Like many folk beyond the Roman frontiers they had been persuaded to take service with Rome and drafted well away from their own area.

The military situation after Maximus thus remains shadowy. If

[1] A change in style does not necessarily mean a change in market.

[2] Late work on the bathhouse at Bitterne, around A.D. 390, together with a timber building behind the town-wall reminiscent of practice in later-Roman forts, is perhaps a sign of activity by Stilicho in a period when troops were commonly billeted in towns (for Bitterne, see M. A. Cotton and P. W. Gathercole, *Excavations at Clausentum, Southampton, 1951–54*, 1958). There is no evidence for replacement of regular units by irregulars on the Wall.

there were no poetic figure of Britain in the pages of Claudian,[1] it would be hazardous indeed to fix upon Stilicho as a figure who had made any impression upon the situation. The literary creation is, after all, a device for enumerating in picturesque fashion the Western spheres of command of Stilicho in order to say that he had deserved well of them. On this showing, the British statement is so general as to read more like an affirmation of duty than a catalogue of performance. If a panegyric can say no more, one is tempted to think that it is telling the truth.

[1] Claudian, *De Laudibus Stilichonis*, ii, 247–55.

5

BRITANNIA PRIMA AND *BRITANNIA SECUNDA*

The division of Britain into four provinces instead of two was the work of the government of Diocletian; and one of the new units, *Flavia Caesariensis*, owed its name to Flavius Valerius Constantius Caesar who recovered the island, while a second, *Maxima Caesariensis*, was named after his fellow Caesar, Galerius Valerius Maximian. The other pair received no honorary name, being called respectively *Prima* and *Secunda*. If, as Bury thought, the capital towns of the Caesarean provinces took the honorary title of *Caesarea*,[1] then it seems likely that this was the first form of the honorary title of London, which would then become *Augusta* when Constantius was elevated to the senior rank and visited the province for a second time in A.D. 305–6.

The geographical boundaries of the provinces are obscure. A consideration of these may start from the point that when the imposing size of *Corinium Dobunnorum*, the modern Cirencester, is combined with the inscription of the *praeses* of *Britannia Prima* found there,[2] it is natural, as Haverfield thought, to regard it as the capital of that province. But Cirencester would hardly have been selected for the capital of a province extending as far east as Kent, and it may therefore be thought that the southeastern corner of the island was included in *Britannia Secunda*. So a general arrangement begins to emerge.[3] If the southeastern

---

[1] J. B. Bury, *Camb. Hist. J.*, i, 1 ff. London must surely have been the seat of the *vicarius* of the diocese of the Britains.

[2] *RIB* 103: the title is *rector*, as in the case of *Valentia*.

[3] J.C.M. points out that this disregards the basic rule: '*Prima*' provinces were derived from earlier Superiors and '*Secunda*' from Inferiors.

cantons belonged to *Britannia Secunda*, while *Britannia Prima* would embrace those of the west, the canton of the *Belgae*, which extends at least as far west as Bath, must be thought of as going with the southeastern group. But this carries with it geographically the *Durotriges* and the *Dumnonii*. The province of which *Corinium* was the metropolis will thus include the west of *Britannia Superior*, comprising the *Dobunni, Cornovii, Silures* and the rest of the Welsh tribes *in formulam redactae*, to use a contemporary phrase. That will leave for *Flavia Caesariensis*, with its capital at London, at least the *Trinovantes, Catuvellauni* and *Iceni*, with possibly the addition of the *Coritani*, in a redistribution of the older areas. *Maxima Caesariensis*[1] embraces the old province of *Britannia Inferior*, with perhaps the *Coritani* subtracted. A division on these lines is not only tolerably balanced in the matter of size, but it comes very close to the traditional outline in literature recorded by Giraldus Cambrensis from a document seen in Rome,[2] in which *Corinium* was the metropolis of *Britannia Prima*, *Durovernum* that of *Secunda* and London that of *Flavia Caesariensis*. The last-named province is by Giraldus equated with Mercia, though it does not include its north-west territory. But the fact that an analysis of the list of provinces and the archaeological evidence, meagre though it is, leads independently to the same general conclusion as the document of Giraldus tends to enhance the value of both.

Britannia Prima and *Secunda* thus seem to embrace between them Britain south of the Thames and west of the Cherwell basin and middle Trent.[3] In considering this area the principal

---

[1] It is worth noting that, in the *Notitia*, *Maxima Caesariensis* is the only British province formed in the early fourth century governed by a *consularis*, which J.C.M. has pointed out was a Constantinian innovation, usually associated with the capital of the diocese.

[2] Giraldus Cambrensis, *De Invectionibus*, ii, 1 (Rolls Series, Giraldus Cambrensis, iii, p. 45) (J.C.M.). J.C.M. thinks its a forgery, meant to bolster the claims of the see of Canterbury.

[3] For another and radically different view see now *Antiquity*, xxxv, 316 ff.: *Britannia Prima* is seen as Wales and part of the West, *Maxima Caesariensis* as the London area. The two northern provinces, centred on Lincoln and York, are not identified.

body of evidence for the fourth century towns comes from four sites, Wroxeter and Caerwent in the area of *Britannia Prima*, Silchester and Canterbury in the area of *Britannia Secunda*. Wroxeter, *Viroconium Cornoviorum*, is a fine town of 180 acres in extent, which owed its expansion and embellishment to Hadrian in A.D. 129–30.[1] About thirty years later the spacious *forum* and *basilica* and adjacent buildings on the main street were burnt down,[2] apparently on a market-day,[3] though whether this was one of those accidental fires which tended to sweep through Roman towns or whether it was due to a local disturbance at a time when there was much unrest, must remain uncertain. Thereafter the buildings were rebuilt and remained in commission until the end of the third century, when they perished in a final conflagration and were not again restored. The *forum* remained completely derelict and its site was treated as an open space with booths,[4] not unlike the untidy areas appropriated for car-parks or hucksters' stalls in present-day towns after bombing or slum clearance. This present-day analogy is mentioned because it must surely induce a cautious attitude towards interpreting the meaning of this change in relation to contemporary life. The fact that the *forum* was burnt down and not again restored undoubtedly marks a serious crisis in the affairs of the town. Indeed this local disaster coincides so closely with the general trouble of A.D. 296 which involved the destruction of the legionary fortress at Chester, and also lies so obviously in the path of Irish raiders, that it is natural to see here another of the events which shook provincial confidence.

The fourth century thus appears to open with the town in sad decay. Yet at other points within the walls there was activity and enterprise. Across the main street from the *forum* a set of public

[1] Graham Webster writes that Hadrian may have been responsible for the *forum* but there is no evidence that connects anything else with him. J.C.M. points out that the Cornovii will have had to *pay* for the *forum*.

[2] The fire seems to have been confined to the west side of the main street (G.W.).

[3] The shops would surely have kept their stocks full at all times, not just market-day (G.W.).

[4] In fact it looks as if there were permanent domestic buildings on the site (G.W.).

baths remained in service at least until the seventies of the fourth century,[1] though built to a simpler plan than before. A great building resembling a market-hall to north of the baths certainly also continued in use, though its fourth-century levels were so destroyed as to be deprived of architectural significance. The occupation of a substantial house not far from the *forum* lasted until at least the reign of Valentinian and a small building further west was then still in active occupation. The impression thus conveyed is that in the fourth century the buildings in this part of the town were considerably simplified but that a busy trading life went on; as if the town had lost or reduced its civic amenities[2] but retained its importance as a commercial centre. But before the close of the century the community had received a severe shock. The two coin-hoards associated with the Baths, one in purse whose dead owner was found by its side, close with coins of Valens and of Gratian respectively: that is to say, they indicate a disaster in the seventies or eighties.[3] From this disaster there was only a weak recovery. Coins on the edge of the main street, where shops existed, run in a very thin stream down to the time of Arcadius, and a few other coins of the House of Theodosius are now known.[4] The fate of the town would seem to be closely connected with the disappearance of the legion from Chester, where the coin-list runs in strikingly similar proportions.

This state of affairs is in interesting contrast with that at Caerwent. Here the earlier excavations, as at Silchester, came too soon to include detailed stratigraphical observations, but more recent work upon buildings close to the centre of the little town in some degree compensates for the loss. The most interesting and

[1] It now seems doubtful whether the baths were in commission in the fourth century, but evidence from one large house suggests that the larger town houses so prominent a feature of the air photographs may be predominantly fourth century (G.W.).

[2] The significant point is that the patronage necessary for the construction of large public buildings had disappeared – a social change (G.W.).

[3] People seem to have been using the ruins of the Baths for shelter and some may have been killed by a collapse: there is little evidence for a general disaster (G.W.).

[4] The coins are perhaps more than a mere trickle. The real end must have come when the manpower to defend the long circuit of walls failed (G.W.).

important building is the aisled hall, 99 feet long by 49 feet wide, which adjoins but does not directly serve a set of public baths. Both hall and baths were still in use after 395, though the hall had by then been slightly modified by the insertion of offices at one end of the north aisle and by the encroachment of the baths upon the south aisle. But it is fair to say that these buildings were in active use until at least the close of the century. Across the main street and to west of the *forum* and *basilica* buildings fronting the main street were occupied equally late. A sizeable courtyard house was in use until about the middle of the fourth century, and was thereafter equipped with a workshop for iron-smelting, associated with coins that include several of Honorius and Arcadius. It is evident that the function of Caerwent both as a commercial and social centre continued important and lasted undisturbed throughout the century. The sole reflection of external dangers is the equipment of the town-wall (in particular, the southern seaward front) with hollow polygonal bastions in the thirties. Later in the century, apparently in the late fifties or early sixties, when raids were becoming more threatening, the bastions were filled up solid, perhaps in order to avoid the burning or rotting of wooden floors: for the structures appear not to have been roofed but to have been true bastions with an open top on the same level as the rampart-walk.

The case of Silchester is more difficult. It is indeed unfortunate that the earlier excavations were conducted with so little attention to stratification. But there are two categories of evidence which are of real help in estimating the general condition of the town in the fourth century. The valuable analysis of coins by the late Mr. J. W. E. Pearce reveals that fourteen per cent of the total yield of 9,000 falls between 312 and 379, while after that the volume is about halved. These percentages are higher than any others in the history of the town except those covering the period of the third-century inflation. It has also been noted that, as at Cirencester, the unusually worn state of the late issues suggests an occupation prolonged for some time into the fifth century. The second class of evidence is provided by the pottery of the late fourth century, which was first detected in abundance at Silchester. Thus, if nothing can be said about the history of individual sites in the town, it nevertheless emerges clearly that the place was active and busy until and beyond the close of the century.[1]

The full story of late-Roman Canterbury has yet to emerge, but meanwhile some significant points have come to light. It is plain that by the middle of the fourth century many of the earlier buildings were in ruins.[2] This phenomenon has been observed in Burgate Street,[3] in Butchery Lane[4] on an extensive scale, and in Rose Lane.[5] But in the large bath-building in St. George's Street matters were different. In the thirties of the fourth century this building was drastically remodelled[6] and, it would seem, simplified, rather as happened at Wroxeter. The reconstructed building lasted until about A.D. 390 and then fell into ruin. On its floor, however, in association with the late fourth-century coins, were 33 *minimi* and 60 *minimissimi*, emergency issues of the very smallest module. These token pieces have been widely assumed to represent sub-Roman attempts to keep a coinage in being, but it becomes evident that, at Canterbury at least, this class of issue had already been put into circulation well before the close of the fourth century. The same phenomenon is observable at Verulamium in the rubbish deposit of the theatre, and it is perhaps most readily linked with the parsimonious mint policy of Magnus Maximus, which seems to have been of the most opportunist kind, depending upon a confiscation of metal objects for melting down and treatment as bullion. A rather earlier application of the same uttering of local issues is seen at Ham Hill, where the large copper issues of Magnentius were cut up for crude local coins.

The picture afforded by the four towns is thus not at all in-

[1] See now G. C. Boon, *Roman Silchester*, 1957, 78 ff., which supports this conclusion.

[2] S.S.F. writes that 'it is very unsafe to conclude that Canterbury was much in ruins before 400'.

[3] This building had a coin of Valens in the collapse (S.S.F.).

[4] No late deposits survived (S.S.F.).

[5] This reference cannot be traced (S.S.F.).

[6] Alterations c. 355–360; burning soon after this (S.S.F.).

consistent. Civic life at Wroxeter had been shorn of its amenities by disaster at the beginning of the century. But the town baths remained in commission, if in simplified form, and the commerce of the town went on, if in much humbler surroundings. Of the civic buildings in the other three towns nothing useful can be said: unaffected by disaster, they presumably continued to function. But while at Canterbury many of the ordinary buildings were in decay and the state of commercial life is unknown, at the other towns trade plainly remained active and even prosperous.

It is the countryside rather than the towns that reveals the brighter side of southern and western Britain in the fourth century. The numerous smaller country-houses of this period can be seen to exhibit at least three kinds of organization. The first is represented by such houses as Brading, in the Isle of Wight, where a fair-sized and comfortable well-appointed house is accompanied by slaves' quarters in an aisled barn. This plainly represents the slave-run farm, with the master and men concentrated in one set of related buildings, a state of affairs which lasted until the time of Honorius. The second type is marked by such a farm as Llantwit Major, in Glamorganshire, where, as already observed, an establishment very like that of Brading existed during the third century. In the fourth century, however, the seignorial house was deserted and only the slave quarters continued to exist: the master was now an absentee landlord and had presumably left the running of affairs to a *vilicus* and his slave *contubernales*. Thirdly, there is the estate of the type discovered at Ditchley, north-west of Woodstock, in Oxfordshire. Here, after amost a century of desertion, the farmhouse and buildings were again occupied about A.D. 300. But whereas the buildings had previously included barn-like quarters for slaves, these were not rebuilt and their place was in part taken by a substantial granary for the wheat which the estate was producing. The farm-house, on the other hand, was enlarged and embellished, although it still lacked the set of baths which were in the Roman world the indispensable accompaniment of a civilized dwelling. It has

[103]

accordingly been suggested that the social interpretation applicable to this state of affairs may well be that of a bailiff in permanent residence subject to periodical visits by the owner. It is, however, certain that the fourth-century arrangement embodies no slave quarters, although the granary-capacity suggests that the farm comprised about 500 acres of corn-land, apart from other necessary developments, all of which would certainly demand a considerable staff. It is thus to be inferred that the labourers on this farm were *coloni* or tied tenants, whose business it was to supply the estate-owner with labour and often with payment in kind. The dramatic representation of such tenants trooping in to the great house with their fish, fowl and game upon the Igel monument in *Gallia Belgica* is well-known and it is of the highest interest to come to grips with the same system in Britain. That the colonate existed and was related to *decuriones* or members of the cantonal councils is clear from the item in the *Codex Theodosianus* dated to 319:[1] but we owe to Mr. Stevens the suggestion that these *decuriones* were natives, bedevilled by an odd form of tenancy inherent in peregrine law.[2]

At least three types of social structure are thus to be seen flourishing side by side in the Romano-British estates of the fourth century and in two of them absentee or semi-absentee landlords are involved. But there were many estates in which the landlords certainly were not absentees but lived on the spot in large and luxurious houses. Woodchester is one of the most famous and is the more interesting because its farm-buildings are to be recognized, segregated from the great house in a special lower court. These buildings, however, are not in themselves noticeably bigger than those of Brading or Llantwit Major, and the conjunction of so sumptuous a house and such relatively modest farm-buildings seems to imply a home farm of moderate size, allied to other main sources of wealth. In fourth-century Britain it is natural to think of sheep-walks, and Woodchester lies at the foot of an extensive hinterland of downs. There were other estates in which a wing or block of buildings were allotted to

---

[1] *Cod. Theod.*, xi, 7, 2.   [2] *JRS* xxxvii, 132 ff.

the fulling or dyeing of cloth, as at Chedworth,[1] Darenth and Titsey, all in close contact with downlands. Many substantial villas, however, like Witcombe (Gloucestershire), Keynsham, Low Ham and Lufton (all in Somerset) or Bignor (Sussex), Lullingstone (Kent) and North Leigh (Oxfordshire) have yet to reveal their economic associations. Meanwhile, however, the obvious culture of their owners is revealed by the remarkable mosaic pavements associated with most of them.

These late-Roman figured pavements, the equivalent of carpets in stone, are particularly notable for their variety and charm. They are closely connected with classical legend and two at least, at Frampton and Lullingstone, embody in their pattern a verse or a song, the former in solemn heptameters, which have an old connexion with singing, the other an elegiac couplet. Neither of them is a first-class piece of poetry. Both are like the nugatory dinner-table compositions in which Roman cultivated society delighted, and such may have been their origin, for neither is a necessary part of the design of the pavements to which they belong. If this is not fanciful, we can recapture for an instant an evening's entertainment in a Romano-British house, when the company made verse on the subject for a new pavement. The figured scenes of Europa and the Bull at Lullingstone and a head of Neptune at Frampton come from the representational repertoire of the Mediterranean world. More common than these are the great compositions whose subject is Orpheus charming a circle of wild beasts and birds; and their widespread popularity in an age which made of Orpheus an allegory of Christ the Redeemer is a point which deserves consideration, even if a definite answer is not forthcoming. The marine pavements associated with bath-buildings at Witcombe (Gloucester) and at Lufton (Somerset), have an unassumingly simple message, of water and its joys, and once more go straight back to Mediterranean analogies. Less common, but very properly reflection of an aristocratic society are the scenes from the circus, as at Colerne

---

[1] The 'vats' at Chedworth were later demonstrated by I.A.R. to be part of a bath-suite. See also p. 147 below.

(Wiltshire) or the hunt at East Coker (Somerset). Bacchic scenes are uncommon – the vine had no great vogue in Roman Britain – but the lost scene representing a so-called surgical operation from Pitney (Somerset) may well be the birth of Bacchus. Hercules and Antaeus at Bramdean (Wiltshire) or the *amorini*-gladiators at Bignor (Sussex) are part of the more normal repertoire, though the nimbed goddess who overshadows the *amorini* is an enigma. But the most remarkable pavement of all is that of the Vergilian scenes from Low Ham (Somerset), illustrating the story of Dido and Aeneas. This matches the fragments of a Vergilian battle-scene on a wall-painting from Otway (Kent) as a testimony to the close connexion between stock Roman culture and the wealthier classes of Roman Britain. But many pavements contain no scene and exhibit conventional patterns, like a less expensive carpet or rug. The elaboration of these patterns is often so subtle that, like a page of the Lindisfarne Gospels or the Book of Kells, they take now one form and now another as the eye or the light catches them. Their design is an illusory play with form which marks the highest skills in pattern-making all the world over and which is well known to have had an immense vogue in the Celtic world. Without claiming that this kind of art actually influenced post-Roman development, it can nevertheless be seen as part of the cultural preparation for it, in an atmosphere of wealthy and tasteful patronage.

How long did this remarkable manifestation of comfortable and cultured life last? On this point estimates vary, and it may be well to collect from the area now under consideration some specific numismatic evidence from villa sites. It must be premised that there are certain districts where evidence is not forthcoming, for example, Devonshire, Shropshire and the Welsh Marches. Warwickshire and Worcestershire supply only habitation-sites: in the former coins to 383 and 380 are recorded from Stratford-on-Avon and Tiddington; in the latter to the end of the century at Tredington, to Gratian at Droitwich, to Valens at Bredon Hill. But in country houses Somersetshire yields coins of Valens or Valentinian from Keynsham, Lansdown, Combe Down, Wellow,

Somerton, East and West Coker and Yeovil: at Chard coins to 380, at Newton St. Loe coins to Honorius. Gloucester produces coins to Arcadius at Sea Mills, to Honorius at Hucclecote, to at least 390 at Bourton-on-the-Water, and to Gratian at Witcombe. In Oxfordshire there are coins of Arcadius from North Leigh, Ditchley and Callow Hill; of the nineties from Hensington, of up to 383 from Headington Wick, of Valens or Valentinian from Wigginton, Stonesfield, Cuddesdon and Wheatley. Frilford in Berkshire should be added as running to Arcadius and Twyford to Valentinian II. Wiltshire offers coins of Honorius from Preshute, evidence of late occupation at Froxfield, coins of Valens or Valentinian from Silbury, Limpley Stoke, Lyneham and Yatesbury: while coins in its ancient hill-forts run to Honorius at Old Sarum, and Valens at Cold Kitchen Hill. In Hampshire or the Isle of Wight may be noted coins to Arcadius at Micheldever, Honorius at Brading, to 383 at North Warnborough, to 380 at Nursling, to 378 at Castlefield, to Valentinian and Valens at North Waltham and Finkley. But there is a noteworthy stop after 350 at such houses as Clanville, Thruxton, Abbot's Ann, West Dean, Holbury and Carisbrooke. In Surrey there is occupation to the close of the century at Walton-on-the-Hill and to 360 at Cobham. Kent comes into the picture of late occupation with coins to Arcadius at Aylesford, Honorius at Greenwich and Hartlip, to 383 at Darenth, Snodland and Keston; while the newly discovered villa at Lullingstone is as late as any in the area.

This list is not complete. But it suffices to illustrate the important fact that while the economy of the villas may have been shaken in the sixties, it continued in large portion intact for another twenty years and that a by no means negligible part of it was still a going concern as late as the end of the century.

It would be easy to use the evidence of coin-hoards to amplify the picture. For there are two sides to the historical consideration of this class of evidence. It can be used to indicate moments of alarm, political or economic; it can also serve as an indicator of the distribution of wealth in the area which it covers. But in a social study sites are of more significance than isolated hoards

and there is an important class of sites which has a special contribution to make to the general picture. These are the temple-sites,
of which late-Roman Britain possesses one really notable example
and others which are typical rather than exceptional and the more
notable for that.[1]

The most spectacular and remarkable site is Lydney, the pilgrim
shrine almost midway between Gloucester and Caerwent, on the
north shore of the Severn. The sanctuary occupies a bold but not
outstanding hilltop, and in view of the fact that no part of it is
earlier than A.D. 364, its elaboration is remarkable. The temple,
with triple shrine, nave, aisles and side-chapels, like that of Pesch
in the Eifel, owes something, however indirectly, to Oriental or
Christian influence. There is a large and imposing guest-hall for
pilgrims, a dormitory for dream-oracles or cures, a good set of
baths. The tutelary god, *Nodens* or *Nodons*, is at once a sea-god and
a hunter. The frontal of a ritual head-dress shows him riding in
triumph over the sea in a chariot of four horses, just as the white
horses of the Severn bore pass the temple twice a day in irresistible
and stately progress. The wealth and attraction of the shrine is
shown not only by its fine appointments and the high rank of its
benefactors, but by the total of over 8,000 coins which the site
yielded.

But Lydney is not the only late foundation. Maiden Castle,
once the principal *oppidum* of the *Durotriges*, became after 364 a
sacred precinct, whose gods included a strange fertility god, half
triune mother-goddess and half bull, of which the *interpretatio
Romana* emerges in an odd statuette. Here the temple conformed
to normal Celtic pattern, a high square building with surrounding
veranda. Repairs were undertaken, as at Lydney, late in the
century, but there was certainly a crisis soon afterwards, when
someone buried a small but valuable hoard of gold about A.D.
405 and did not return to retrieve it. Apart from new shrines old
ones held their own. Chanctonbury Ring, perched high on the

---

[1] See M.J.T. Lewis, *Temples in Roman Britain*, 1966, 139 ff.: there were in fact
among dated structures four times as many founded in the third century as in the
fourth.

north escarpment of the South Downs, north of Worthing, contains one, if not two, temples, with coins to Valentinian I, and issues of barbarous type. Weycock, midway between Reading and Maidenhead, is a large polygonal temple, again yielding coins of Honorius. Frilford, west of Abingdon, is shown by the character and state of the coins which it yielded to have continued attractive to worshippers well into the fifth century. Pagan's Hill, at Chew Stoke, halfway between Bath and Weston-super-Mare, carries a large polygonal temple associated with late fourth-century pottery. Evidence for late fourth-century occupation is not, however, forthcoming from all such sites; as in some villas an earlier end, about the middle of the century, is suggested at Worth (Kent) and Harlow (Essex),[1] but these sites were much robbed and a *caveat* that the evidence may be incomplete is therefore required.

Closely connected with religious centres were fair-grounds, for the holding of large temporary marts at occasional important seasonal dates. Reference has already been made (p. 87) to the existence of this kind of place as a frontier institution upon Hadrian's Wall, but in civilian districts such fairs must have been more common. In this connnexion the Oxfordshire site of Woodeaton deserves special note.[2] It lies somewhat aside from the main road between Dorchester and Alchester, but close to regions well sprinkled with estates and villages. The area productive of Roman remains is well over fifty acres in extent, but the remains themselves, though including relics from a shrine or shrines, do not exhibit the substantial features of a town, and suggest rather a casual arrangement of less permanent buildings connected with workshops and commerce. The evidence for commerce lies partly in the large number of scattered coins which the site has yielded: over 1,300, exclusive of hoards, are on record and run from the first period of Roman occupation, when there is no doubt that the site had been already long inhabited, to the

---

[1] Recent work at Harlow is reported in *JRS* liii, 138; lv, 214; lvi, 210, but no evidence relating to the end of the site is given there.

[2] Recent finds, including votive letters, are reported in *Oxoniensia*, xxviii, 89.

very end of the fourth century, though the last heavy deposits belong to the seventies. In addition, the area has yielded a quantity of small bronze objects, many in mint condition, suggestive of manufacture or retail. The place was plainly an emporium for the village communities of the lower Cherwell valley, but it never grew into a small town. Perhaps a temple[1] was here the focus of the activity: and the possibility of the headquarters of a temple-estate taking very much this place in the social life of the district cannot be overlooked. Whether the site at Swalcliffe, west of Banbury, which covers much the same area, is of the same order is less certain. Our knowledge of it, as of Woodeaton and so much else in the detailed record of Romano-British antiquities, is due to the indefatigable labours of Miss M. V. Taylor. But at Swalcliffe the systematic gathering and study of coins and small objects has not been undertaken and vitiates any attempt to define the site more closely.

The whole trend of the foregoing evidence is to reveal continuing paganism, increasing in fervour as dangers beset the province. Christianity had not yet made any deep impression upon general religious life: and as to the character of Christianity in the province, little can be added to current views.[2] The church at Silchester remains the sole edifice which can safely and securely be recognized as a Christian church, though an atrium enclosing the laver in front of the narthex must be added as an essential element not recovered by the excavators.[3] The buildings at Caerwent and in the amphitheatre at Caerleon, which have been acceptably identified as church and *martyrium* respectively, belong to sub-Roman times and to early Welsh Christianity rather than that of the Roman province.

[1] For the temple and site see now Lewis, 21 etc. (especially 129, discussing the possibility that there was a border market between the *Dubunni* and *Catuvellauni*).

[2] See now M. W. Barley and R. P. C. Hanson (edd.), *Christianity in Britain, 300–700*, 1968.

[3] Re-excavation by I.A.R. in 1961 revealed that the laver was enclosed by a separate small building (? baptistery) and that the main building was constructed not earlier than *c.* 360. The details revealed in 1961 strongly support the identification as a church (*JRS* lii, 185 f.).

Britannia Prima *and* Britannia Secunda

But in the Canterbury area the late Sir Alfred Clapham considered that there was no reason to doubt the Venerable Bede's specific statement that at St. Martin's outside the walls and at Christ Church Cathedral within them, ruined Romano-British churches existed in 598 and together with other buildings of the same kind were available for restoration.[1] If Canterbury, as Giraldus Cambrensis records, was the capital of *Britannia Secunda*, it might well be expected to have contained at least one church. But the existing buildings, even at St. Martin's, do not embody any such work, closely though they may copy it. There is also evidence from the villas which must be accepted as undeniable proof of the Christianity of their owners.[2] The Frampton mosaic, from Dorsetshire, on which a Christian monogram occupies the most prominent place in the design, cannot be dismissed as a work in which the emblem was slipped in unbeknown to the patron. If it is an original feature, it indicates a Christian owner who did not dissociate himself from pagan decorative patterns or poetry and there were many such even at much later dates. If it is a later insertion, the addition is the more deliberate and significant: it would then match the way in which at Chedworth an ornamental water-basin or *nymphaeum* is specifically exorcized by a cross carved on each of the four corners of its rim. These indubitable examples of Christian action by owners of country estates are more valuable testimony than the table furniture or *objets d'art* because they cannot be explained away as possessions whose owners tolerated but did not deliberately order the Christian symbolism. But equally, there are certain articles of British provincial manufacture which were manifestly intended for a market where Christian allusions were no longer unwelcome. In such a category must be placed the large lead tank or butt from Wiggonholt in Sussex, decorated with the Christian monogram, like that from Icklingham in Suffolk. Again the table-service of pewter, from Appleshaw in Hampshire, like the pewter dish

[1] Clapham (*English Romanesque Architecture before the Conquest,* 1930, 14) thought it unlikely that much of the buildings remained that was usable.

[2] Lullingstone and Hinton St. Mary now have to be added to the list.

from Welney (Norfolk) and the much more elaborate collection of table silver from Mildenhall, Suffolk, indicates a Christian owner, and there is no doubt that pewter vessels are British products. In addition, there is the fourth-century inscription from Cirencester, recording the restoration of a sacred column erected by the 'old religion', which does imply a conscious opposition to existing Christianity on the part of the governor of *Britannia Prima*.[1] The easiest though not the only possible explanation is that this belongs to the period of Julian (A.D. 361–3); if so, it must be regarded as an antidote to Christianity already established within the towns under favour of official recognition. It is not necessary to suppose either that Christian worship had made large strides outside official circles, or that every official had embraced it. But it is interesting to observe that with Christianity came attendant heresies. Gnosticism, the unfruitful compromise between pagan and Christian theology, is represented by the very remarkable mosaic pavement from Brading (Isle of Wight) and by signet-rings from Silchester[2] and Castlesteads on Hadrian's Wall.

In conclusion, something may be said of economics, with particular reference to the specialities of the area with which we are concerned. It is well known that the development of wool production culminated in this century: and it has been shown by Professor Hawkes that certain dykes upon Cranborne Chase, comparable with those at Bitburg in the Eifel, belong to ranch enclosures. The official reflection of this activity is found in the Imperial *gynaecium* or weaving-shed established at *Venta*, by which *Venta Belgarum*, Romano-British Winchester, is undoubtedly meant.[3] But apart from the state-controlled industry it is clear that there was much development of sheepwalks and their products by private enterprise. As there is reason to suspect at Woodchester, this was one of the prime sources of wealth among Romano-British landowners. The island created capital. Early in

---

[1] *RIB* 103. [2] *EE* ix, 1342 (I.A.R.).
[3] W. H. Manning (*Antiquity*, xl, 60 ff.) argues persuasively for considering *Venta Icenorum* (Caistor-by-Norwich) as a possibility.

the fifth century an inscription from the Adriatic coast mentions a Dumnonian[1] lady who was a senator's wife, implying an immense dowry derived from British sources. Overseas capital investors were also attracted. Melania, the pious and wealthy senatorial lady who was a friend and admirer of St. Jerome, had British properties among those which were scattered all over the Roman West. It should be emphasized that in modern terms these rich ladies belong to the millionaire class.

In the mining industry an altogether new interest was being taken in British tin, following the decline of the Spanish tin-mines, about the middle of the third century. In Cornwall good evidence for a new interest in the territory at this moment is afforded by milestones of Gordian (Gwennap),[2] Volusian (Tre-thevey),[3] and Postumus (Breage)[4] and activity on the roads was continued under Constantius (St. Hilary)[5] and Licinius (Tintagel).[6] There is also evidence for the actual mining, associated with coins of the middle and late third century and even with a coin of Valentinian. It seems clear, however, that the workings were not large and it may be supposed that they were let out to small-scale contractors or *conductores*.[7] Support for this view is afforded by the Ravenna list, which mentions in the West Country two *stationes*, one on the river Tamar and the other to east of it.[8] The second is presumably connected with the South Dartmoor tin, where, as Mr. Salzmann has shown, the Golden Dagger and Swincombe deposits were extensively worked in the twelfth century. Such *stationes* were the centres for collection of dues from lessees, and their existence implies that a system of letting was in operation. An interesting effect of the developing exploitation of the tin is the introduction of pewter on a large scale for table services, which in the homes of less wealthy provincials took the place of silver and copied its form. Notable groups or examples

---

[1] *CIL* iii, 9515: see C. E. Stevens, *Trans. Devon Ass.*, lxxxiv, 172 (I owe this reference to S.S.F.). J.C.M. points out that the inscription may read 'Pannonian', an opinion with which J. J. Wilkes concurs, to whom I owe the reference.

[2] *RIB* 2234.   [3] *RIB* 2230.   [4] *RIB* 2232.   [5] *RIB* 2233.

[6] *RIB* 2231.   [7] This was true even in the large Spanish mines.

[8] See *Archaeologia*, xciii, 17.

of such vessels have been found, as at Appleshaw (Hampshire), Manton (Wiltshire), Shapwick (Somerset) in the south[1] and frequently in East Anglia.[2] Small vessels of pure tin are not unknown; they went as far afield as Hadrian's Wall at Carrawburgh and beyond it at High Rochester.

But pewter implies the use of lead in quantity. Here it is necessary to face the curious fact that the most important lead-mining centre in south-west Britain, at Charterhouse-on-Mendip, has produced no evidence of operations much later than the thirties of the fourth century. Since no other source of the metal exists in south Britain, it is impossibly difficult to suppose that the mines were not still kept at work, and it might be suggested that, as in Bosnia, the administration passed to the *curiales* and free miners. In this connexion the occurrence of lead slag in a villa at Whatley (Somerset) might be considered relevant. Even more valuable and important was the silver production, by cupellation from the lead. This was a sphere in which the late-Roman government had a deep interest, as the London ingots show. But the organization and manufacture must come under the same considerations as lead, a field in which the older organization was no longer working. The extraordinary abundance of late fourth-century silver hoards in south-western Britain was long ago observed by Mommsen as a phenomenon both remarkable and peculiar to the province. It cannot, of course, be directly related to silver production, but if the *curiales* or wealthy local *conductores* were in charge of the silver-works, then the profits may well have come back to them in the form of coinage, and the provincial preference for silver as a money of account is a very old Romano-British tradition of which, for example, Carausius took advantage.

Iron production was also widespread. Activity was intense in eastern Glamorganshire in the early part of the century, when streets could be metalled with iron slag in the fort at Cardiff, and

---

[1] And now at Appleford (Berkshire).

[2] The odd situation in East Anglia, far from centres of production, *may* be due to the high density of settlements in the Fens and their comparative poverty. They were unable to afford much silver but were at a level above the native settlements of the north. At an earlier period they had imported much samian.

the smeltery active in Caerwent in the nineties, if not later, has already been noted. The important working centre for the Forest of Dean deposits, at Ross-on-Wye (*Ariconium*), shows very marked prosperity up to the middle of the century and was working until the end of it, though with a heavy decline in the volume of coins. There is no need to stress the activity in the Weald.

The whole picture is an impressive one. The wool and mineral production of the south and south-west could enrich the native capitalists and attract investors in real property from abroad. Despite the shocks of the sixties, the system remained in substantial working order until the end of the century. In the towns the emphasis of life had certainly changed, but administration was not their sole function and commerce still played a part in the life of the community. Knowledge of the landed estates is as yet too fragmentary to piece together the whole story. The absentee landlords may imply either a move back to the towns or fortified townships, or the concentration of wealth in fewer and richer hands. But this is a matter for which the spade, having provided the grounds for posing the question, may in due time furnish a solution.

6

FLAVIA AND *MAXIMA*
CAESARIENSES

In discussing the fourth-century subdivision of the British *dioecesis* or vicariate, the result reached was that *Flavia Caesariensis* is considered to have received the city of London as its capital, while its boundaries are seen to have included at least the cantons of the *Trinovantes*, *Catuvellauni* and *Iceni*, with the possible addition of the *Coritani*. *Maxima Caesariensis*, on the other hand, is seen to embrace the *Brigantes* and the *Parisi*, with the possible subtraction of the *Coritani*. In further comment it may be added that to name *Flavia Caesariensis*, with its metropolis at *Londinium*, after the Caesar Constantius was wholly apposite to the historical situation. Constantius chose the relief of London as the subject for his famous medallion as *redditor lucis aeternae*, while Eumenius laid special stress upon the same theme in his contemporary panegyric, delivered in A.D. 296.[1] The province named after the Caesar Maximian, whose sphere of activity was the East Roman world, was the northern *Maxima*, appropriate but in purely civilian terms less important.

The town of which most is known in the Flavian area is *Verulamium*, the capital of the *Catuvellauni*. This important place, like Wroxeter, had begun to blossom into full civilization under Agricola and had steadily grown over the next fifty years. During the third century the town has been thought to have been in decline, but recent excavations do not corroborate this view. All, however, are agreed that at the beginning of the fourth

---

[1] *Paneg. Constant. Caes.*, 17: the relief does seem surprisingly accidental.

century, in the closest numismatic association with the restoration of 296, there was a thorough-going restoration of the public buildings.

The theatre was rebuilt almost from the foundations and was substantially enlarged by the addition of an outer ring passage and by the contraction of the orchestra. The stage and curtain in front of it were reconstructed, new and enlarged rooms were added in the wings. This rebuilding gave to the theatre its maximum size and elaboration. But tradition was not neglected. A return was made to the use of the orchestra for some kind of display which involved a tethered victim. The orchestra could thus sometimes be used as an arena.

A new triumphal arch, tall and with single passage, linked the theatre architecturally with another elaborately reconstructed building on the opposite side of the main street. This was the second triumphal arch to be erected in *Verulamium* and it breathes the same confidence as the first in the beginning of a new age.[1] The adjacent building was a market hall which now received a massive arcaded front, a vaulted nave and side aisles. Its size, 78 feet square, gives it an area not very different from the Caerwent market hall. The centre and end of the nave were occupied by massive foundations for statues or shrines. The design of the building, in bold vaulting and blind arcading, is strongly reminiscent of the contemporary architecture of the new audience-hall in the Imperial palace at Trier. Gaunt and functional, it no longer hid the structure of the building below an outer casing or decorative façade. The rougher quality of the walls, which would be entirely concealed by their stucco rendering, is no criterion of the general effect.

The market-hall, to judge from associated coins, remained in commission until the eighties. It is significant, and wholly decisive for the date of disuse, that not a single issue of the nineties came from the building. Across the way, the theatre was apparently in service until the sixties. It then began to be put to a

---

[1] Another arch, dated not earlier than 160/190, was excavated in 1961 further north along Watling Street (*Ant. J.*, xlii, 153 ff.).

totally different use. The orchestra was filled to a depth of four feet with rubbish-laden refuse deposits in two main layers, each containing minor ones, which yielded between them over two thousand coins, continuing to Honorius and Arcadius but comprising principally the issues of the House of Valentinian and earlier. The deposit of this money-laden refuse, remarkably free from building rubbish, seems like a continuous act in two phases, of which the second cannot have come into operation before the early nineties. The material, a mixture of vegetable refuse, broken crockery and coins, is such as can have come only from the regular cleansing of a garbage-strewn open market, and the choice of the theatre as the refuse tip indicates that the popularity of the stage had come to an abrupt end about the seventies. Christian divines had for some time been fulminating against the snares and obscenities of Roman theatrical performances. They cannot have failed to represent the disasters of 367–9 as a demonstration of divine wrath. *Verulamium*, one of the principal Christian centres of the province in 426 may very well have renounced, perhaps in spectacular fashion, the heathenry of the theatre. Behind the theatre lay a temple, one of the oldest stone buildings known in *Verulamium*. This too had been drastically reconstructed at the close of the third century, when colonnades were added both inside and outside its precinct wall, while the temple itself received a pair of side rooms. In the eighties the east entrance to the temple precinct behind the theatre was blocked and replaced by a western entrance. The fate of the theatre is thus not unrelated to the continued use of the temple. Had the temple now become a Christian church?

The domestic buildings of *Verulamium* so far explored lie in the south-east quarter of the town.[1] There is good evidence for their restoration under Constantius I, sometimes in quite ambitious style. Among the new buildings was a sausage factory,

---

[1] Excavations in the centre of the town in the fifties and early sixties by S. S. Frere examined a number of domestic buildings showing *e.g.* major domestic building *c.* A.D. 370, occupation into the fifth century and civic activity (a water-main) to the mid fifth century (*see e.g. Ant. J.*, xl, 1 ff., esp. 21; xli, 72 ff., esp. 77).

apparently utilizing horse-meat. But late-Roman levels were almost everywhere absent. Only one house produced evidence of re-occupation as late as the eighties. That this sparse occupation of the area is not chance, but represents something like the true state of affairs is demonstrated by the record of fourth-century coins from the soil covering the area. These are notably few; a bare 200 as compared with 140 from the temple at the theatre and 67 from the small triangular temple. The inference would seem to be that the late-Roman town was contracting towards its north-west end. Here, as the scavenging activities of the nineties show, there must have been abundant life and commercial activity. But it is plain that detailed evidence for the character of this latest social phase will be excessively difficult to come by upon so heavily robbed a site.

Compared with the record from *Verulamium*, the evidence from other towns is scanty. London has as yet yielded virtually no information about its fourth-century archaeological history. The town wall received bastions, in two series. There is a set of hollow drum-towers extending from Ludgate to Bishopsgate and commanding the higher and drier approaches to the city. A second set of solid bastions extends from Bishopsgate to the Tower, covering the wetter and marshier ground. There is little doubt that the latter set are late-Roman in date,[1] though no precise dating is available, but the western group is not quite certainly Roman, though one piece of evidence would support a date of about A.D. 350.[2]

Inside the city the mint established by Carausius continued to produce copper coinage until about 324. It was then closed down and was not revived until the time of Magnus Maximus, when the mint mark bore the fourth-century name of the town, *Augusta*,

[1] See R. Merrifield, *The Roman City of London*, 1965, 70.

[2] A coin of Constans (see Merrifield, *loc. cit.*, for this and for doubts on the Roman date of the hollow bastions). A bastion since discovered (no. 11a: *JRS* lvii, 191) is said to be undoubtedly medieval, and from it similar bastions near the W. gate of the Roman fort (no. 14) and in the Aldersgate re-entrant (no. 15) are argued also medieval. A detailed account is given in W. F. Grimes, *The Excavation of Roman and Medieval London*, 1968, 71 ff.

as in the title of the chief officer of the diocesan treasury recorded by the *Notitia*. But these facts are a poor substitute for structural evidence.

At Caistor-by-Norwich (*Venta Icenorum*) there is evidence that houses erected about the beginning of the third century continued in use until the close of the fourth, both pottery and coins extending to the nineties. A glass-furnace, however, which was active throughout the earlier part of the century seems not to have continued in use beyond the sixties. A largish half-timbered house yielded evidence of habitation until the late nineties or the early fifth century, followed by massacre and conflagration. At Lincoln, evidence for developments inside the walls during the fourth century is lacking. In the Flaxengate area, there were drastic changes of plan, but the remains were too fragmentary to reveal their import.

At York there were important changes in the architecture of the legionary fortress, a magnificent towered front being added on the riverbank, with huge polygonal angle-towers and six close-set bastions. In the *colonia* there were also great changes. The area of the baths was completely re-planned. New bath-buildings were developed to south-west of the demolished monumental building of the third century, which was covered with new structures on the same orientation but at a higher level and of much smaller scale. But the most remarkable relics of fourth-century York are the remains from the cemetery. The very great variety of objects denotes not merely a wealthy population, but indicates some currents of trade. The volume of imported Rhineland glass is large. There is also a large amount, notable in quality as well as quantity, of ornaments made from the jet obtainable from Whitby and known to Solinus,[1] whose information was versified by Priscian and condensed by Isidore of Seville. So much jet is present and so well worked as to raise the question whether the Rhineland jet, which often equals it but never surpasses it in quality or workmanship, is not in fact of British origin and perhaps the product of York workshops, evidence of actual

[1] *Collectanea rerum memorabilium*, 22, 11.

working in York having been found. The highest technical skill is lavished upon the interlocking pliable jewellery for the neck or arm, and upon the charming family-portrait medallions, whose subjects are arranged in fourth-century style.

At Aldborough, the capital of the *Brigantes*, which lies seventeen miles north-west of York, the north-west angle of the town wall was fitted in the early fourth century with a huge external bastion, sixty-five feet wide and obviously imitating the enormous multangular bastions of the fortress at York. Others of smaller size filled other parts of the circuit.[1] Inside the town portions of numerous fourth-century houses have been discovered, but no systematic excavation has been undertaken. The total impression, however, is of a town of considerable prosperity and wealth. One of the most curious manifestations of the social scene is the remarkable series of mosaic pavements. The conventional patterns are bold and many are plainly a local brand of geometric pattern, bolder and more garish than the average, dealing much in long thin lozenges. But far more startling than the patterned pavements are those with figured scenes, which deserve more attention as social phenomena than they have received. The first and most famous is that of the Wolf and Twins, now at Leeds.[2] Under a stark and scantily leaved fig-tree stalks a gaunt grey wolf. She is nothing like the real animal: her hind-quarters resemble those of a horse, her eyes gleam like buttons, here mouth gapes with a broad grin like a Cheshire cat. Her breasts are entirely missing and below their vacant place a pair of elf-like twins seethe in bewilderment. No wilder travesty of the foundation legend of Rome exists, except upon barbarous copies of the well-known coin type. Equally bizarre was a similarly composed panel of a great lion, couched below a tree, to judge from the surviving portion, though the unintentionally comical human element is here lacking. Much more ambitious and unusual was an important pavement which filled an oblong room and an apse beyond it, though unfortunately only the wreck of it survives. One end

---

[1] Recent work on the defences is reported in *JRS* lv, 204; lvi, 200.
[2] See *e.g.* J. M. C. Toynbee, *Art in Roman Britain*, 1962, pl. 220.

was filled with a row of highly schematized busts, most probably the personified days of the week. The other exhibited a row of standing figures in panels. There now exist only two of the figures and the borders of 4½ panels across one half of the apse imply nine in all: but one, holding a scroll, stands next to a rocky mass, labelled in blundered Greek lettering *ΕΛΗΚΩΝ* which is thus revealed as the Boeotian Mount Helicon, and we can be sure that the figures were the Nine Muses, whose abode Helicon was. Fragmentary though the pavement is, it has an indisputable claim to rank among the more remarkable of Romano-British mosaics.

But pride of place is taken by the fourth-century pavement of the same school in the country house at Rudston, near Bridlington. This hardly less ambitious composition has at one end a panel of flowering plants growing from pots, between which is set a crude garlanded bust of Mercury, identifiable through his winged staff. It looks as if the artist had mistaken grape-bunches and the wings of Mercury's hat for flowers. The main composition is a roundel, surrounded by lunettes and quadrants. Each quadrant cages a gaily-plumed bird. Each lunette encloses a wild beast, two specifically labelled as 'the man-killing bull' and 'the speared lion', while each spandrel between them contains a hunter, bearing weapon or snare. The central roundel portrays Venus, or Diana, surprised at the bath. She is furnished with mirror, flower and, rather unexpectedly, back-scratcher, and attended by a triton. The choice of subject is credible enough, though it may be felt that the connexion between the hunters and the central theme is somewhat weak. But the execution is crude to the point of farcicality. The scenes are comparable only with the treatment of some human figures upon Castor ware or the stone relief of Venus at the bath from High Rochester.

This raises the question of the origin of these curious pavements. That the work is in each case native there can be no doubt. But the inspiration is wholly classical. The Lion and the Wolf and Twins are obvious pattern-book pieces, very closely akin to the stone panel of the dog and lion from Caerleon. The Nine Muses, with their Greek inscription, form a late-Roman composition of which the form is matched in such tapestry works as the Cybele and Bacchus panels in the Metropolitan and Hermitage Museums or the *Hestia* panel from Dumbarton Oaks. So the spectacle is presented of Romano-British workmen in the fourth-century north copying expensive contemporary patterns such as would be obtainable in York, and finding their subjects within ambition but beyond capacity. The good fortune which has preserved these pavements gives us a phenomenon in late Romanization un-paralleled in the Roman West. As already hinted, however, manifestations of this kind appear in the military sculpture of Roman Britain. If circles of the same kind took to mosaic work this is precisely the kind of art which they might be expected to produce: vigorous, ambitious and virile, deriving its themes from classical myth and legend, and obviously steeped in the appreciation of both, but toally incapable of endowing them with the grace and beauty native to their southern home.

The smaller centres evince signs of another type of activity. The large towns had by now long ago been fortified, many of them in the third century. In the fourth century this precaution was extended so as to embrace sooner or later all the smaller centres. The process was not new: evidence has already been cited to show that the fortifications at the small roadside post of Great Casterton belong to the early third century. But in other places, the step came later. The little settlements of Ancaster,[1] Caistor and Horncastle in Lincolnshire received fortifications of fourth-century type, with strong masonry wall and solid pro-jecting bastions. Ancaster, where Ermine Street crosses the Slea-ford gap, was certainly a civil site, to judge from the character of the remains which it has yielded. Neither Caistor nor Horncastle occupies positions suitable for a fort, being blind to seaward, the direction from which danger was expected, and both sites have

[1] Excavation in 1963 and 1964 showed that the town-wall and bank was not later than *c.* 275: the outer ditch was probably late second-century and the wall may be contemporary (*JRS* liv, 159; lv, 205). Further work on the defences is described in privately-circulated interim reports for 1965, 1966 and 1967, and in *JRS* lvii, 182.

yielded abundant civilian remains. They therefore seem to bear witness to a consistent policy of fortifying the minor civil centres of Lincolnshire, whether posting-stations, as at Ancaster, or small local market-towns for the people of the Wolds, as at Caistor and Horncastle. Further inland, the fortification of posting-stations probably came later still. *Margidunum* received a defensive wall and new buildings in the late sixties, probably in connexion with the restoration of Count Theodosius.[1] But the design is so unorthodox as to suggest that this was local work uninspired by military architects, the most notable feature being the total absence of bastions.

But not all small centres lasted so late. There is a complete and striking dearth of late fourth-century coins from Brough-on-Humber, where it appears that the site was now virtually deserted.[2] The final fortification, with bastions of fourth-century type, seems to belong to the earlier part of the century and it might well be considered doubtful how far it represents a town. The *Notitia Dignitatum* records that the garrison of Malton consisted of a unit once stationed at *Petuaria* and bearing its name: and it may be wondered whether the original stationing of the garrison marked the end of *Petuaria* as a civil centre and the transfer of tribal government to another spot. Not much is yet known of the township at Norton, across the Derwent from Malton, but its flourishing activity in late-Roman times certainly contrasts abruptly with the scene of decay and desertion at Brough.

Turning now to the countryside, the villas of the two eastern provinces have not yet yielded anything like the amount of evidence that is forthcoming from those in the south and west. But some significant sites must be noted.

There are two houses, situated at widely distant points, where there is detailed evidence for a comparatively early end. At Park Street, south-west of St. Albans, on a fertile terrace of the Ver, a

[1] But see p. 162, n.1 below.
[2] In the 1958 excavations a considerable quantity of later fourth-century pottery was found, especially in the robber trenches for the town wall (*Ant. J.*, xl, 64).

medium-sized house had been substantially enlarged during the fourth century. It was the centre of an estate which produced corn and barley, dried when harvested in a very large corn-drying kiln at the back of the house. Although the house had a heated wing it was in no sense a luxurious dwelling and evidence for elaborate mosaic floors was entirely lacking. The end came in the sixties, certainly not later than A.D. 367, possibly a little earlier. It involved the destruction of the house by fire and its subsequent desertion.

A rather similar story comes from Norton Disney, close to the Fosse Way on the western border of Lincolnshire. Here the third-century barn-like building had been substantially improved in the fourth-century by the addition of a bath-building, attached to the small dwelling-house in such a fashion as to show that the barn-building had become the more important unit. The end came with violence. The establishment was burnt down and eleven skeletons were found on the topmost floor-level, one of them knifed, in association with coins running down to 361.

That the end came elsewhere about this time is suggested by coin-finds from houses at Castledykes, near Ripon, North Newbald (Yorkshire, E. Riding), Apethorpe (Northants), Bartlow (Cambridgeshire) and Hadstock (Essex). It seems equally certain that destruction at this time was not general but sporadic. Not only did many houses continue in existence unscathed, but new ones might even be built. An important and interesting example of new construction is Denton, some seventeen miles due south of Norton Disney, where an aisled barn-like dwelling, comfortably appointed with mosaic floors, was built after 369, as is proved by a coin of Valens underlying one of the pavements. Occupation continued until at least 383. The same state of affairs is revealed at a rather similar building which belongs to the latest phase of the Great Casterton house, where coins from the floor covered by the burnt wreck of the final destruction include a coin of Valens not issued before A.D. 375. This house also is a late one, not built until after 324, and it may be noted that the coins from it include only two before A.D. 340. At Lockleys near Welwyn

(Hertfordshire) a house which had been inhabited since pre-Roman times was burnt down late in the third century or early in the fourth and, after lying derelict, was reconstructed in the thirties. The new building was a slight structure certainly half-timbered and not enough of it remained to denote the architectural type, but it lasted until after 378.

Among the older houses which still continued in occupation the most northerly is at Old Durham, where the bath-house belonging to a farming establishment has yielded pottery later than A.D. 369.[1] At Langton, near Malton (Yorkshire), the modest farm-house had been destroyed in A.D. 367-9, but was thereafter rebuilt and continued in vigorous occupation until 395. At Rudston, on the east fringe of the Wolds and only six miles from the sea, occupation continued until at least the eighties, while at the northern end of the Vale of York the bath-house of a medium-sized establishment at Well was still in use to judge from pottery into the last quarter of the century. The same kind of evidence is forthcoming from Wetherby, above Tadcaster, on the Wharfe. Finally at Nobottle (Northamptonshire) a house in need of further excavation yielded coins running into the nineties.

This interesting and widely distributed evidence of farms occupied till late in the century can be supplemented by coins recorded in older and less precisely observed excavations. At Hovingham, west of Malton (Yorkshire), the coin-list runs to Valens and Theodosius; at Claxby and Ulceby, at the north end of the Lincolnshire Wolds, to Honorius and Theodosius; at Medbourne (Leicestershire) the same; at Market Overton (Rutlandshire) to Honorius; at Cotterstock (Northamptonshire) to Valentinian I; at Comberton (Cambridge) to Gratian; at Ridgewell (Cambridge) to the nineties; at Boxmoor (Hertfordshire) to Arcadius and at Purwell Mill, in the same county, to Valentinian II; at Coddenham (Suffolk) to Valentinian and at Icklingham to Honorius. The list has not the density of that from

---

[1] The reports (*Arch. Ael.*, 4th ser., xxii, 1 ff.; xxix, 203 ff.; xxxi, 216 ff.) show no sign of pottery later than 367.

the south and west, but its distribution is both wide and tolerably even.

Equally consistent is the evidence for late occupation from the countryside at large. At Seamer, west of Scarborough, native huts yielded abundant late fourth-century pottery. At Elmswell, on the Yorkshire Wolds near Driffield, a wide and straggling village settlement, inhabited from the first century A.D., continued to exist with remarkably little change until long after the close of the fourth century. The coins run into the nineties and late fourth-century pottery abounds: but it is succeeded by hybrid British and Saxon pottery and by purely Saxon pieces and a barbarous coin much resembling a *sceatta* in style. Here, it would seem, is a place in which Saxons settled side by side with Britons and presently commingled ways and fashions. Such a discovery prepares us in some degree for the hybrid Britto-Saxon sherd in the house at Great Casterton, which must, however, belong to a much earlier phase of Saxon activity.

In Upper Wharfdale, there is interesting testimony of two kinds. The caves continue to be inhabited during the first half of the fourth century. The stronger and later evidence is for life in the valley-farms: and in the Grassington area these settlements, associated with the extensive field system which fills this part of the dale, yielded surface finds of late fourth-century pottery, showing a peasantry still active in agriculture. But in Skipton, where the Roman road from the Aire Gap forded or bridged the Haw Beck on the way to Aldborough, the inhabitants of the district observed the ancient custom of throwing coins into the stream. A selection of these in the Skipton Museum reveals an interesting point. Bronze coins of Honorius are included in the series, but in a state so worn as to be barely recognizable. In this out-of-the-way corner of the Pennines Romano-British everyday customs plainly continued well into the fifth century.

The less vocal but no less valuable evidence of pottery for habitation of native dwellings down to the close of the fourth century is also forthcoming from Edlington Wood, near Doncaster, where the native villages on the magnesian limestone yield late fourth-century pottery, though their coin-hoards belong to a century earlier. In North Lincolnshire the two native villages at South Ferriby and Winteringham on the Humber attest occupation until the nineties. Beltoft in the Isle of Axholme yields pottery of the late fourth century. Occupation of the Kirmington village in the sea-plain south of Barton runs to Gratian and Valens. Thealby, the ironstone mining village on the Scunthorpe Oolite, and Dragonby, further south, have produced coins to Valentinian II and to Magnus Maximus respectively, while Flixborough, overlooking the Trent, offers late fourth-century pottery. It is evident that here an active life of production continued till the close of the century, and this must have a bearing upon the military protection of the Humber estuary for which there is as yet no late fourth-century evidence.

In the Derbyshire hills the story is not quite the same. Here the cave-sites, which, as at Edlington, have yielded third-century hoards, again produce much pottery of the first half of the fourth century. But the typical wares of the period after 369 are entirely lacking and this is true of forts in the heart and on the fringe of the area, as at *Navio* (Brough-on-Noe) and at Templeborough. It looks as if, after 369, the folk of the Peak were left to themselves and remained cut off from the normal currents of exchange. This is reflected in the evidence from the Derbyshire mining area for fourth-century activity, which, while somewhat tenuous, is not entirely absent for the opening of the century at least. Cowley Crake mine, on Elton Moor near Winster, has produced a coin of Constantine and pins, vaguely suggestive of workers living on the spot, as at Great Orme's Head. In the same district, nearer Bakewell, searchers in lead waste found a hoard of Constantinian coins: and a similar hoard was unearthed at Crich. There is just enough material evidence, therefore, to suggest that the mines were at work during the first half of the century, while the neighbouring forts were still in commission. Objects of the later fourth-century are not forthcoming, though systematic exploration of a lead-working site has never been undertaken.

The corn-growing district of the Fens was also certainly active for most of the fourth century, but not enough is yet known about its ultimate fate.[1] Here the physical changes which have been observed by Professor Swinnerton on the Lincolnshire coast[2] may now have begun to operate, and may well have combined with the climatic deterioration, observed by Professor Van Giffen on the other side of the North Sea,[3] to produce a drowning out of the dyked areas.[4] But as late as the sixties Britain had corn to spare, in spite of the tendency to convert tillage to sheepwalks observable in the southern downlands. The granaries built in Germany by the Emperor Julian, of which the submerged Dutch site of Brittenberg is almost certainly an example, were for customary corn-supplies from Britain, not merely for temporary relief of disaster. This is a fact of prime importance. For the first time since Strabo's day, British corn is definitely described as an article of export across the Channel.[5] It becomes possible to see how the economy of the fourth century provinces was working out. If the two eastern provinces, with cornlands stretching from East Anglia to Yorkshire, could produce enough wheat and to spare, then the southern province of *Britannia Secunda* could the more readily devote itself to wool-production; while the lead and silver production of Derbyshire went on matching that of the Mendip area for the first half of the century at least, there being no evidence as to what happened later.

This difference in economic emphasis reflects itself substantially in the character of later Roman civilization in the two areas. It

[1] The pottery goes down as late as Roman pottery anywhere else in Britain and the same is true of the coins. But there is no more evidence of production of a corn-surplus for the fourth century than for earlier periods. The chief difference – in the seaward Silt Fens – was a tendency towards fewer and larger settlements.

[2] *Lincs. Nat. Union Trans.*, ix, 100; xiii, 239 f.

[3] For a modern survey of work on sea level see S. Jelgersma, *Holocene Sea Level Changes in the Netherlands*, 1961.

[4] There is still no evidence for sea-banks in the Wash region.

[5] As R. G. Collingwood (*Roman Britain and the English Settlements*, 1937, 243) pointed out this was an *annona*, or a forced levy, not commerce. Nothing was probably received in return and no benefit gained for Britain. See Zosimus, iii, 5; Ammianus Marcellinus, xviii, 2, 3; Eunapius, 15. Ammianus emphasises that the supply of grain from Britain was regular, and it may be assumed to have been part of normal taxation.

cannot be an accident that in the south and south-west the relative density of discovery of villas is much greater and that the country-houses themselves are, generally speaking, much richer and larger in one area than the other. As in medieval England, the wool-trade was surely the factor that made the difference. But if this was so, and wool was so profitable an investment, why did the development and its results not spread to East Anglia and on to the Yorkshire and Lincolnshire Wolds where it so impressively benefited the medieval world a millenium later? It would seem that the answer to this question is to be found in the fact that the British *annona* was in the fourth century expected to supply not merely the army of Britain but the Lower Rhineland as well. In this government-planned economy, wherein taxation was ever more closely related to raw commodities, it must have been necessary to relate production to a budget of requirements and to concentrate corn-growing in the districts suited for it. The establishment of fixed quotas of production of given commodities for different regions would automatically influence the economic activity of the district concerned. If the quota for one type of commodity were set at a high figure a switch to another kind of production would be impossible no matter how intrinsically profitable such a change might be. This is, moreover, exactly the position which must have been reached in relation to British corn production if the diocese was now expected to meet official requirements not only for its own area but for others: and the smaller margin of profit in corn as against wool reflects itself in the degree of civilization of the eastern and northern provinces which we have been studying both in quality and in density of distribution. Where there are pockets at a higher level, special local resources may be suspected to be affecting the picture.

Two pockets of this kind may be noted. In North Lincolnshire, there is a small group of rich country-houses set on the edge of the Scunthorpe Oolitic and Chalk ridges of the Wolds. The former are closely related to the ironstone deposits which are now shown by much evidence to have been **worked extensively** throughout the fourth century. Evidence for occupation of the great houses after the sixties is not forthcoming but it must be emphasized that the record from them is not from excavation but rather from casual finds,[1] and that systematic examination might well alter the picture. That the native villages in the neighbourhood were occupied until at least the nineties there is no doubt. The western group of richer houses, as Mr. Dudley has suggested, might thus be connected with the ironstone deposits and their *coloni* working them.[2] The eastern example at Horkstow, with its fine chariot-racing mosaic and the rich horse-pastures of the Ancholme at its doors, may not inappropriately be linked with horsebreeding.

The development in the Brigantian town of Aldborough is less easy to diagnose. Here was concentrated the administration of the canton and it is conceivable that in a canton where there was less land favourable to large estates in proportion to its area than in others, the tribal aristocracy may have concentrated in the capital rather than elsewhere. Such a movement might in itself suffice to account for the interesting group of late-Roman pavements already discussed. But if local factors of supplementary enrichment are to be considered there are three possibilities. The Pennine hinterland with its prosperous and active village-life may have been specifically related to old aristocratic family properties: for the client relationship of Celtic tribal society is surely likely to have lasted here as long as anywhere. The lead mines of Nidderdale and perhaps Swaledale were still in production, for lead spindle-whorls and other objects abound in the peasant villages. Lead concessions may therefore have had a contribution of wealth to make. Lastly, the York cemetery so abounds in linen shrouds, which have left their impress in the

---

[1] Winterton has now been excavated, but the published reports (*Ant. J.*, xlvi, 72 ff.; *JRS* lvi, 202; etc.) do not suggest how long it continued in occupation. I. M. Stead however writes that the coin list indicates occupation at least till 394–5.

[2] For Roman smelting sites see H. E. Dudley, *Early Days in North-West Lincolnshire*, 1949, 194 f. J.C.M. points out that the *coloni* were *farmers*, not industrial workers.

gypsum-filled coffins or sarcophagi, as to attest an area of linen production. Flax growing is well suited to the Vale of York, where the low-lying land well watered by streams will have also favoured not only the crop, but the processes of soaking and scutching.

With these remarks our survey of third- and fourth-century Britain may be concluded. It is well to end upon a note of uncertainty, directing attention to the many problems that call for solution. But there is also much gain. Two generations ago, when the same subject was treated in these lectures by Professor Haverfield, the chronological subdivision now made between late-Roman and early-Roman developments would have been impossible. Only the advancing tide of archaeological progress has made it possible now: and the advance is a reality, however numerous the gaps and however great the need for further knowledge. For this we have to thank, and particularly so in Oxford, the tradition which Haverfield founded, the critical judgment which he brought to the task and the power possessed by his thought and writings to inspire later workers.

II

THE J. H. GRAY LECTURES
(1952)

THE ROMANO-BRITISH
COUNTRYSIDE

I

THE COUNTRY ESTATES

The earliest known examples of Roman villas in Britain are those at Lockleys near Welwyn and Park Street near St. Albans, in the territory of the allied tribe of the *Catuvellauni*. Both are known to stand upon the remains of earlier native buildings, at Lockleys round in plan, at Park Street rectangular; both have remarkably similar plans and both, finally, belong to about the same date, the later years of Nero.

The plan of the two houses is so simple as to have attracted little attention. Both buildings were half-timbered erections standing as do many prefabricated houses, upon low stone walls, and they comprise a row of four rooms, one being subdivided, and all presumably furnished with interconnecting doors now vanished. Their plan is thus not at all unlike that of the Pembrokeshire farm-house of Garn, Llanychaer, dated to the seventeenth century, recently discussed by Sir Cyril Fox.[1] Not that such a comparison can suggest the remotest actual connexion between them, but it can and does illustrate the point that similar needs in different ages may produce similar effects. When the simple farming folk of Jacobean West Wales or of the Neronian *Catuvellauni* wanted a modest building capable of meeting their elementary notions of convenience and comfort, this was the type of house which they chose to build: and, simple though it was, this Romano-British house represented quite literally a world of difference between itself and its purely British forerunners in solidity, amenity and finish. The Pembrokeshire

[1] In *Aspects of Archaeology in Britain and Beyond: essays presented to O. G. S. Crawford*, 1951, 125 ff. and especially fig. 29.

analogy may, however, render the valuable service of checking any tendency to over-elaboration of the contrast. It illustrates the important point that there is no necessity to erect upon such a ground-plan a two-storeyed house. Upper floors, if they existed at all, need not have been more than lofts.

Lockleys and Park Street thus represent a phase enucleated in few other provinces of the Roman Empire, namely, the architectural form representing the earliest conversion of native farmers to Roman provincials. That these houses were in fact farm-houses, the dwellings of owners of agricultural estates, is abundantly clear from the later history of Park Street villa, so ably disentangled by its excavator. As soon as the establishment grew, its intimate connexion with farming became manifest in all phases. If further and more formal proof were wanted it is usefully provided by an air-photograph of Little Milton, in southeast Oxfordshire, showing a very similar house, with outbuilding, set in the midst of its rectangular paddocks and fields. The only significant difference is that this Oxfordshire house has acquired a front corridor.

An important stage in development next apparent is one by which the amenity of the building is greatly increased. A house with the first feelings after elegance is seen at the well-known Roman farm at Ditchley, where a slightly larger house, of similar plan to Lockleys and Park Street, has been furnished with a large projecting room at each end of the front. The introduction of these large isolated rooms seems plainly to connote a desire upon the part of the owner for greater personal privacy and for social life not shared by the entire household. In other words, the household is in process of transformation into a graded society as opposed to a purely family concern between blood relations. This is one of the differences between Celtic and Roman society,[1] and its reflection in the house-plan is a sure indication of the advancing tide of Romanization.

The type of villa thus developed at Ditchley is one which

[1] In view of the slave-chain from pre-Roman Park Street (H.M.S.O., *War and Archaeology in Britain*, 1949, 22) this statement is perhaps questionable.

belongs to the common heritage of Western Europe. It is much in favour in the Rhineland and in the Danube provinces, where it was studied by Swoboda, who first defined it as a type, naming it the *Eckrisaliten-villa*.[1] But it is in Britain that its evolution, out of the simpler farm-house, is recognizable; and this can be said without any suggestion that Britain was the original scene of such a genesis. Indeed it need hardly be doubted, in view of the history of such German villas as Mayen,[2] that the development was proceeding upon parallel lines in the other northwestern provinces of the Empire. In Britain, however, the distribution of these houses is widespread, ranging from Glamorganshire and Cornwall to the Isle of Wight, the middle Thames, Norfolk, Nottinghamshire and Staffordshire. Further, it is in several cases possible to review the kind of farm-buildings that are associated with such houses and to show that the house in is fact a farm-house or *villa* in true sense, the dwelling of the owner or administrator of a farm.

The first example may be Ditchley itself, now to be considered as a whole.[3] Here a Flavian timber house of rectangular plan was succeeded by a stone dwelling house of the early second century which stands inside a (rectangular) walled and ditched enclosure, containing a well, a threshing-floor and at one end a large building, 70 feet wide and 280 feet long. This wide barn, of which the eastern half at least had been inhabited, must have been divided into nave and aisles by posts, and plainly formed the working quarters of the farm, which has evidently been approached by an open passage through it. In the fourth century, after about a hundred years of disuse, the dwelling-house was restored without the working quarters, which were replaced by a substantial granary, 36 feet square, capable of containing, it is calculated, the produce of a thousand-acre farm. On the presumption that

---

[1] The reference is perhaps to K. Swoboda, *Römische und Romanische Paläste*, 2nd ed., 1924: I owe this reference to D. J. Smith.

[2] See *e.g.* O. Brogan, *Roman Gaul*, 1953, 122, fig. 20.

[3] *Oxoniensia*, i, 24 ff.: see also A. L. F. Rivet, *Town and Country in Roman Britain*, 1958, frontispiece.

the estate had always been the same size but was now worked by
tenants or *coloni*, it is instructive to reflect that this size of estate
goes with this relatively unostentatious establishment.

Two more northerly examples may now be taken, the first
being Mansfield Woodhouse,[1] on the limestone ridge between
the Idle and the Don basins. Again the house starts as a timber
building of the Flavian age, replaced in the second century by a
house exactly resembling Park Street and Lockleys. In the third
century this house was converted to a dwelling of the Ditchley
pattern, with the difference that there is a front corridor or veranda
running between the two wings, and a large room, 24 feet
square, attached by a vestibule to one wing. This last feature is
reminiscent of the billiard room so often added to the small
country-house of a well-to-do owner in the nineteenth century:
and without going beyond the evidence of the plan, it might be
guessed that here also it was added for comfort or recreation.
The area in front of the main house is flanked by a considerably
large barn-dwelling, of which the ends and large portions of the
sides have been divided off into long and narrow rooms fitted into
the original aisles. One set of rooms certainly forms a cramped
and uninviting bathing-suite, which a wealthy man would
certainly view much as Seneca viewed the baths of Scipio's
villa at *Liternum*.[2] The other set reads like quarters for bailiff
and slaves. It is difficult to see, however, how the rest of the
internal space could be given up to anything but human uses or
habitation. There is no place in the internal disposition of the plan
for animals: only the three isolated rooms at one end of the building would hold them. Here, then, is a small farm with comfortable
owner's house, and a barn-dwelling for the working-staff, their
vehicles, agricultural implements and draught-animals, whether
horses or oxen. Less systematic though the planning is, the size
compares not ill with Ditchley, and might fit a comparable estate.

[1] V. E. Nash-Williams' illustration *Arch. Camb.*, cii, pt. 2, 131, fig. 16, gives a
useful set of villa plans and includes Mansfield Woodhouse.

[2] Seneca, *Epist. Moral.*, lxxxvi, 4: *balneolum angustum, tenebricosum ex consuetu-
dine antipua.*

The second north Midlands villa is Norton Disney. A little stone house with front corridor and one wing-room only (after the fashion of the later Lockleys) replaced a timber dwelling at the close of the second century, and was associated with a large barn-dwelling. In the early third century both buildings were rebuilt after a fire and a threshing-floor was introduced in the space between them. There is no need to stress the essential resemblance between this establishment and the other developed examples already described.

A less purely utilitarian aspect of life is reflected at the well-known site at Brading, in the Isle of Wight, where a small house of the Ditchley type was developed for a well-to-do owner, whose individuality is reflected in his choice of mosaic floors. These comprise a remarkable series connected with Gnosticism and including Abraxas in his holy place, Thales the wise and the legend of Triptolemus. A further stage in Romanization is marked by attaching to the back of the house a large dining-room, with a pair of smaller rooms on each side. This compact and comfortable dwelling stands at the back of a walled court, embellished by a fountain or shrine and flanked by two large barn-like buildings. One of these has the open plan of a Dutch barn; the other is a triply-divided barn-dwelling of the type now becoming familiar, and its upper end has been partitioned off into separate rooms which still clearly convey the distinction between nave and aisles. This pleasant combination of buildings has an air of somewhat greater wealth than is apparent in any of the examples so far considered. The farm buildings are more extensive and the house is both more comfortable and more refined in its appointments. But the house was never divorced from the economic activities of the estate. Late in its history, a corn-drying kiln, interpreted by the excavators as a subway, was inserted into the front corridor or veranda.

The last establishment in the series under consideration is in striking contrast to the rest and much more grossly utilitarian. This is the estate of Hambleden, in south-west Buckinghamshire. The main house is a little larger than any so far considered, though clearly related to earlier examples. The increased size is largely due to a duplication of veranda and wing-rooms, which appear both at the front and back of the house, as in some *villae* of the *agri decumates* in Roman Germany. The effect, however, of the arrangement in relation to the rest of the Hambleden establishment is as if the house had turned its back upon the walled courtyard over which it presides. This is not surprising, for the courtyard, though representing in fact a systematization of an earlier and more scattered arrangement, must have presented a sufficiently sordid scene. It is flanked by barns and a silo, but its whole area was packed with wooden buildings, containing numerous corn-drying kilns and many hand-driven flour-mills, disposed with little trace of order or arrangement. It seems clear that the operatives engaged in the work were slaves, including many of the females to whom such work fell, for infant-burials in large numbers were a feature of the area. If, then, the house accommodated either an owner-manager, or an Imperial *procurator*, or the bailiff of an absentee landlord – to take the appropriate possibilities – these functionaries will hardly have wished to contemplate the activities over which it was their will or their lot to preside. Thus, although the scale of Hambleden comes tolerably close to that of Brading, the establishment presents a very different picture. It was plainly a centre where corn was collected for drying from an extensive estate, and, while stored and ground for current use on the spot, was in major part evidently retailed, since there are no granaries, as at Ditchley, in which to store grain in bulk. The fiscal policy of the third century onwards will suggest that Hambleden was a government establishment for bulk collection and distribution of the *annona*, whose operatives were used for production only, regardless of amenity or humanity, even as then understood. Its entirely exceptional nature can be appreciated by a comparison with other estates.

Out of the examples of *villae* so far considered there thus begins to emerge a type of smaller Romano-British estate. Its principal buildings comprise an owner's house and a barn which was partly a dwelling for slaves, partly a shed for implements and tools and sometimes no doubt a stable or byre for stock as well. The distinctive feature of the agricultural concern is indeed often the barn-dwelling, and this is frequently recognizable as the common factor which links the type of establishment so far discussed with examples which bespeak a lower or a higher scale.

That a barn-dwelling could continue to subsist as the sole element upon an estate is well shown by the later history of the villa at Llantwit Major. This Glamorganshire farm began its existence in the second century as a larger establishment than any of those so far considered, in which an owner's house, evolved from the Park Street type, included from the first not only a set of baths and an entire extra wing, but also a barn-dwelling and four sets of sheds, stables or byres. But at the close of the third century the main house was burnt and deserted, while the barn-dwelling continued to exist for another century as the working quarters of the estate. This building thus emerges as the essential heart and core of the villa as a working concern, demonstrably intended to accommodate the farm-servants now managed by a bailiff. The land-owner has gone elsewhere, either to another estate or to the safety of a walled town. It so becomes clear that (in the economic scale) the villa worked by slaves or servants only might very well comprise solely a barn-dwelling without an owner's house. As has recently been pointed out by Professor Hawkes,[1] an establishment of exactly this kind existed in the third century at Iwerne, Dorset, which was succeeded in the fourth century by a farm like a medieval long house, in which three rooms and an attached grain-store or silo formed the living quarters, the third room being actually half byre or stable, with the appropriate drain occupying its long axis. This is plainly something very close to what would have been called in medieval times a grange. A more sophisticated establishment of the same kind is at Clanville, near Weyhill, where walled stock-yards or the like, bordered by outbuildings, are associated with a good example of the developed barn-dwelling. The ends of nave and aisles are partitioned off into rooms, but the original system of

[1] In *Arch. J.*, civ, 27 ff.

posts is still sufficiently preserved to denote the architectural character of the building. Whereas, too, the average villa is without significant written records, Clanville has furnished an interesting inscription, a dedication to the Caesar Carinus of A.D. 282–3.[1] This is so rare and out of the ordinary as to suggest that the place may have been a Government establishment, and the dedication part of a series forming its official decoration.

North Warnborough is another Hampshire villa of substantially the same kind as Clanville, but it is better planned. An attempt has been made to tack wing-rooms on to the end of the barn-dwelling and these are attached to a comfortable self-contained bath-house. The working-quarters have in fact come to be combined with an owner's dwelling, and in terms of Roman society one is tempted to think of a *vilicus* who became a *libertus* and bought his way into ownership and land-owing society.

We may now turn to consider the higher end of the scale. No known villa in Britain is larger or more sumptuous than Woodchester,[2] with its great dining-room and its comfortable heated wings, symmetrically disposed about a large garden-court. Yet imposing though the outer court is, with monumental triple gateway, the buildings flanking it are both of the barn-dwelling type. It is of the greatest evidential value that these workaday buildings should be associated with so princely an establishment, since they declare plainly that not even the largest of country-houses is divorced from the workaday life of an estate. In this respect the large Romano-British villa is the counterpart of the rich and productive estates in Roman Africa. For Woodchester is not isolated. The same conditions obtain at Bignor, where the great house is again equipped with an outer court containing a large barn-dwelling and out-buildings. Even North Leigh, which until recently had seemed a singularly self-contained luxurious country-house, is now shown by air-photography to lie alongside the yards and buildings of an extensive farm. It is interesting also

[1] *RIB* 98.
[2] Except now Fishbourne, which is unlikely to have been a purely private establishment.

here to observe how the prosperity and size of the house increased, after a comparatively modest start in the second century.

To the large villas a return will presently be made. Meanwhile, it is important to realize that there were farms much lower in the scale of Romanization than this. The villas at Park Street and Lockleys, which served as a start for this study, themselves grew out of primitive British farms, of which the form derives from the sordid and insanitary homesteads of pre-Roman days. Little Woodbury is a well-known pre-Roman example of the type:[1] the first habitation at Iwerne was of the same kind, but continued in existence until the close of the second century. Archaeologically the distinctive feature of such sites is the quantity of storage-pits and corn-drying kilns, insubstantial and relatively ephemeral structures in themselves, which over a long occupation are used several times, disused and then replaced by new ones. When this process is repeated over the centuries the result is a site honey-combed with pits and drainage-ditches, which give the illusion of a large and crowded community – that is, a village – rather than a small community active for generations. It is thus essential to recognize that many of the sites hitherto classified as villages are in fact farmsteads whose remains represent the sum total of all activity capable of leaving an archaeological trace that has ever been carried out on the site. Such, for example, as Professor Hawkes has demonstrated,[2] are Woodcuts and Rotherley in Cranborne Chase, Wiltshire, and as such may be recognized the scores of so-called village-settlements in the Winchester area, in the Thames Basin, in the Fens,[3] the Yorkshire Dales or the Westmorland fells. It is, indeed, clear that for one villa of Romanized type there are very large numbers of such native farmsteads,

[1] See J. G. D. Clark, *Prehistoric England*, 1945, pl. 24, for an excellent air photograph.

[2] See above, p. 144, n. 1.

[3] Excavation at Hockwold-cum-Wilton in 1961–2 showed that at least some of the Fenland sites could be villages, not single farms, since the whole site seems to have been occupied at the same time (*Proc. Camb. Ant. Soc.*, lx, 56). It looks probable that in the particular case of Hockwold the village was attached to a villa, and there is at least one other probable example of the same phenomenon nearby.

and it would be rash indeed at this stage of knowledge to hazard a figure of proportion. The cleavage between the two is on the whole not a social distinction between farmers who owned *villae* and villagers who lived in native fashion: it is rather an an economic distinction between those who could or would afford to Romanize their establishments and those whose farms were too small or too profitless to warrant such expenditure. The result is thus a state of affairs not at all unlike the picture in lands where smallholdings in a field-pattern of Celtic type have survived today. The well-to-do farms and the larger estates exist, but they are islands in a countryside of older pattern.

This, it may be prophesied with some confidence, is the picture which air-photography will in due time afford. At present, however, its results have tended to illustrate one side of the picture only. They have not yet included a large villa with its contiguous estate. But such hints as exist point in the expected direction. At Little Milton in south-east Oxfordshire a large and strictly rectangular field-system is related to the Romanized house and it is interesting to observe that both the new house and the new field-boundaries overlie remains of an older, less regular system of much smaller fields. So also at Ditchley,[1] where new rectangular enclosures, contemporary with the Roman house and its compound, overlie a smaller and non-rectangular field pattern. Again, at Northfield Farm, Berkshire, the regular fields or paddocks associated with a Roman house overlie the huts, pits and garths of an older steading.[2] If these changes had not taken place, the older remains would have continued to fit well enough into the general picture of the Romano-British countryside. It is this general pattern that is so very well attested in so many areas by air-photography. A Cambridge audience does not need to be reminded of Fenland discoveries, but Crawford's map of the Winchester area,[3] published in 1924, is now so old as to be worth

[1] *Oxoniensia*, i, pl. iii.
[2] *Oxoniensia*, v, fig. 10: the chronology and exact significance of the crop-marks may emerge from fresh excavation in the near future.
[3] *Geog. J.*, May 1923, following p. 366.

recalling and comparing with such areas as Grassington (York-shire) or Combe Down (Somersetshire) or Fyfield. It is a land of little fields, long and winding lanes and small primitive farms, matched in remoter Wales or western Ireland where the Celtic world which gave it birth still survives.

In relation, then, to the tribal society of Roman Britain the state of affairs which we have been tracing has significant impli-cations. It becomes evident that within the tribes all who could afford to do so set out Romanizing their houses and estates. It was to these wealthier landowners that such a campaign of Romanization as is described in the *Agricola* was directed. Not a few of the items, *domus, balineae, conviviorum elegantia,*[1] belong just as much to the country as to the town. The simplicity which can be seen to mark some of the early examples of such action, however, indicates that the desire for the new civilization was not confined to the wealthiest members of the tribe, but spread some way below, well down into the middle stratum of wealth. This is important in relation to the '*segnitia*'[2] or 'lazy reluctance' to take the step, which Tacitus also notes, because it suggests that in the long run this was an attitude which did not subsist. But, secondly, it is beyond doubt that the cultural transformation on the lower limit of architectural achievement was not high in the Roman scale, though a very great improvement upon native standards. It is difficult to suppose that Roman culture meant much to the family crowded into the Park Street or Lockleys *villae*, though Roman comfort plainly meant a great deal. And it must not be forgotten that at the lower stage still, where building *more Romano* is absent, steadings like Woodcuts and Rotherley produce abundant wall-plaster, indicating the penetra-tion of the material comfort which it represents much lower down the scale than the more expensive carpentry and masons' work. This does not at all imply dislike of Romanization, as has sometimes been suggested; but there can be no doubt that it denotes sheer economic inability to go far along the path.

[1] Tacitus, *Agr.*, 21.

[2] Tacitus, *Agr.*, 21: *laudando promptos, castigando segnis.*

Another economic factor in this general picture of a land of small-holders is the inability, well known in the ancient world, of such a class to withstand the buffets of fortune and to remain completely independent. In relation to the richer land-owners such farmers will generally have tended to become tenants. Indeed, when it is recalled that the Celtic tribe was normally permitted to fit its social customs intact into the framework of the Roman provincial *civitas*, it becomes manifest that many of the small farmers must already have been *clientes* and related as vassals or tenants to the aristocracy of the tribe. This will imply that, while most *villae* had their own estates, many will in addition have drawn dues in money, in services or in payment in kind from a wider area. At the worst, small-holders will have tended to disappear, in the ineluctable process of bad fortune familiar to all students of Greek or Roman agrarian history.

The last process, or something uncommonly like it, has left its traces in certain parts of Britain. On the Berkshire and Wiltshire downs the characteristic later-Roman development is the construction of stock-enclosures for cattle or sheep. These are usually large and normally situated so as to enclose a spring for watering the stock, and sometimes, as at Lowbury Hill, Berkshire, they enclose also shielings for the stockmen. But in two instances at least, Soldiers' Ring and Knighton Hill, which lie in the great triangle of downland between the Ebble and the Wiltshire Avon, the systematic lines of the enclosures cut across earlier field-systems which they have obliterated. This state of affairs represents the substitution of cattle-ranches or sheep-farms for agriculture and it must have been accompanied, as in more modern days in the Cheviots or the Highlands, by the removal of small-holders. As Professor Hawkes has observed,[1] the boundary-work known as Bokerly Dyke seems to be the westward boundary of this great ranch, which is presumably Imperial domainland. But elsewhere, as at Lowbury Hill, where a cattle ranch is specifically indicated, private ownership must be taken into account and in such cases it will have been the fate of the small man to suffer. In

[1] See p. 141, n. 1 above.

this connexion the situation of Woodchester will be recalled. It lies in a rich valley-bottom, but behind it and in front of it rise fertile and famous sheep-downs. The farm-buildings at Woodchester are indeed of some size but they are not of consonant size with this huge villa:[1] those at Brading, for example, are as large. A second source of wealth is therefore to be sought and it is natural to find it in sheep-farming and the wool-sales or cloth manufacture which were its product. Closely akin to the source of extra prosperity inferred for Woodchester is the Chedworth fullery first identified by the late George Fox.[2] This is a late development in the life of that villa, which appears to destroy some of the pleasantest and most ambitiously planned south-facing rooms; and the impression conveyed is of an attractive country-house converted into an estate factory. Iron-working on an impressively large scale was in progress there, as well as the fulling. If this view is correct, it will recall another tendency among wealthy families, ancient or modern, namely, the tendency to die out in the male line, with a consequent concentration of wealth in the hands of heiresses. When estates were by such conditions united, a family seat might well be converted to new uses. Of the two other *villae*, at Titsey and Darenth, associated by George Fox with Chedworth and by him supposed to have been similarly used, it will suffice to say that the resemblances are not convincing and that the heating arrangements in several rooms can now be recognized as corn-drying kilns, as if both establishments had in fact been engaged in more conventional activities.

But the sources of wealth were many, and it is impressive indeed to note how certain districts of Britain flourished throughout the fourth century, when external dangers are reckoned to have been severe. In particular the Somersetshire *villae* show a degree of wealth and comfort which raises them above the average, and

[1] Woodchester could have been the luxury country-house of a magnate connected with the presumed fourth-century provincial capital of Cirencester, and not necessarily have had a large estate attached (cf. *Proc. Camb. Phil. Soc.*, n. ser., xiii, 35 f.).

[2] (*Archaeologia*, lix, 207 ff.). Later re-examined by I.A.R. and proved to be a bath-suite.

the rich hoards of late fourth-century silver coins associated with the area attest that until the last it was receiving in exchange for its produce an abundance of good silver coinage in fresh condition.

This, as Mommsen long ago perceived, is a phenomenon which requires a special explanation: the most probable reason for the wealth in silver is the exploitation of the Mendip mines. Until the close of the third century these had been run by the Government from the centre at Charterhouse-on-Mendip. In the fourth century, however, activity at this site came to an abrupt close. On the other hand, the abundance of fourth-century pewter in Southern Britain[1] shows that lead was still being mined in quantity, and that silver was accordingly still available by extraction from it. The inference would then be that in Britain, as in Bosnia, the mining concessions had been handed over in the fourth century to the *curiales*, that is to say, to the principal citizens of the *civitas* concerned. From the silver thus received the State would pay back a fixed percentage, and so bring about the exceptional flow of good silver coinage into the hands of the Somersetshire land-owner *concessionaires*. The chain of evidence is completed by the abundance of lead ore noted in association with the *villae* of south Somersetshire.

Other land-owners went into horse-breeding. It is a remarkable fact that Horkstow, one of the richest *villae* in North Lincolnshire, should have produced a spirited pavement with circus-racing of a kind reserved for skilled amateurs, and should at the same time lie on the edge of the rich river-meadows of the Ancholme, ideal for horse-pastures. Across the valley westwards from Horkstow the rich *villae* of Roxby and Winterton lie close to the North Lincolnshire iron deposits which were worked in late-Roman times and probably under the same tendency towards delegation of responsibility for production to members of the local authority.

The vigour with which these enterprises were working until late in the fourth century or early in the fifth, as associated coin-finds show, may serve to dispel some of the gloom which

[1] See now *Proc. Camb. Ant. Soc.*, lx, 19 ff.: the industry seems to start *c.* A.D. 250.

attaches to current accounts of Roman Britain, which picture a collapse in A.D. 367–9 from which the province hardly recovered. It is true that a number of *villae* do at that moment go out of commission. But the number which produce coins that take us to the 80's of the century is very large, and of these a high proportion continue until the 90's, when ready supplies of coinage failed. There is also a substantial number of *villae* which received repairs after a sack in A.D. 367–9 and at least one, at Denton in South-West Lincolnshire, which was not built until then. It is interesting and perhaps significant that it should be a well-equipped barn-dwelling, a workaday house of the type associated with operatives rather than owners. But it indicates an appetite for investment in real estate and a confidence in the future which belies the impression that the province was in despair and private enterprise exhausted. The rise of the villa system may indeed be counted one of the most steadily successful achievements in the Romanization of Roman Britain, and one of those most intimately connected with the indigenous population.

2

THE VILLAGES

It has recently been recognized that the great majority of the so-called 'villages' of Roman Britain are in fact homesteads, of which the apparently complicated plans represent the total effect of an occupation lasting for many generations.[1] This raises the question what kind of villages in the generally accepted meaning of the term existed in the province at all, and how numerous they were. The matter is not unimportant for an understanding of the Romano-British countryside, especially in view of the fresh classification which is necessary.

It is not easy to base a discussion of this question upon material from the southern area, where the excavated sites look like villages in plan and normally turn out to be farmsteads upon analysis.[2] But there are some instructive northern examples which suggest that some farmsteads at least grew into groups recognizable as a family settlement on a scale large enough to be defined as a hamlet. One of the most instructive of these is Greaves Ash, a site in the south-eastern foothills of Cheviot, which was inhabited in both pre-Roman and earlier Roman days. The main settlement, forming the nucleus out of which all else developes, comprises about twenty huts clustered inside a double walled enclosure planned concentrically, the outer ring subdivided, as if for stock

[1] This idea originated with G. Bersu's excavation of an early Iron Age farm at Little Woodbury (*Proc. Prehist. Soc.*, vi, 30 ff.) (whose precise relevance for the Roman period may perhaps be doubted) and developed after C. F. C. Hawkes' re-interpretation of Woodcuts (*Arch. J.*, civ, 27 ff.). It has most recently been re-stated by L. Alcock (*Antiquity*, xxxvi, 51 ff.).

[2] This does not seem necessarily to be true of the Fenland: see *Ant. J.*, xliv, 19 ff., and *Proc. Camb. Ant. Soc.*, lx, 39 ff.

enclosures, the inner circle forming the dwelling-space. It is difficult to imagine that all these dwellings represent the residence of a single family: on the contrary, they have all the look of a small hamlet. Yet, as the hamlet grew, the additions to the plan suggest that it was the splitting off of new families that in due time conditioned the enlargement. Such a new cell is recognizable on the northeastern rim of the original settlement.[1] Another spreads somewhat further northeastwards. Finally, a second small group is founded about two hundred yards away. The agglomeration cannot but recall the still existent farmstead-villages of the Borders, formed though they were in much later days. Bowness-on-Solway or Long Burgh in Cumberland; Glanton or Ingram in Northumberland are composed of just such groups of small-holders clustered together for mutual protection in troublous days and continuing as an intermarried social group in the generations that followed.

This was well enough for settlements in good agricultural area. In the thinner lands, which favoured stock-raising rather than agriculture, the basis was similarly family life, but the effects were different. Such a development is well shown in the Westmorland valley of Lyvennet, where one settlement, at Ewe Close, exhibits excrescent groupings strikingly like those at Greaves Ash, and a second additional farmstead of a type closely resembling the first. But subsequent swarmings spread over the entire head of the dale, manifesting themselves in little steadings like Ewe Locks, or slightly larger and more systematic settlements like Burwens, until in effect the whole area was full. At Waitby, on the shoulders of Smardale Fell, a rather closer grouping is perceptible on the rich grasslands that the limestone supports; and it is associated with a series of boundary-banks which divide up the pasturage into sizable grazing-grounds, whose connection with the settlements seems sufficiently evident. In the second century A.D., when for about a generation the Roman government gave over

[1] Though confused by the presence of a pre-Roman site this interpretation of Greaves Ash as a developing village is borne out by recent work (see *Arch. Ael.*, 4th ser., xlii, 44).

to *pastores* the evacuated military zone between the Vallum and Hadrian's Wall, it was just such hamlets that their herdsmen built, the excavated example being Milking Gap, whose resemblance to the original settlement at Ewe Close is striking enough.

The large native village, however, in Roman North Britain is a rarity. In this respect the contrast with Roman Wales is striking. When the Welsh tribes were left to themselves, not later than A.D. 140, by a withdrawal of Roman garrisons from all but especially important strategic or economic positions, the tribesmen began to flock back to their old hillforts, packing them tight with new villages.[1] Here the only restriction exercized concerned the nature of their defences, if so they should be called, which were slight enclosure-walls, mere hedges when compared with the massive ramparts of the pre-Roman Iron-Age *oppidum*. But the villages, comprising both homesteads and rows of huts, represent a synoecism on a scale never seen among the Brigantes: and it thus looks as if in the Welsh area, regarded as loyal, large villages were permitted, while among the Brigantian hill-folk large communities were disallowed, the permissible unit being the farmstead or hamlet. Where a general pattern can be discerned the effect is striking; and Dr. Arthur Raistrick's[2] map of Brigantian settlements in Craven gives a sociologically interesting picture of a land of steadings in which the old native hill forts, from which the tribe had been governed in its *pagi* or subdivisions, have been destroyed. *Divide et impera*: the new settlements remain of family size only. Beyond the frontier no such restriction reigned: the Scottish villages of later Roman date are again large.

Just as, however, in the country estates it was possible to distinguish a higher and a lower grade of economic well-being, upon which the Romanization of any given estate was in large measure dependent, so among the villages of the North there can

---

[1] In fact the evidence for a wholesale military evacuation of Wales in the second century is thin, and only 3 hill-forts show definite evidence of second-century occupation (Braich-y-Dinas, Dinorben and Sudbrook): see G. Simpson, *Britons and the Roman Army*, 150 ff.

[2] Perhaps *Yorks. Arch. J.*, xxxi, facing p. 214 (strictly a map of Roman roads and finds).

be discerned more advanced types. Many of these are closely linked with the garrison posts and in favourable conditions they may grow to large size.[1] In general, such settlements have been little excavated. That of Housesteads on Hadrian's Wall has yielded, however, useful samples of the types of building included therein. Aerial photography also, in particular that fostered and forwarded by the Committee for Aerial Photography of this University, has revealed a great deal about the planning of this settlement. It becomes clear that it covered an area of at least ten acres, well over twice as large as that of the fort itself. The planning is not regular. Ribbon development is clearly discernible along the roads leaving the fort. The intermediate space between the southward and eastward roads is also well filled with buildings, although the street-plan with which they are connected has been largely wiped out by later agricultural terracing. The buildings themselves were half-timbered structures, almost always long and narrow shops, taverns or workshops. Their open fronts were normally divided by a central pier and often closed, like shops, by shutters working in grooved stone thresholds. The ground-floor of such buildings, as the structural remains disclose, is mostly given over entirely to supplying the needs of customers.[2] The owner or his agent must therefore have inhabited an upper storey over the ground-floor establishment, for no buildings of domestic character afford the requisite accommodation elsewhere on the site. The architectural type is portrayed upon Trajan's Column in the stations on the Danube, comprising both independent townships and settlements outside the walls of forts. It is natural enough, then, that the god much worshipped at the Housesteads settlement should be Mercury, the patron of mercantile enterprise.[3] But sometimes other deities in the guise of everyday folk appear,[4] affording an unexpected glimpse of the

[1] See Salway, *Frontier People, passim.*

[2] This seems in general true, but there are exceptions, *e.g.* Housesteads Building viii (Salway, *op. cit.*, 168, fig. 10).

[3] It cannot be proved that any civilian made such a dedication.

[4] *E.g. JRS* xxiv, 190 (*Arch. Ael.*, 4th ser., xi, 190 f.; xii, 187; *Latomus*, xxviii, 460).

villagers, as one might meet them at dusk, so stoutly clad against
the wild and broken weather of the district, that it is difficult
even to distinguish their sex.

Housesteads is in no way exceptional. Precisely the same kind
of village development appears outside the south gate of Chesters
(*Cilurnum*) amid an irregular street-plan which the buildings
plainly follow as best they may. It is noteworthy that very few
of the visible buildings deviate from the characteristic shop-plan.[1]
Again, at Chesterholm (*Vindolanda*), similar groups of buildings
are plainly visible skirting the branch road which links the west
gate of the fort with the arterial Stanegate. The only building in
which a complicated series of rooms occurs is the bath-house of
the fort. But at Chesterholm the settlement extended much further
west than is shown on the photograph, and produced a crude but
politically important communal dedication. This is an altar[2] to
Vulcan for the welfare of the Imperial House and the spirits of
present and departed Emperors by the *Vicani Vindolandesses*,
showing that the settlement was officially styled a *vicus* and that its
inhabitants had the specific corporate status of *vicani*. This securely
establishes the meaning of a much more fragmentary inscription
from Housesteads, recording something done *d[ecreto] vica(norum)*;[3]
it also demonstrates that the description of such settlements as
vici refers to their regular official status. If further proof were
required, it is provided by a third inscription,[4] from Old Carlisle,
which mentions a *vic(o)mag(ister)* or village headman as the
authority responsible for making the dedication involved, this
being an altar to *Iuppiter Optimus Maximus* and Vulcan on behalf
of the Emperor Gordian. At this fort also an aerial photograph
reveals a large and flourishing extramural settlement spreading
along the roads which emerge from the fort or pass close beside
it. Once again, the predominant type of building is the long
and narrow shop or tavern. Another equally large settlement

---

[1] Except for the presumed *mansio* (Salway, *op. cit.*, 78, fig. 8).

[2] *RIB* 1700: significantly the dedication by *vicani* from Old Carlisle (*RIB* 899)
is also to Vulcan, underlining the probable importance of industry in these
settlements.   [3] *RIB* 1616.   [4] *RIB* 899.

surrounded the fort of Old Penrith (*Voreda*), extending for a quarter of a mile to north and south.

Sometimes, as at Brougham (*Brocavum*) in Westmorland, it is possible to descry beyond the limits of the external settlement something of the adjacent field-system. One of the tasks of such settlements must certainly have been to feed themselves and to raise a steady supply of fresh vegetables for sale to the garrison of the fort. This means that every *vicus* must in fact have been ringed about by agricultural land which both fed it and provided a livelihood for retailers. Many of these retailers were no doubt native cultivators, and it is an interesting point that Brougham, where a field-system of native pattern is discernible, has yielded a little group of folk with native *nomina*: Audagus,[1] Annamoris,[2] Lunaris[3] and Vidaris[4] are all names of native men and women resident outside the fort.

The question of land-settlement leads on to another aspect of the extramural *vicus*. It is noteworthy that at Housesteads the maximum development of the *vicus* belongs to the first half of the fourth century. On the other hand, it is clear that a very substantial village had already established itself there in the third century. It is at this earlier date also that the beginnings can be discerned of two actions by the Imperial Government which must have had a profound effect upon the growth of such villages. The first step is the wholesale introduction on the British frontier of the *numeri* or irregular units of tribesmen levied from territories outside the Empire. Free Germany was particularly prolific in such units, where they were quite frequently exacted by way of punishment following a frontier war, just as *Brittones* were transported for service on the German frontier in the same way. These units differed from the older auxiliary regiments in that there was no intention that their members should disperse or return home after their period of service was over. They were to settle in the frontier area allotted to them, with the expectation that they and their families should provide the stock for a new frontier *militia*. In the same period, under Severus Alexander,

[1] *RIB* 774.   [2] *RIB* 784.   [3] *RIB* 786.   [4] *RIB* 785.

came the second step – the allotment of leaseholdings in the frontier districts to serving soldiers whose sons would also serve.[1] This creation of a territorial frontier-force and a hereditary caste of landed soldiery must automatically have given a new importance to the extramural village and may often have provided the reason for its very existence. The troops of the *numeri*, administered from the forts but in northern Britain not normally stationed in them, would look upon the *vicus* as their market-village, and this surely explains the overwhelming predominance of shops.[2] The combination of such market villages and presence of *numeri* can often be demonstrated. Housesteads, where the *cuneus Frisiorum* and the *numerus Hnaudifridi* share a village shrine to their own imported deities is a particularly striking case.[3] But the *vexillatio Germanorum* at Old Penrith,[4] the *vexillatio Sueborum* at Lanchester (Co. Durham)[5] or the *equites Stratoniciani* at Brougham[6] provide other excellent examples, and this is not the time and place to linger over them. Very occasionally it is possible to trace the interest of such new landed settlers in the surrounding countryside. In the fertile area north of Lancaster and the river Lune, an ex-decurion from the cavalry-garrison of the fort set up an altar to *Ialonus*,[7] the Celtic god whose name means 'He of the meadowland', at a spot not far from the northward road hallowed by a copious spring. At Greetland in the West Riding of Yorkshire a *magister* set up an altar to *Victoria Brigantia* and the *numina Augustorum* on a bluff overlooking the river Calder in A.D. 205.[8] This man was a Roman citizen before the *Constitutio Antoniniana* and comparable citizen-dedications came from Longwood[9] and

---

[1] This is strongly disputed (see Salway, *Frontier People*, 33 f.): Aemilius Macer, writing after 217 and very likely under Alexander Severus, says that soldiers were forbidden to hold land in the provinces in which they were on active service.

[2] Surely the fact that regular troops were now allowed to marry had some effect on the growth of *vici*. It is by no means proven that most of the strip-buildings were shops.

[3] *RIB* 1576, 1594 (*cf*. 1593).   [4] *RIB* 920 (*cf*. 919).   [5] *RIB* 1074.

[6] *RIB* 780.   [7] *RIB* 600.

[8] *RIB* 627, where I.A.R. is cited re-dating the stone to A.D. 208. The man seems to have been *magister sacrorum*.

[9] *RIB* 623.

Castleford[1] in the same river basin. If at Lancaster it is possible to detect an ex-decurion invoking the blessing of local deities upon the lands which he intended to exploit, in the Calder Basin there are veteran-settlers of which at least one holds a village-headman's post. These dedications in the *vici* and the countryside may be contrasted in form and intention with the remote moorland shrines of *Silvanus* which the high Pennine has produced. The Bollihope altar of Veturius Micianus, praefect of the *ala Sebosiana*,[2] the Eastgate altar of Aurelius Quirinus, praefect of the First Cohort of *Lingones*,[3] the Scargill altars and shrines erected by the praefect and a centurion of the First Cohort of Thracians[4] indicate the enjoyment of hunting in the wild hill-country and a due veneration for its presiding deity. There is an indication of habitual use of these hunting groups in the inscriptions. At Bollihope a fine boar, hunted by successive officers in vain, was caught at last: at Scargill *Silvanus* is equated with the local deity, *Vinotonus*. The carefree hunting and the long-unmolested shrines give a vivid glimpse of a land where the Emperor's peace reigned in its wildest corners.

Before leaving the North, there are other districts to consider. The canton of the *Brigantes* was not all hill-country: in particular, the Vale of York supplied not only a natural line of penetration, but a great plain where agriculture might flourish and furnish the amenities of civilized existence. Even today to cross the Tees southwards is to enter upon a new and richer cultural area. Within the Vale of York the tribal capital lay at Aldborough (*Isurium*), but it is clear that there were also other centres, no doubt corresponding to different *pagi* or subdivisions of the tribe. The most northerly of these lay at Catterick, the ancient *Cataractonium*, where the North Road crossed the Swale. Here is still visible a Roman defensive wall, first planned in detail in 1851 and now shown by aerial photography to have enclosed an irregular street-plan in which the main element is formed by the North Road itself. The buildings are again principally long and narrow

---

[1] *RIB* 628.   [2] *RIB* 1041.   [3] *RIB* 1042.
[4] *RIB* 732, 733 (cf. 735, 736, 737, 738).

shop-like buildings, and there is always the possibility that the place may have developed out of the *vicus* of a fort,[1] like Heddernheim (*Nida*) in Germany. Indeed at Piercebridge, where the North Road crosses the Tees only 10 miles further north, just such a *vicus* is seen in process of emergence. At Catterick, the fort may be expected to have occupied the higher ground at the west end of the site,[2] now covered by the large farm of Thornborough, and no trace or hint of its presence has as yet emerged. Yet, whatever its early history may have been, the community which ultimately emerged at Catterick is a small local township of a kind which in size or extent much more closely approximates to what is nowadays meant by the term village.[3] A second Brigantian site about which very much less is known is Adel, north of Leeds, of which the ancient name and plan alike have perished. But there is a sufficiently large number of finds, mainly of civilian character, from a tolerably extensive area to suggest that here also lay one of the minor centres of the *Brigantes*. And these centres lasted long and late.[4] *Cataractonium* is still called a *vicus* by Bede[5] and gave refuge to James the Deacon when Penda and Cadwallon wiped out the early Christian Kingdom of Edwin in 633. Adel lies in the heart of the British Kingdom of Leeds, which had lasted independent until Ethelfrith absorbed it early in the seventh century. It can be seen how, when central authority broke down, these smaller places attained greater significance.

The second area deserving of attention exhibits a political organization which is of peculiar interest among the British cantons. The East Yorkshire tribe of the *Parisi*, whose territory embraced the East Riding and ran somewhat beyond it towards the north, had for its administrative centre the township of *Petuaria*. When this place received defences, in the middle of the

---

[1] Excavations in 1958–59 are shown in *JRS* l, 217, fig. 20. There is some variety of buildings.

[2] It is now almost certain that the fort did lie at the west end (*JRS* l, 217).

[3] Yet it was walled, apparently not before the mid third century.

[4] It was still flourishing at the end of the fourth century (*JRS* l, 218).

[5] Bede, *Hist. Eccles.*, ii, 14.

second century,[1] they enclosed an area of only 13 acres, inside which such buildings as have been discovered were of the simplest character. It is not therefore surprising that, on an inscription recording the gift of a new theatre-stage, the place should be called officially *Vicus Petuerensis*.[2] If the occurrence of a theatre at so small a place should seem surprising it may be recalled that the 35-acre township at Great Chesterford also boasted a theatre. To be reminded, however, of the essentially Celtic character of its inhabitants it is necessary only to consider the grave-gods of a local magistrate or priest, whose ritual bucket was adorned with a delightful representation of a Petuarian. Politically, the point of importance is that this tribe was in fact administered from a *vicus*,[3] and in estimating the significance of the situation, the name of the place is itself full of meaning. Derived from the ordinate form, *petuarios*, of the number *petor* or *petru* and thus meaning 'Fourth', it denotes that the place was one of a number of such centres, connected with the division of the tribe into *pagi* or *curiae*. As is well known, divisions of the kind are in fact contained in Gallic tribal names such as *Petrucorii* and *Tricorii*. It may then be assumed that each division of the *Parisi* had a village centre comparable with *Petuaria*, but that *Petuaria* was regarded, as Ptolemy indicates, as the administrative centre of the whole tribe. They were, in fact, in exactly the same political condition as the Gallic *Allobroges* in the late first century B.C., who are described by Strabo as living 'in villages', one particular village, *Vienna*, serving as the metropolis.[4] It is possible, further, to identify at least another of the tribal centres, which lies just across the river Derwent from Malton, the sole permanent military centre known in Parisian territory, at Norton. Archaeological investigation has not yet systematically defined the limits of this *vicus*. But it is

[1] The first town defences seem to fall within the period A.D. 125–45, the second, enclosing a smaller area, 150–180+ and the stone wall not earlier than *c.* 180 (*Ant. J.*, xl, 61 f.)

[2] *RIB* 707, where VICI PETV[is expanded *vici Petu[ar(iensis)*.

[3] It is not proven either that *Petuaria* was the administrative centre of a *civitas* or that the Parisi were a Roman *civitas*, though Ptolemy, *Geog.* ii, 3, 17 may suggest it.

[4] See p. 68, n. 4 above.

known to have had defences enclosing an area of much the same size as *Petuaria*, and it was a busy centre of pottery production. Its buildings, so far as yet recovered, appear to be of the shop or workshop class.

The *Parisi* thus differed from the normal Romano-British *civitas* in their lack of a major administrative centre, in which a developed town-life set the pattern of Romanization. Why was this? The early history of *Petuaria* and the adjacent native settlement at North Ferriby indicates that the tribe was not hostile to Roman influences. Roman imports were pouring in from Claudian times onwards;[1] and when Cerealis advanced upon the *Brigantes*, the *Parisi* afforded the line of advance. Again it is in their territory that the village-site at Elmswell near Driffield has yielded one of the loveliest hybrid objects of Britto-Roman art. Such a record supports the deduction to be made from their geographical position that they were allies from the Claudian settlement onwards, and that this allied tribe earned for its services an immunity for its ancient way of life. One might compare the treatment accorded to the simple folk of *Novempopulana* in the organization of Roman Aquitaine.

The number of villages which can be recognized as minor tribal centres is in fact very large, and an enumeration would here be out of place. But certain further examples illustrate special points which it is worth while to note. In the first place it is evident that the Imperial government regarded such centres as important elements in the cantonal organization, since it normally look the trouble to see that they were secured by a town wall. This differentiates them sharply from the *vici* outside the military stations, which in extremely rare cases only are provided with walls. Secondly, it seems clear that in many cases it was the Roman government which picked the site for the *vicus* and that it did not grow automatically out of older native villages, but was specifically related to the Roman road system. This was certainly so at

[1] Surely the contents of Lexden tumulus and other finds from *Camulodunum* demonstrate that cultural penetration need have little to do with political affiliations.

I. The Roman Fenland: Bullock's Haste, Cottenham, from the east. The Cambridgeshire Car Dyke is visible as a depression on the near side of the lower hedgerow. It is approached by a lane, flanked on the left by the enclosures of the settlement and on the right by earthworks formerly thought to be the substructure of granaries.

Petuaria, where the *vicus* lay at the Roman Humber crossing and was allotted, at the moment of integration of the tribe into the province, the site of a military work of Petilius Cerealis. At Alchester, in Oxfordshire, a new Claudian 27-acre site was founded adjacent to native villages. It was supplied with earth-work defences at once and received a stone wall under Hadrian.[1] Little is known of internal buildings, except that a large colon-naded courtyard occurs at the main cross-roads and a temple-like building associated with it is clearly visible on an air-photograph. Closely comparable with Alchester is Dorchester, where the road from Silchester to Alchester crossed the Thames. The size of the Claudian foundation here is not known, though an abundance of relics attest its existence. The known settlement, $13\frac{1}{2}$ acres in size, received a wall under Hadrian,[2] presumably at much the same moment as Alchester. Here, as at the northern *vici,* there is ample evidence for a long-lived site, which not only outlasted Roman days but was sufficiently important in the seventh century to attract Birinus to found there an episcopal see. Its late-Roman prosperity is well attested by good imported glass and a little hoard of silver spoons. In the third century it was the quarters of a *beneficiarius consularis,*[3] whose duties were probably connected with supervision of official traffic and the collection of the *annona.* The existence of such an official points to the value of the place as a centre for the collection or forwarding of taxation in kind, which must always have formed an important part of the tribute expected from Romano-British communities.

Another pair of very similar foundations are Caistor-on-the-Wolds and Horncastle, in Lincolnshire. Both are protected by walls of fourth-century type and it has sometimes been suggested that they are military posts. The position of both however, and very particularly Caistor, does not support the suggestion that they are of military purpose, and it is easier to suppose that they

---

[1] This certainly needs re-assessing in view of what we now know of general trends in defences.

[2] The pottery from recent excavations suggests a date *c.* A.D. 270 for the stone wall (Frere, *Britannia,* 252).   [3] *RIB* 235.

are walled *vici*. Both remain local centres of some importance today and Caistor became the seat of an important Saxon monastic church. In the locality of Roman times they would represent minor centres of the *Coritani*, isolated from the main tract of tribal territory by the colonial lands of Lincoln.

Quite another type of *vicus* is seen at Wilderspool on the Mersey, just south of Warrington. Here the site of a Roman fort of the Flavian period was covered with workshops engaged in iron-smelting, in pouring window-glass and in the production of coarse pottery. The works are associated with coins of the late first and early second century and undoubtedly represent the conversion of an abandoned fort-site into workshops for official needs. Iron-working of the same type was undertaken on the site of *Margidunum* after its disuse early in the second century. But the specifically industrial sites have been little examined. Pentre Ffwrnddan, near Flint, a lead-smelting centre of the second and third centuries, has been sampled rather than explored. Charter-house-on-Mendip, much larger and more important, still awaits the spade; so also does the iron-working centre at Weston-under-Penyard.

Finally, there are the *mansiones* or posting-stations on the main roads. These arise directly out of the organization of the Imperial Post which conveyed Government despatches and officials. The convenience of catering for extensive commercial and private traffic side by side with the official travellers led to the accumulation round the official post-houses of numerous non-official stables and inns for the service of the ordinary traveller. The result was a small village. As at *Margidunum*, such places normally remained open settlements and received no walls until late in the history of the province. The incidence of such provisions is, however, sufficiently lacking in uniformity to suggest that varying degrees of importance were attached to the *mansiones* and that they probably came to combine different functions. *Margidunum*, for example, received no wall until after 369 and then a small circuit,[1] suggesting that it remained a simple *mansio*.

[1] In 1966 a ditch, said to be contemporary with the wall, was found to contain

The Villages

Chesterton near Water Newton (Northamptonshire), the Roman *Durobrivae*, grew into a 33-acre township from which milestones were measured, as if from a centre of local government, though when it received its wall is as yet unknown. Great Casterton, (Rutlandshire) where Ermine Street crosses the Gwash, received a wall in the third century which enclosed some eighteen acres. Wall (*Letocetum*) remains a small 12-acre *mansio* on Watling Street.[1] The elaboration of the ditch-system which begirts it might at first sight suggest that, like *Margidunum*, it occupied an early fort. But at Stretton (*Pennocrucium*), the next *mansio* to the west, the *mansio* occupies one site and the early fort another, yet the *mansio* is furnished with a no less complicated set of ditches. The truth may well be that, as disclosed by excavation at Alchester (Oxfordshire), more than one series of ditches is represented.

The term village is thus seen to cover in Roman Britain both a great number and a great variety of settlements, so different from one another that a recapitulation of the facts seems required. In the native areas of the North and Wales they tend to be agglomerations of farmsteads clearly so assembled for purposes of mutual protection. But between the North, subject to military occupation, and Wales, almost entirely free from it, the important difference emerges that in the military area large native villages do not appear nor are the villages themselves defended, while in Wales the reoccupation of ancient hill forts was permitted[2] and accompanied by small-scale fortification. It seems a legitimate inference that these differences represent genuine differences in the treatment officially accorded to the two areas.

Side by side with the native settlements in the North there grew up, however, large villages, officially known as *vici*,

in its silt Central Gaulish samian (*JRS* lvii, 183). No fourth-century wall was found on the supposed line.

[1] Excavation in 1961 defined the walled area as 5 acres and suggested that the walls dated from the second half of the third century (*JRS* lii, 170). There is some possibility that a fortress of the XIVth legion was situated here under Ostorius Scapula (G. Webster and D. R. Dudley, *The Roman Conquest of Britain*, 1965, 141). The walled enclosure, which Webster and Dudley put in the fourth century, did not enclose all of the civil town and its exact purpose is uncertain.

[2] See p. 152, n. 1 above.

[163]

forming extramural settlements at the forts. While such settlements often began their existence in the second century, they grew to large size only in the third and fourth centuries. They consist very largely of shops or taverns, and are to be brought into connexion with the supplementation of the normal auxiliary garrisons by irregular troops recruited from beyond the borders of the Empire. The close relationship between the new soldiery and the villages is proved by their shrines, which occur in the villages themselves. The conversion of the frontier troops into soldier-cultivators also resulted in fixed settlement upon the land and the need for market villages at the forts became greater. The new land-settlement[1] has as yet left few traces, but it is to be detected here and there by means of dedications scattered over the countryside.

Another class of village is the local centre for a subdivision of the tribe. Among Brigantian examples of these are Catterick and Adel, while the neighbouring tribe of the *Parisi* furnishes an example of native communities left at the level which they desired without pressure to Romanize themselves further. But these villages, while serving the needs of tribal administration, were nevertheless founded on sites of Roman choosing and specifically related to the Roman road-system. Their relation to the fiscal policy of Rome thus becomes evident, and is well illustrated by such Oxfordshire centres as Dorchester and Alchester, or the Lincolnshire villages of Caistor and Horncastle.

Industrial villages seem closely connected with early fort sites, but the larger and later industrial village sites await exploration, while the posting stations or *mansiones* exhibit a variety of treatment which suggests a variety of subsidiary uses.

In short, there are many sides to the picture of the villages in Roman Britain and not all of them are well or clearly illuminated. Yet it may be claimed that in this sphere, as in not a few others, British archaeology has taken us further along the path of knowledge than it is possible to advance in most provinces of the

---

[1] The evidence for land-settlement is extremely unconvincing (see Salway, *Frontier People*, 33 f.).

Empire. And with this augury it is possible to hope that subsequent generations, each making its new contribution of knowledge, will both see the picture more comprehensively and appreciate it in greater detail.

3

THE SOCIAL CENTRES

In the *De Excidio Britanniae* Gildas, mentioning the pagan shrines of Britain, lays stress upon their very large number and adds that in some there could still be seen the weathered statues, standing stiff and menacing in and about the deserted buildings.[1] Unintentionally, he thus affords a glimpse of a British countryside still exhibiting its ancient temples and emphasizes the fact that in the British province at large, religious buildings had occupied an important place in the landscape. They had also a great hold upon its people and were among the most important of its rural social centres.

Much the most common form of shrine, as will presently appear, was the native type of temple.[2] This, as is well known, comprised a small sanctuary, usually square but sometimes round, often of modest scale, but capable, in Gaul at least, where these types also reigned supreme, of reaching a great height and towering above the colonnade or veranda which normally surrounded the building. Such was the native temple, and it is normally found to be constructed in Roman fashion. But the plan was long pre-Roman. The war-time discovery, as yet unpublished,[3] of an early Iron-Age village on Hounslow Heath containing a timber temple of precisely the same type, indicates that,

[1] Gildas, *De Excidio*, 4 (i, 2).

[2] See now M. J. T. Lewis, *Temples in Roman Britain*, 1965, *passim*.

[3] See Lewis, *op. cit.*, 10, n. 5 for references. W. F. Grimes suggested that this temple was of classical and not Romano-Celtic type, and Lewis points out that there is an awkward gap of 150 years between it and the earliest temple known in the Celtic world. Lewis argues for a Belgic importation of the type, perhaps *c.* 50 B.C.

while the style of building and the architectural embellishments of such temples might be Romanized, the plan itself was of pre-Roman origin. The Hounslow temple stood on a village green, bordered by the huts and enclosing earthwork of a small community. Evidently these people cherished their guardian deity in their midst. But many of the older holy places lay apart and took the well-known form of sacred groves. For such sanctuaries the Gallic and British term was *nemeton*, which occurs in Strabo[1] in the compound form δρυνέμετον, 'the oak grove', and is glossed in a much later source '*sacra silvarum*'. The word also occurs in several Romano-British place-names,[2] widely scattered through the province: in Cornwall west of the Tamar, in Nottinghamshire at Willoughby-on-the-Wolds, which lies on the Fosse Way, at Buxton in Derbyshire, and in Scotland, not far from the middle point of the Antonine Wall. The word is also associated with the rivers Mole and Yeo in Devon, and with the Newe[3] in Scotland. The groves could be used for feasting as well as for sacrifices and shrines, and there is a grim and horrific account of the grove of the war-goddess *Andarte* in the Greek description of the Boudiccan revolt.[4] But most famous of all were the holy groves of Anglesey, the high seat of Druidism in Britain. Here a very remarkable collection of votive objects was recovered during the recent War and studied by Sir Cyril Fox.[5] Its source was the pool of Llyn Cerrig, in which the material was deposited either as offerings, or, less probably, as rubbish when the groves were destroyed by Roman orders. Be that as it may, the group as a whole tells a remarkable story of war-booty brought to a sacred shrine. Significantly enough, the material is derived from the three aggressive tribal groups of pre-Claudian Britain, and from

[1] Strabo, xii, 5, 1 (I.A.R.).

[2] Also on the Continent and in Ireland: see T. G. E. Powell, *The Celts*, 1958, 138 ff.

[3] There is a gap here in the typescript: I owe the suggestion to R. M. Ogilvie. For a discussion of *nemeton* in Scotland see W. J. Watson, *History of the Celtic Place Names of Scotland*, 1926, 246 ff.

[4] Dio, lxii, 7, 3. The name is in fact given as *Andate*.

[5] Fox, *A Find of the Early Iron Age from Llyn Cerrig Bach, Anglesey*, 1946.

the Irish offshoot of the north-British group: and it represents a god's share, the non-Roman equivalent of the *sortes Herculis*, of the most valuable things captured in war; horses and chariots, war trumpets, weapons, and finally, the gang-chains which conveyed the human victims of a savage cult.[1] Nothing could illustrate more strikingly the Druidical power or the political need for its suppression.

Mona had been a sacred island, and there were others which were reckoned so in Britain, as Plutarch records,[2] and some of their holy names found their way into geographical sources:[3] Arran, known as *Man(an)na*, the home of *Manannan* the god of the sea; *Minerve*, a western Isle, one among the many which were held to be the abodes of spirits. But such islands lay for the most part either outside the Roman world or on its extreme fringe, and they represent the survival of old beliefs rather than a Romanization of new structures. To see the Roman adaptation of groves it is necessary to come back to the heart of the Roman province and to its first religious centre, Colchester.

While the *colonia Victricensis* became the centre of the Imperial cult for the province of Britain, its vicinity exhibits shrines which attest not only the survival of the old order but the existence of wealthy native cults. The outstanding feature of these temple precincts is their large size and the lack of prominence given to the temple in the over-all plan. The temples do not occupy a dominating position: on the contrary, they stand to one side or even in one corner of the enclosure in such a fashion as to suggest that the main position was occupied by a grove containing features incapable of leaving readily recognizable archaeological traces. The great trees of an ancient grove might in fact perish unrecorded, without leaving even such indications as might be seen in an air-photograph. Accordingly, it becomes possible to suppose that the extensive enclosing walls, surrounding what

[1] It is equally possible that the material was votive offerings collected in a sacred grove and either thrown in by the Britons to save them from the Romans or by Agricola's troops erasing traces of the Druids.

[2] Plutarch, *Moralia*, 419E.

[3] *Ravenna Cosmography*: see *Archaeologia*, xciii, 39 and 41.

looks like unoccupied space, were in reality surrounding sacred groves, in which the natural features and the portable or impermanent monuments connected with them had been the main feature, while the holy edifice or shrine was the deity's dwelling-place when worship was either not in progress or in a minor key. This implies both a calendar of worship and a substantial body of worshippers.

The most remarkable of these suburban sacred places is, however, at Gosbecks Farm, about 2 miles southwest of Colchester. The chief religious structure on the site is a rigidly rectangular enclosure, bounded by a broad ditch. Only the southeast corner of the area thus hallowed is occupied by a temple, which is of second-century date, while the ditch contains pottery going back to pre-Roman times, and must clearly be connected with a native sanctuary. When the temple was built the ditch, which belongs to the oldest and holiest fashion in sacred boundaries, was not filled up but was enclosed by a double *porticus* of Roman style, no doubt still respecting the grove or comparable features which occupied the main part of the enclosure. The outer portico provided shelter for the users of a festival ground, which may well have existed before, but was now equipped with festival buildings in the Roman manner, including a great theatre, in the style of such Gallic sites as Sanxay. It is easy to imagine such a priesthood in the hands of the local aristocracy of *Camulodunum*, beginning with those who were *incolae* of the *colonia*. The priesthood and the entertainments upon festival days could then be turned to advantage on the occasion of elections to local magistracies. Who the god here worshipped may have been is not completely certain: but a substantial bronze statue of Mercury, discovered in the immediate vicinity of the shrine, represents the likeliest of deities to be connected with a much frequented native sanctuary, not merely in his own right as the god of traders, but especially in view of his popularity among those concerned with the *interpretatio Romana* of native deities. Just such another *Mercurius* with native appellation is known from nearer the town.[1]

[1] *RIB* 193 : *Mercurius Andescociuoucus.*

The Social Centres

It thus becomes evident that close to the very centre of official Roman worship in the province the native cults persisted, and in time came to employ the material advantages of Roman structure to perpetuate and maintain their ancient social and religious forms substantially unchanged. At a minor site in North Berkshire very much the same effect is also discernible. At Frilford, 3½ miles west of Abingdon, a rectangular native temple of normal type lies close beside another circular enclosure. The rectangular temple was a Romanized building erected on top of an earlier timber hut, of which the sacred character is possible but not demonstrable. But the circular shrine, 36 feet in diameter, over-lay, and followed with remarkable fidelity, an early Iron-Age structure enclosed by a wide ditch. The native building had been a broad and shallow structure consisting of three pairs of post-holes, set in two lines about five feet apart and eighteen feet long. The front row is a little wider than the back, as if the object of the building had been to shelter and display images of the gods, and perhaps offerings as well.

The continuous occupation of older sacred sites is thus seen to be a feature of the Roman province. In some cases these gods were expressly connected with the ancient hill-forts, the most famous example being Maiden Castle. But the dating is here as curious as it is certain. The erection of Roman-built shrines on the hill belongs to the late fourth century and there is a long period during which the ancient stronghold was deserted. Does this represent the consecration of the fortress to a deity, who was perhaps already represented in less substantial form? It is difficult otherwise to comprehend why or how the spot should have become sacred. When the sanctuary was built, after A.D. 364, it was well equipped, and a priest's dwelling was built close beside it. The deities wor-shipped were rural enough: this is no case of a new sanctuary erected for protector gods as times became dangerous. From the temple came a silver plaque of Minerva, possibly from a ritual crown, a remarkable votive bronze in which a three-horned bull, the emblem of *Taranis* the Celtic sky-god, who was lord of the thunder, is associated with a triple deity, one bust having disappeared, the others representing respectively the busts of goddesses, one of them furnished with bird's wings. In the priest's dwelling was found the base of a marble statue of a hunting goddess in the Roman guise of Diana, whatever her native name. These gods and goddesses of the chase and the sky belong to the welfare of everyday things which were of popular appeal. Other ancient sanctuaries of the kind reflect rather the same story. At Chanctonbury Ring a large late-Roman temple occupies the ancient hill-fort. Harlow Hill, in the Stort valley, a low hill ringed by a ditch in the marshes, is occupied by a third.[1]

But there were some hills which were occupied late and where a previous occupation dissociated from social gatherings or religious enclosures can be demonstrated. The outstanding example of this is Lydney, where the sanctuary of *Nodens*, another hunter god, was built on the site of third-century iron-workings, which can hardly have been associated with any religious occupation of the hill. Both the date and the situation are highly remarkable. The establishment did not come into existence until after A.D. 364 and it is situated on the north shore of the Bristol Channel, where Irish raiders had already begun their devastations under Carausius and Allectus. That a great pagan shrine should have been erected so late is interesting enough: it is still more remarkable that it should have been designed as a capacious pilgrimage shrine, with a guest-house, bath-house and porticoes capable of accommodating pilgrims of high or low degree. For this implies not only peace but faith in its continuance, the place being unfortified and in full view of the Severn waterway. The easiest comment upon this is the inscribed pavement from the sanctuary itself, which was laid down by a *praefectus reliquationis*,[2] or chief of a naval repair-depot, with a member of his staff. Here is reflected the naval activity which kept the western approaches safe and made the existence of the *Fanum Nodentis* possible.

---

[1] Recent excavation has revealed a complicated history and plan: see *JRS* liii, 138; lv, 214; lvi, 210 – they should be read in conjunction with *VCH Essex* iii, 139 ff.

[2] See p. 91, n. 2 above.

The name of *Nodens*, the presiding deity, refers to hunting, and several of the votive offerings are hunting-dogs, including one magnificent wolf-hound. He was also a finder, or restorer of stolen property, since at least one leaden tablet calls upon him to afflict a suspected thief.[1] But his ritual objects, the crowns with which his priests or their attendants were adorned, are concerned either with fighting or with the sea. It is thus evident that *Nodens* was a marine deity, as well as a god of the chase, and the best preserved of his priestly crowns exalts him riding in majesty over the waves. It is not difficult to find at Lydney a natural phenomenon which connects hunter and sea-god. Twice every day, in full sight of the sanctuary, is enacted the startling miracle of the Severn bore, which comes racing in like a pack in full and inexorable cry. Well might a hunter god be thought manifest in such a tidal wave and so come to be the god of the estuary, fitly claiming the worship of the naval officers who had their stations upon it.

But the arrangements for pilgrims imply that *Nodens* also possessed oracular or healing powers. There is no sign of an oracle. His temple is designed open and with side aisles or ambulatories and niches, which invite a tour of inspection and the collection of votive offerings. The main division of the buiding is an arcaded nave terminating in a triple shrine or *cella*, as if *Nodens* had companion deities, though we do not hear of them. The whole design has sometimes been compared with that of a Christian church; and indeed it would not be surprising if late fourth-century paganism borrowed something, consciously or unconsciously, from its ascendent rival. But, despite their difference in size, it may be remarked how close is the resemblance between the Lydney shrine and the principal temple of Caerwent (*Venta Silurum*) the centre of the canton in which Lydney was situated. The Caerwent building is also arranged in nave and aisles, but its nave is apparently screened off and its sanctuary is an apse. There is therefore perhaps no need to look far afield for analogies to the Lydney temple, and the Caerwent example is no more than a

[1] *RIB* 306.

variant of the common Celtic type. Later in its history, however, the Lydney temple acquired a series of new features. Three out of the five large niches in the ambulatory were turned into separate shrines, arranged so as to hold offerings or dedications. The arcades of the nave were also closed, rendering the resemblance to the Caerwent temple closer than before. The final trend of the changes is thus away from Christian architecture rather than towards a closer *rapprochement*, if there was at any time any conscious imitation at all.

On the social side the accommodation for visitors to the shrine is both commodious and well-planned. The main guest-house is a large courtyard building with common dining-room in the centre of the main range and suites of rooms on one side. The front range is a large clearing-hall, highly reminiscent of the reception hall in the great military hospitals. The other side of the building is planned more spacious and less regular and may be recognized as servants' quarters. The bath-house of the establishment is so arranged as to serve not only the guest-house but others using the long portico behind the temple. This, as has been observed, has all the characteristics of the temple porticoes in which cures were wrought during sleep or by dreams, as at Epidaurus and other famous healing sanctuaries.

The establishment and furnishings at Lydney introduce the richer sanctuaries and their appointments, and afford the clue to the setting of a series of sites which have yielded relics but not structures, either because these have been later stripped of their building materials or because chance discoveries have not been followed up by systematic excavations. Such a site in East Anglia is Cavenham Heath, in Suffolk. Here were discovered, not long before 1925, three very remarkable priestly headdresses.[1] The first two are crowns, evidently temple furniture intended for use by different persons at different times, since they have adjustable head-bands. Both had been richly decorated with silver plaques

[1] *cf.* the Wilton head-dresses (*JRS* xlvii, 211: for a discussion see J. M. C. Toynbee, *Art in Roman Britain*, 1962, 178); and the fragments of a crown from Deeping St. James (*JRS* lvi, 203).

soldered on to them, shaped as *aediculae* upon the more ornate piece, and including winged figures on the simpler example. The third object was a head-dress of plaques and chains, so arranged that a diadem was suspended from a central ornament at the top of the head by four sets of chains. Ritual head-dresses of this kind are no doubt a heritage from prehistoric Britain, and part of one has been recognized, as Miss Claire Fell tells me, in an early Iron-Age context in the Museum of Archaeology and Ethnology.[1] It becomes clear then that Cavenham Heath has yielded a hoard of ritual headdresses belonging to a shrine of considerable wealth and these imply ceremonies attractive to a large body of worshippers. Other comparable hoards of silver plaques have come from the shrines of *Mars Alator, Teutates* and Vulcan at Barkway (Hertfordshire), and from Stony Stratford (Buckinghamshire), which also yielded a chain head-dress exactly comparable with the Cavenham example.

Another site which obviously has much in common with those so far cited is Woodeaton, from which the small bronzes have recently been studied in detail and published for the first time.[2] This is a very large site, covering some fifty acres, and compares with such widespread festival sites as Gosbecks Farm near Colchester. The area has been prolific in coins: well over 1000, exclusive of two hoards, have been recorded. On this basis it has been suggested, with great likelihood, that the place was a fair-ground or mart. But the character of the bronzes also makes it very evident that Woodeaton was a cult-centre. The bronze figurines of Venus and a Celtic goddess, whose charms are perhaps improved by being half hidden, the plaques with an *amorino* and a strangely attractive if infantile rendering of a divine figure, the fragment of leaf from the decoration of a shrine or headdress, point unmistakably towards a religious explanation of the site. In addition may be mentioned model axes and an unusual number of mountings in the form of eagles. This does not supply sufficient information to identify the deities worshipped, but it at least attests their existence. The Lydney

[1] At Cambridge.   [2] *Oxoniensia*, xiv, 1 ff.

cult furnishings thus make it possible to fit into a context many
isolated objects and to recognize in them the evidence for other
religious centres.

The size and elaboration of the Lydney establishment, however,
is outstripped by that other class of social centre, associated with
curative waters. Two of these spas are known in Britain, the
widely famous Bath, whose deity was *Sulis Minerva*, and the
much less renowned Buxton, whose tutelary goddess was
Arnemetia. The decorative remains from the temple of *Sulis* are so
familiar as to be almost hackneyed and many views concerning
Romano-British art have centred about the pedimental sculpture
known as the Bath Gorgon. This figure, which is an emblem
within a *clipeus*, has often been described as a male Gorgon. But
if it represents, as its position in the design would indicate, the
powers with which *Sulis* was endowed, her apotropaic emblem
corresponding to the Gorgoneion of Minerva, then it may be
related to an indigenous legend of a magical head, such as, for
example, the Head of Bran the Blessed. But content apart, it is
clear that in form the head may owe much to the Hellenistic
tradition of grotesque heads such as occurs upon the great dish of
Mildenhall. But apart from this strange and dominating variation
on a classical theme, the remaining architecture of the temple is
Roman[1] and exhibits those interesting variations of the Composite
Order which kept design and development from stiffening into
the rigid forms which eventually deprived the style of life. The
detail has much in common with the idiom of *Belgica* or of
Northern Gaul, and in fact at least one North-Gallic mason,
Priscus, son of Toutius, from Chartres was at work in Bath.[2]
If they are closely compared, the work of the Moselle valley
tends to carry off the palm: for the British work is often stiffer
and less gracious, as if the artist were following his pattern more
rigidly and with less assurrance. But there are, nevertheless,
moments when work at Bath equals or surpasses the products of
Belgica. In either case the style employed is purely classical, and
it is evident that the temple of *Sulis* was built for worshippers

[1] See now B. Cunliffe, *Antiquity*, xl, 199 ff., especially figs. 1 and 2. [2] *RIB* 149.

who were either Romans or philo-Romans of highly Romanized taste. They included at least one *collegium* or chartered cult-organization.[1]

The classicism of style applies even more strictly to the great thermal establishment associated with the hot springs over which *Sulis Minerva* presided. An early date for their use is afforded by their occurrence in Ptolemy,[2] whose sources for southern Britain are at the very latest Vespasianic, and is confirmed by a fragmentary inscription of A.D. 77.[3] The foundation date of the existing establishment, however, is not securely established and it can only be said that it exhibits from the first a plan of which the greater part forms an evident unity, centred in the Great Bath. The impressive feature of the building is its size, which far outstrips, for example, such a spa as the North African *Aquae Flavianae*, where the arrangements are not unlike a smaller edition of *Aquae Sulis*. As time passed the establishment grew more elaborate, and was furnished with facilities for the normal type of hot baths, side by side with the curative waters of the hot springs. These accessory units evolved gradually and grew ever larger. That at the east end of the range had at least three stages of growth. The western heated baths are often accepted as part of the original building, but the plan does not display a really convincing homogeneity. The most recent architectural survey, by the late W. H. Knowles, suggests that these too are in large part additions.[4] The impression of growing luxury and regard for convenience is heightened by the architectural development of the Great Bath. This had commenced its existence open to the sky, with arcaded walks along each long side, probably surmounted by balconies, and only the smaller baths beyond each end of it appear to have been roofed. Eventually, however, it was determined to cover the Great Bath with a vaulted roof, forty feet in span. In preparation for this, the main piers were almost trebled in size towards the front and were further strengthened at the back by smaller pilasters, whose main function was

---

[1] *RIB* 141.   [2] Ptolemy, *Geog.*, ii, 3, 28.   [3] *RIB* 172: dated there to A.D. 76.
[4] *Archaeologia*, lxxv, 1 ff.

II. Hadrian's Wall: a length on Sewingshields Crags as newly-uncovered and consolidated in 1958.

to carry arches that would serve as veritable flying buttresses. The roof was then carried upon a series of ribs composed of hollow tiles, and there must have been large lateral lunettes occupied by windows to carry off the steam. This is much the most ambitious of surviving Roman architectural schemes in Britain. The minor edifices associated with the baths were also of some pretensions. There was a portico of the Seasons and a pediment of the Moon Goddess suggestive of a balanced astronomical composition in which the Sun and Moon took the principal part.

In the end the baths attracted about themselves a little town, of which the walls enclosed some 22 acres. But that was not the manner in which the establishment had started. Bath was at first a Claudian fort, guarding the point where the Fosse Way crossed the Avon Gorge and was joined by the early road from St. Albans and Colchester. The first discovery of the site will thus have been made by soldiers and inscribed and sculptured stones[1] show that they continued to frequent the place in later days in search of cures or pleasures.

The second Romano-British spa is Buxton. This place also had been the site of a fort, established in Flavian times where the main road from Manchester to Littlechester, near Derby, meets the cross-road from Brough-on-Noe. The fort lay on high ground, significantly known as Silverlands. Below it rises today St. Anne's Well, immediately opposite the Pump Room which contains the springs, and there is enough evidence to show that when the modern Baths were constituted, in the eighteenth and nineteenth centuries substantial Roman remains were discovered, including at least two large lead-lined baths. Scanty and ill-recorded though the evidence is, there is, as Haverfield indicates,[2] enough to show that a Roman curative spa existed. Here the presiding deity was also feminine, and her name appears in the Ravenna list as *Arnemetia*. The name itself is interesting: it is a personal name formed, in the manner of the Welsh *Arfon*, from the words *are-* and *nemeton*, meaning 'at' or

[1] e.g. RIB 146.   [2] VCH Derbyshire, i, 222 ff.

M   [177]   R.A.A.

'before' and 'the sacred grove', so it seems certainly to suggest a pre-Roman regard for the place as a holy spot. It may be presumed that *Sulis* was similarly worshipped at Bath in pre-Roman times as the deity of the spring, although her name is not in itself specifically indicative of a holy place.

Sometimes these ancient tutelary deities survived as huge cartoon-like figures carved or cut on the hillsides. The most famous of these is the Uffington White Horse in Berkshire, one of the few pre-Roman sacred horses to have survived. He cannot but remind us of the famous horse dedicated to the Gallic deity *Rudiobus*, whose processional bronze image, from Neuvy-en-Sullias, is one of the treasures of the Museum at St. Germain. Less renowned but certainly not less impressive is the Cerne Giant, cut on the hill above Cerne Abbas, north of Dorchester. If the White Horse is designed in accord with the artistic conventions of the Iron Age, the Cerne Giant equally clearly exhibits the hybrid art of Roman Britain, in which the human form is so often expressed largely in outline rather than in full modelling. For the style there is an apt comparison in an interesting and little known Romano-British version of the contest of Apollo and Marsyas comes from the same district, where it decorated a villa at Lenthay Green. As to the *interpretatio Romana* of the Cerne Giant there can be no doubt: he is certainly equated with Hercules. But it must be borne in mind that in Celtic religion Hercules, whose popularity in Gaul was great, does not figure in the character of a hero and benefactor of mankind. His activities are connected with the underworld and Pluto: and this kind of association still clung to the Cerne Giant in the thirteenth-century, when his name was recorded as *Helith*, a name connected, as Professor Piggott has pointed out, with the early mediaeval French *Helequin*, in English *Helethkin*, a club-bearing giant leader of a band of lost souls.[1] So it is indeed the Gallic type of Hercules who is so strikingly perpetuated at Cerne, a god of death and the underworld, and in mediaeval times popular festivals were still conducted by his side about a may-pole, while the new religious

[1] *Antiquity*, vi, 214 ff.; 323 ff.; I owe this reference to S. Piggott.

centre of Cerne Abbas lay at his feet. His local function is not wholly clear. Close beside him lies the enclosure of an ancient shrine or sanctuary where the later may-pole was erected. But the plateau which he surveys across the valley, and whence he was presumably intended to be contemplated, is full of Romano-British fields and homesteads. He thus either commands the worship of a community or surveys the lands of a temple-estate. He was not the only god whose feet so trod the hills of Roman Britain. There is a well-authenticated tradition of a very similar giant who gave his name to the Gog Magog hills in our immediate neighbourhood, and who may be recognized as belonging to the same kind of religious manifestation, without attempting to detect its ancient form amid the detail of mediaeval legend with which it is overlaid.

Thus far the country gods and shrines considered have been the pagan deities whose shrines Gildas could still see. Is it possible to distinguish any trace of Christian pilgrimage sites? It is at least worth while to recall two points in native tradition concerning the British church of the fourth century, relating to the tombs of martyrs or saints. The tradition in Gildas concerning the proto-martyr, St. Alban, is vivid and based upon authentic topographical detail.[1] The inference would seem to be that his place of martyrdom was well known and venerated, as Bede also indicates in his account of the mission of St. Germanus to St. Alban's.[2] Similarly it will be noted that at the close of the sixth century St. Augustine found outside Canterbury a Romano-British church of St. Martin, which Queen Bertha was already using before his mission arrived. This would best be explained as a church connected with a cemetery or tombs which were venerated by the Christian community.

Doubtless there were others, and it is curious at least that the sole archaeological trace of such a tradition yet recovered should be directly referable to the two western martyrs recorded by Gildas, whom Bede copies, Iulius and Aaron of Caerleon.[3]

[1] Gildas *De Excidio*, 10 (i, 8).
[2] Bede, *Hist. Eccles.*, i, 18: this was in A.D. 429.   [3] Gildas, *loc. cit.*

When the amphitheatre or *ludus* outside the legionary fortress was excavated, no trace of late-Roman occupation was associated with it except at one point. In the ruined cell on the short axis of the building, where there was direct access to the arena and where beasts or victims may alternatively have been kept, a tiny apsidal shrine was inserted at a date when the arena was filled high above its original level with accumulated rubbish and silt. It was difficult to date the structure, and still more difficult to associate it with the active use of the amphitheatre. It has all the look of an insertion long after the building was in disuse. It has therefore been suggested that it was a small *martyrium* or commemorative chapel connected with a cult of the martyrs Iulius and Aaron, which Gildas knew and connected with the last and severest of the anti-Christian persecutions, and the traditions which it had produced. Even so, its date must remain uncertain, and it may in fact be connected with the beginnings of Welsh Christianity rather than the end of the Romano-British phase. But in either case it belongs to an age when Britons still thought of themselves as *Romani*, and it may serve as a curious and problematic tail-piece to a consideration of social centres in the Romano-British countryside.

III

OTHER PAPERS

I

HADRIAN'S WALL[1]

The most dramatic part of the Hadrian's Wall[2] is the central sector, which we know as the Crags and which the geologists know as the Whin Sill, where it reminds us of one of the earliest descriptions of the Wall 'Verily I have seen the Wall rising and falling'.[3] The highest portion now standing anywhere rises to some eleven feet, on the slope of Hare Hill in Cumberland. Ordinarily we see it standing from six to eight courses high; yet this enables us to appreciate its thickness and solidity better than we could if we were not, in fact, able to look over the top of it (plate II). In front of the wall, when there are no crags, there is a ditch so large that a cart-track can run down the middle of it. If we think of the two works together, a space of about twenty feet separates the wall from the inner lip of the ditch, while the material dug from the ditch is piled on the counterscarp so as to give no cover to an enemy, while the wall is so placed that from its top one can see right into the ditch.

The Wall was manned first by patrols based upon milecastles, and between every pair of milecastles (1520 yards apart) is a pair of turrets. When we wanted to recover the turrets and the milecastles in the western sector where the whole work has been destroyed by agriculture we trenched along the back of the

[1] This lecture has the air of being a verbatim report of what was said, hence the rather colloquial style – however the typescript has corrections in Richmond's hand and it has been printed here as corrected. It was given at the annual conference of the Museums Association at Newcastle upon Tyne in 1963.

[2] See now J. Collingwood Bruce, (ed. I.A.R.), *Handbook to the Roman Wall*, 12th ed. 1966; E. Birley, *Research on Hadrian's Wall*, 1961.

[3] Holland's translation of Camden, *Britannia*: see Birley, *op. cit.*, 6.

wall at intervals and found eventually the side walls of a turret. Measuring from the centre of the turret to the next milecastle position we dug a trench at the appropriate point, from north to south, and found we were right in the middle of the gateway. Although one thinks that in such indented country this accuracy would not be easy, milecastles are always placed so exactly.

In the first planning of the Wall the western sector, of eighty Roman miles from milecastle 49 to milecastle 80, was built in turf, and although here the turrets were of stone the milecastles had turf ramparts with timber buildings. This is a point to remember in the comparison I am going to make between Hadrian's Wall and other frontiers. There were several changes during the building of the Wall, the most important being the change from a wall with milecastles and turrets and with forts lying behind the wall, to receive forts on the line of the wall itself. The earlier forts were on the line of the Stanegate, an Agricolan road; they were of varying sizes and occurred at intervals of about 2½ to 3 miles, and the intermediate forts are small blockhouses, such as the one at Haltwhistle Burn which could take about a *centuria* of men. The larger forts such as Chesterholm, capable of holding a cohort, are like the early forts of the German *limes*. When the forts were moved forward to the line of the wall they were larger and of singularly interesting plan. We know they are secondary because the line of the wall and ditch and turret 27a lie beneath them.[1] Most of them project from the line of the wall so that you have not only the north gate, but also the west and east gates in front of the line of the wall, so that the garrison can make a rapid sally when it is necessary to intercept the enemy. The Wall was not designed as what we used to call a 'thin red line' from which people were fighting; half the usefulness of the Roman armour and tactics would have been destroyed if that had been the case. These forts, together with the milecastle gateways, were used as the basis for a pincer movement which would develop as the enemy approached the

[1] *i.e.* under Chesters fort: there is a similar situation with turret 36b under Housesteads fort.

wall and drive him up against the very barrier he was attempting
to cross.[1] Of course the system was not applicable anywhere.
Where you have the fort on the edge of a cliff, as at Housesteads,
you could not, of course, make it project, and so the fort there is
designed in relation to the wall and is of more normal design;
but still there is the large gateway and the way leading down to
the country in front of this line.[2] From one of these secondary
forts on the line of the wall we got the beautiful inscription[3]
which is now in the Museum of Antiquities at King's College.[4]
This dates the change as taking place under the same governor
(Aulus Platorius Nepos) as was responsible for the original
erection of the milecastle there; everything was done very
quickly.

Once you had put forts on the line of the wall you could
consider putting a barrier behind them, and it is that barrier
which has been known since the time of the Venerable Bede
as the Vallum[5] – not, perhaps, the most logical name, as when he
called it the Vallum he was thinking of the mound but the most
prominent feature is the ditch. I have heard Commando officers
say that they would have no difficulty in getting their men across
a ditch like that, but this obstacle was not designed to deal with
Commandos but with everyday people. The ditch is 25′ wide at
the top, but the Olympic record for the long jump is 23′ 4½″.
The sides are very steep and cut in stiff slippery boulder clay, and
the flat bottom of the ditch is 8′ wide. Another point is that if
you were caught on the wrong side of an obstacle like this you
couldn't pretend you had not noticed it. Yet it is not a defensive
work, because the first essential of a defensive work is that it
should give advantage to one side rather than another, and that is
exactly what this doesn't do. It is a perfect example of the frontier
obstacle and corresponds exactly to the rows of barbed wire
which one sees round an ordnance depot or an airfield where

---

[1] This theory seems very doubtful.
[2] The present sharp drop outside the north gate is due to modern clearance.
[3] From Benwell: *RIB* 1340.   [4] Now the University of Newcastle.
[5] Bede, *Hist. Eccles.*, i, 5.

pilferers are expected. It runs quite close behind the wall, and when it comes to a fort it makes a divergence and comes to a point opposite the south gateway where there is a permanent causeway of undisturbed subsoil with revetted stone sides and a gateway across it. There is only one case of a fort which was added after the Vallum, at Carrawburgh,[1] a point where aggression was not immediately an obvious thing to be resisted, and this was almost the last touch of the work.

Let us consider for a moment how the Wall compares with other Roman frontiers. We used to think that in Scotland we had a wall[2] which was of turf and on which the garrison was housed entirely in forts; now we are learning that between the forts there were structures uncommonly like milecastles in size and disposition.[3] There is more on the Antonine Wall that is like Hadrian's Wall than we were at one time disposed to think; we have yet to learn if there were at any time any turrets there.

If we compare the wall with the German *limes*[4] the first thing we notice is that the extent of the *limes* is five times as long as that of the Wall. It too has been subjected to alteration; there was an original line and the *limes* as we have it now came a little later, but the rest was a Hadrianic creation, and this inevitably calls for a comparison between the two works. The history of the German *limes* is no less complex than our own. The earliest element, the palisade, was later on replaced by a rampart and ditch; similarly, small towers with a smaller ditch round them were later replaced by larger wooden towers and ultimately by stone towers. The long history behind these things has not by any means been fully worked out. We have the great series of volumes[5] illustrating the

---

[1] It covers the gap between Chesters and Housesteads, a particularly difficult stretch of country to patrol. The Vallum runs under the fort and is readily visible from the air.

[2] See A. S. Robertson, *The Antonine Wall*, 1960; K. A. Steer, *JRS* 1, 84 ff.

[3] See Frere, *Britannia*, 143 ff.: it seems quite likely that there was not a regular series of fortlets.

[4] See W. Schleiermacher, *Der römische Limes in Deutschland*, 1959.

[5] E. Fabricius, F. Hattner and O. von Sarwey, *Der Obergermanisch-rätische Limes der Römerreiches* (ORL).

limes, but the sad story is that a great deal of the work was done far too early and that a great deal of it will now have to be done all over again – and nobody realizes that better than the German scholars who are today working on the problem. So we have a restoration here which includes two elements where you ought to have one – the palisade and the ditch and rampart – the point being that the palisade is a modest thing intended to break up infiltration through the woodland, the ditch and rampart belong to the moment when cavalry raiding was the problem as in the late second and early third century when the work was designed. So the change corresponds to a change in tactical requirements.

The history of a German fort on the *limes* is also highly complicated. A Hadrianic fort with buildings in timber inside it is overlaid later on by a great stone fort, which also had developments before the building of the later wall. When we come to the lay-out of the German *limes* at one of its most typical points we see that it was very cleverly laid out on the watershed, just as Hadrian's Wall was laid, and also very cleverly laid out in relation to the native population as represented by its great hill forts, which is nearly all neatly contained within the *limes*. That is exactly what did not happen on Hadrian's Wall, where there was the populated district of Southern Scotland right outside the *limes* and sufficiently far away for no-one on the line of the Wall to be able to exercise effective supervision. That is why these changes come, why the reaction of the natives to the new frontier was to attack it again and again, and in response to this aggression the forts were moved forward. The problem on the two frontiers was entirely different, and therefore this reflects itself in the design and the scale of the frontier.

Then we have the long Danube frontier. Although we know much of this in Austria and Hungary, political conditions have not been conducive to a study of the works between Belgrade and the Dobruja,[1] so for our illustrations of the Danube frontier we go to Trajan's column, where we see the watch towers and

---

[1] Richmond did later visit Romania, but died before putting any of his observations there into print.

the blockhouses and the signalling beacons. The Dobruja is a very remarkable frontier indeed. There are three works involved; a native work, the small rampart which runs behind, the larger rampart, and a stone wall belonging to the late-Roman period which follows a slightly different line. It was argued that because the Roman legions moved forward along the line of the Danube in front of this frontier, therefore it must be earlier than those movements in the reign of Trajan. But to anyone who knows the Dobruja and has seen what the country is like this is not an answer at all. The mouth of the Danube is easy to cross, it is shielded from the line of the river by a line of hills which make it imperative that you should be able to stand at the critical point of any turning movement that was attempted at the frontier, because at this point you have a choice of routes; so it is necessary always to have a barrier at this point, even in the fourth century.

The forts on the slopes behind the line seem at first sight to be set very close together, but the great Wall was at some time enlarged by cutting not only the ditch in front, but the new scoop behind, running through some forts which must have then been out of use and not through others, cutting off little structures which remind us of milecastles. There are features about this frontier not at all unlike Hadrian's Wall. If we were to see that the structures which looked like milecastles were in fact turrets, wooden towers standing in an earthwork, this would begin to make sense, and this is the sort of thing for which perhaps we may look. As Roman frontiers go it is just as complicated as Hadrian's Wall, though it doesn't have the rearward Vallum.

Then there is the African *limes*,[1] which has turrets on the line of a stone wall. The difference between the frontier here and the closed frontiers of the Dobruja and Hadrian's Wall is that here we have a frontier which is in a curious way both closed and open, because it is related entirely to the moving of flocks at given times of the year out of the desert regions into the mountains which the Romans controlled. Again and again the frontier here encloses

[1] See J. Baradez, *Vue-aérienne de l'organisation romaine dans le sud-algérien 'Fossatum Africae'*, 1949.

the mountain area; this is most unexpected and we can hardly understand it as a frontier in our sense of the word, and yet it is just the way to control the problem.

So we have an immense variety, and I want to emphasize in closing that it is the local problem that calls for the design. You may make a blueprint for it in a military establishment well behind the scenes, but sooner or later if you have got it wrong the local conditions will compel you to put it right. That is what we see producing those complications on the Dobruja, complications on the German *limes* and complications on our own Hadrian's Wall, and that, when we see the terrain tomorrow will become evident and apparent.

2

SPANISH TROOPS IN
ROMAN BRITAIN[1]

Although the number of Spanish auxiliary regiments in Britain do not make up a high proportion of the whole, they are sufficiently numerous to afford an admirable example of the Roman principle of using the levies from one province as the garrison of another and to illustrate the type of task in which such troops were engaged.[2]

The employment of Spanish troops at the early stage of the conquest of Britain is well illustrated by the occurrence of the *ala Vettonum* at Bath,[3] which had developed by Flavian times into the spa of *Aquae Sulis*. This unit was then transferred to Wales where it occupied the fort at Brecon Gaer,[4] one of the most important strategic road-junctions in the chain of garrisoned roads by which Wales was dominated. In this fort can be detected the *basilica equestris exercitatoria* or riding-school, crossing the *via principalis* in front of the *principia*. Another Spanish unit in Wales was the *cohors II Asturum* at Llanio, on the river Teifi where it guards the river-crossing again in a significantly strategic position.[5] Centurial stones of the unit suggest that it took a share in building or re-building the fort.[6]

As in Spain itself, it was the mountainous districts of the province that demanded a garrison, policing the districts and

---

[1] This paper was given on the occasion of the tenth anniversary of the re-opening of the German Archaeological Institute, Madrid.

[2] E.B. points out that it is important to realize that units were moved from fort to fort in the course of the occupation.

[3] *RIB* 159.   [4] *RIB* 403.   [5] *RIB* 407, 408.   [6] *RIB* 409, 410, 411.

ensuring their response to taxation and recruiting. The district of
Wales is small as compared with northern Britain, where the
frontier-walls, the forward areas beyond them and their hinterland required a still larger garrison. Here there were some distinguished Spanish regiments. Hadrian's Wall, itself inspired by the
greatest of Spanish Emperors, was designed in tactical relation to
cavalry regiments, and two of the *alae* on the Wall are of Spanish
origin, the *alae I* and *II Asturum* at Benwell[1] and Chesters[2]
respectively. At Benwell a dedication to the *Matres Campestres*
reminds us of the *campus*, or drill-ground over which they pre-
ded.[3] At Chesters the siting and planning of the gateways emphasizes their tactical use and the intercepting movements in
which the garrison would take part, while the placing of the fort
shows that it, like the others, was a secondary improvement in
the design of the Wall. The arrangement of the rearward boundary ditch is obscure at Chesters but the gate on its causeway at
Benwell is one of the finest, and illustrates how the Wall-zone
was enclosed and protected from pilferers (*latrunculi*) at the rear.
Not all forts were for cavalry. Great Chesters, held by *cohors II
Asturum*, was an infantry fort and of smaller size.[4] In the area
north of the Wall Ardoch illustrates both the Flavian and Antonine occupations of Scotland. Its sole tombstone commemorates
a private from a first-century Spanish unit, but with recruits
which it had acquired in Egypt during its stay there.[5] But the most
notable forward post is High Rochester (*Bremenium*) held in
the third century by the *cohors I fida Vardullorum*,[6] which had
previously garrisoned Lanchester[7] behind the Wall. This unit
held a strong-point, at which the evidence for artillery is of
particular interest, since it can be worked out in relation to the

---

[1] *RIB* 1334, 1337, 1348. There is in fact no evidence that any Spanish units
formed part of the *Hadrianic* garrison of the Wall (E.B.).

[2] *RIB* 1462–6, 1480.   [3] *RIB* 1334.

[4] *RIB* 1738.

[5] *RIB* 2213: *cohors I Hispanorum* – E.B. points out that Ammonius was in fact a
centurion; and need not have been recruited in Egypt.

[6] *RIB* 1262–3, 1272, 1279–81, 1285, 1288.

[7] *RIB* 1076, 1083.

terrain. The fort was the headquarters of *exploratores*[1] or frontier-scouts. It is matched by Netherby in the west, with its *basilica equestris exercitatoria*.[2]

In the hinterland of the Wall Lanchester is a good example of a road-patrol post, but Binchester, the third-century home of the *ala Vettonum*,[3] was a great road centre of the kind particularly suited to a cavalry garrison. Ribchester is of exactly the same kind.[4] Maryport on the other hand is part of the Cumberland coast defences.[5]

Brough in Derbyshire is a fort of a different kind, intended to police a district wild in itself and full of lead mines worked, as in Spain, both by lessees and by the State. The size of the fort suggests that its garrison, *cohors I Aquitanorum*,[6] was dispersed in the lead-mining area. The regiment had been transferred in A.D. 158 from Carrawburgh[7] fort on Hadrian's Wall, after having established there the goddess *Coventina*, who is also known in northern Spain. Nothing could illustrate better the variety of duties which might fall to the lot of auxiliary troops like those from Spain in one of the frontier provinces of the Empire.[8]

---

[1] *RIB* 1262, 1270.

[2] *RIB* 978: set up by the *cohors I Aelia Hispanorum milliaria equitata* – cf. *RIB* 976–7, 979. There may have been two units numbered *cohors I Hispanorum* (see *Arch. Camb.*, cii, 19).

[3] *RIB* 1028, 1032, 1035.

[4] *RIB* 586: *ala II Asturum* – presumably at some time in the second century (E.B.).

[5] *RIB* 814–17, 821–3, 827–9, 855: *cohors I Hispanorum*. Recent excavation is reported in *JRS* lvii, 177.

[6] *RIB* 283: except that the Aquitanians were partly Iberian in origin and neighboured on Spain, the relevance of this unit is not clear.

[7] *RIB* 1550: none of the dedications to *Coventina* are in fact by *cohors I Aquitanorum*.

[8] E.B. supplies the names of several other Spanish units known to have been in Britain:

> *cohors I Asturum* (*CIL* viii, 9047, third-century: *Not. Dig. Occ.* xl, 42 seems to give the same unit, as at *Aesica* (Greatchesters)).
>
> *cohors II Vasconum c. R.* (*CIL* xvi, 51 and 69; ii, 1086, where it is described as *equitata*: first- (probably) and early second-century).
>
> *cohors III Bracaraugustanorum* (*CIL* xvi, 48, 69, 70, 93 – all of the first half

of the second century – and perhaps *CIL* vii, 1230; *EE* ix, 1277; both from Manchester).

cohors I Celtiberorum (*CIL* xvi, 51, 69, 93 – all of the first half of the second century).

cohors I Bracaraugustanorum (if the unit number is correctly to be restored as *I* in *ILS* 9002).

The reader may also be referred for further details of garrisons to J. Collingwood Bruce (ed. Richmond), *Handbook to the Roman Wall*, 12th ed. 1966; V. E. Nash-Williams, *The Roman Frontier in Wales*, 1954, 106 ff., and 9; E. Birley, *Arch. Camb.*, cii, 9 ff., *Arch Camb.*, xci, 58 f.

3

ROMAN MILITARY ENGINEERING[1]

The military engineering of the Roman Empire had a long tradition behind it. From the second century B.C. onwards it was well appreciated in the Mediterranean world, that while the Roman army as a fighting force might vary from time to time in quality and might prove a little slow, yet ultimately very sure, in adapting itself to new conditions, its successes were repeatedly won by dogged engineering feats. All are familar with the long siege of *Numantia*, its immense circumvallation which ringed the desperate garrison about and reduced it to cannibalism and suicide. Less well known is the almost contemporary story of Gracchus, who induced those who boasted a ten-year store of provisions to immediate submission by the bland statement 'Then I take you in the eleventh year';[2] and nothing could better attest the impression made by the determination and efficiency in siege engineering which was already becoming a formidable tradition.

The foundation of disciplined and systematic work which made such engineering possible is older still. Already in the third century B.C.[3] foreigners noted, at first with puzzlement and very soon with respect, the temporary camps, systematically fortified and methodically planned, in which the Roman army

[1] See also Richmond, 'Roman Britain and Roman Military Antiquities', *Proc. Brit. Acad.*, xli, 297 ff. The present paper was given as a Discourse to the Royal Institution on 16 November 1956, and an abstract published in *Proc. Roy. Inst.*, xxxvi, ii, no. 163, 487.

[2] Frontinus, *Strat.*, iii, 5, 2.

[3] This should perhaps, as E.B. points out, read *second* century, if I.A.R. was thinking of Polybius.

on the march bivouacked for the night. They were ditched and
further defended by a rampart crowned by stakes, and each
soldier took his allotted part in their erection. When Josephus, the
Jewish historian of the late first century A.D., saw this traditional
operation in progress, he was left astonished. The work went up
θᾶττον ἐπινοίας, 'quicker than the mind could grasp'.[1] The
speed and the efficiency imply not merely good discipline and
high morale but painstaking and systematic organization. The
men needed tools of standard pattern, of which the performance
could be calculated in terms of time and man-power. And while
the larger tools elude us, the smaller abound.[2] First and foremost
was the *dolabrum*, a highly effective wrought-iron pick-axe used
for clearing scrub and lopping timber and for picking earth.
The axe-blade had a handy standard sheath, of which the metal
parts in bronze or iron are frequently found. Next comes the
entrenching tool, of a pattern closely resembling that used in
our own army in the first world war, and reminding us of how
early man often discovered the unchanging pattern of the right
tool for the job. The stripping of turf from the ditch is another
task for which spades or turf-cutters are required and these too
appear in the archaeological record as well as in literature. Nor is
the actual portrayal of such work lacking. We are fortunate in
possessing the sculptured record of Trajan's campaigns in *Dacia*,
fought between A.D. 101 and 105, in which a vivid series of
kaleidoscopic scenes are deliberately composed to lay equally
heavy stress upon the martial prowess and the engineering
capacity of the Roman Imperial Army.[3] First come the men
themselves, crossing the Danube on a bridge of boats into enemy
territory. They are not in battle array, but are marching with full
kit slung on the poles which distributed the burden. Among the
medley of objects can be distinguished a heavily reinforced leather

---

[1] Josephus, *Bell. Jud.*, iii, 84 (I owe this reference to E.B.) (*cf.* v, 509, of the
siege works at Jerusalem: τὸ τάχος δ᾽ ἡττᾶσθαι πίστεως.

[2] *e.g.* J. W. Brailsford, *Hod Hill I*, 1962, figs. 12, 13; J. Curle, *A Roman Frontier
Post and Its Peoples*, 1911, pl. lvii.

[3] See C. Cichorius, *Die Reliefs der Trajansäule*, 1896–1900, for illustrations; (for
more modern publications see D. E. Strong, *Roman Imperial Sculpture*, 1961, 84).

tool-bag, and presently the tools are seen in use. In a curiously
turbulent and powerful composition, can be seen the lopping and
felling of woodland. The crowding and confusion obscure the
essential orderliness of the task, in the anxiety to convey its
strenuous speed and vigorous intensity. Much more methodical
is the scene of turf-cutting, where the stripped ground, the sods
cut but not yet lifted and the turves cut and lying ready for
carrying away form the foreground of a scene of camp building.
In the background the rampart of turf, here schematically rendered like blocks of stone, is in process of erection. One rampart is
half built, the other has received the wooden duck-board walk or
corduroy which crowned it, and of which the log ends, fastened
between two running spars of timber, can be clearly seen.
Ditch-digging is also hinted at, in the figure handing up a basket
from well below ground-level. But a much more striking treatment of the theme of ditch-digging, appears in an adjacent scene,
where, in front of a fort in process of erection, two soldiers are
seen in the very act of comparing their achievement in digging as
measured in baskets-full of earth. We cannot indeed here recon-
struct the rough and sturdy phrasing of the *sermo castrensis*: but
there will be many in the audience who can achieve a translation,
even if their version would not pass the Lord Chamberlain. Yet
this lively conversation piece introduces us to one of the secrets of
Roman military engineering, that organization in gang-work
which got the maximum effort in the best way by inducing
rivalry between the working units, whether large or small;
and it is in fact a picture of gang-work[1] and its effects at which we
are looking, not an idle or pointless field-sketch.

A glance at the field-works themselves will give a swift idea of
their orderliness, and as for the speed involved in construction,
a few calculations will suffice. To erect a camp for a legion,
some 40,000 square feet of turf must be cut, and about 100,000
cubic feet of earth must be moved. But if that is translated into
terms of man-power, it means that each of 4000 men, out of

[1] The distance-slabs on Hadrian's Wall and the Antonine Wall are a vivid
record of such gang-work.

the total strength of 5,500, is to shift only 10 square feet of turf and to dig only 25 cubic feet of earth, while over a thousand men are still available for other tasks. That the work could go quickly, once laid out by the advance party, is thus readily demonstrated.

Closely connected with road-work come the bridges, and these were often part of the preparations for campaign as well as part of the consolidation of results. By a curious chance it is a dictionary item which states that the Roman army had supplies of boats and chains with which temporary bridges of large or small size could be constructed.[1] It is a less freakish matter that the artist of Trajan's Column should have chosen to portray their manufacture in a log corral amid the woodland. For this was a fine opportunity to illustrate the striking specialism in army organization with a scene calculated to grip the imagination of the beholder. It was the same instinct for arresting detail that led him to give us the only representation in antiquity of Roman field-artillery, used in support of troops in battle. But to return to bridges, it is again Trajan's Column which affords the most detailed picture of a great bridge of boats, seen from down-stream. Each boat exhibits one of its steering oars lashed in position against the steersman's platform, while in the background amidships is seen the stout caisson which carried adjoining sections of the bridge whose massive railings contrast with the minor rails surrounding the steersman's platform. It will be recalled that the purpose of this bridge was to span the Danube where it is over a mile and a half wide, and at all times a turbulent stream. Something special and out of the ordinary was called for both in size and quantity of materials. No less impressive was the permanent bridge which in due course crossed the river and linked the new provinces of *Dacia* with the Roman world. It was, indeed, sufficiently remarkable to be mentioned in literature, which is normally silent upon such matters.[2] It was some 1,500 yards long,

---

[1] Vegetius, *De Re Militari*, ii, 25; iii, 7.
[2] Dio, lxviii, 13: the superstructure was removed by Hadrian.

150 feet high[1] and had 20 stone piers. The superstructure was of wood, and could be dismantled if required. The Column has a view of this work also. As in presenting the bridge of boats the artist gives a condensed view, and shows, so to speak, a sample only. There is little attempt at perspective, and such as is made has the weaknesses often apparent in ancient work: so we are given what is almost an elevation. The first most notable feature is the cantilever strutting in the haunches, by which the weight of the roadway is made to balance the thrust of the arches. The second is the building up of the arches in segmental form and in short lengths of timber. It is, of course, certain that in this bridge many more than four segments must have been used for the 170-foot span between the twenty piers. The delineation is a simplified version. But in the average bridge four segments in ten-foot lengths would be a very reasonable span, comparable with the 33-foot spans of the Tyne bridge at Chesters, and about half the size of those on the Rhine bridge at Mainz. The illustration is in fact the basis of reconstruction applied to all such bridges. It is interesting to reflect that the timber segmental arch had its influence upon the form of ancient permanent architectural works in stone. In the amphitheatre of *Emerita Augusta* and in the bridge of Alconetar, both structures readily associated with military architects, the segmental arch appears majestically, though it had little influence upon monumental architecture as a whole until the engineer came into that field again in the nineteenth century.

[1] This was the height of the piers: the total height is unknown. The piers were 60 Roman feet wide.

4

FAME AND IMMORTALITY
IN THE ROMAN WORLD[1]

In the eclectic religious atmosphere of the Roman world, it would be rash to claim that a generally accepted or clearly defined notion of immortality existed. Fame, on the other hand, was an objective sought by all, and it is beyond doubt that there was a close connexion between the two concepts. Nor is it difficult to adduce archaeological evidence in apparent support of such a link. Yet to those conversant with art-history and its studies the trap is seen to yawn wide. He who would interpret the meaning of an artistic representation is all too often confronted by the question whether the scene literally means what it appears at first sight to say, and is to be taken solely at its face value and no more, or whether there is a deeper inner meaning which those in tune with the thought of the period would not fail to perceive. And it might be said that the major achievement of the art-historian in our century has been to demonstrate the significance of representational art in the light of the literature contemporary with the artist. The effect has been to emphasize the supreme value of the classical outlook, in which the two modes of expression were knitted more closely and more clearly together than in other ages, with the result that in the light of contemporary interpretation we may be guided in our own approach. No apology is therefore

[1] This lecture was given at the Warburg Institute on 25 October 1961 as one of a series of lectures on the theme 'Fame and Immortality'. At the end on that occasion I.A.R. seems to have given an impromptu discourse to accompany his slides of archaeological examples illustrating the points made in the text. No record of what he said survives among his papers.

required for an approach through the literary tradition. On the contrary, the possibility is a matter for rejoicing. The flight into remote periods, unembarrassed by such guidance, is one of the symptoms of a dictatorial age, bent upon interpreting the ancient world in terms of ideals or dogmas which that world did not share and would indeed have regarded with mistrust and even abhorrence. It is, however, necessary to take into account an inherent characteristic of the literary tradition of the Roman world, which differentiates it sharply from literature of the present day. It was not directed to a large general public, drawn from all classes of society with very widely differing standpoints of judgment, but to a much more restricted upper class: a class that was highly intelligent, highly individual yet schooled in the same highly stereotyped education, which attached the greatest importance to the art of rhetoric, meaning the presentation of a convincing case stated within the limits of well-recognized conventional terms. The effect of this state of affairs was so to mould literary expression that a writer inevitably found himself directing it towards an upper class: and it was perhaps only the innate Roman leaning to realism, expressed in art by verism and in literature by satire, which saved Latin literature from the extreme artificiality certainly observable in some of its manifestations. Yet the total effect of these restrictions and trammels was that literary presentation of serious thought and practical action had to face a highly intelligent and critical audience well used to distinguish the authentic and convincing statement from the false. The mode or tone in which this was expressed, or the characterization of the social *milieu* from which it purported to come, must therefore have rung true, if success was to have been assured: and this was a powerful inducement to veracity of expression, effectively imposing probability as the prime operative criterion. Thus, while Roman literature imputed to its creations a wide variety of sentiment, attached to very different circumstances and uttered through many different types of character, the statements as such must have carried conviction if they were to have made a mark in themselves and above all a reputation for their author. It is often objected that in ancient literature the set speech is not what was actually said on the given occasion: but what is important for an evaluation of the thought is the essential requirement that it should not in itself have rung false.

Once these terms, which flow from the social *milieu* that produced them, are understood, it is possible to regard the literary evidence as firm ground upon which to build; and the objection that an earthy novel was not written by a groundling author, as, for example, the *Cena Trimalchionis*, has no value. But we can begin from the top and not from the bottom, with Tacitus, whose noble statement of the connexion between fame and immortality deserves full citation. I will venture to translate it.

'If there is any place for the spirits of the righteous; if, as the wise are pleased to think, great souls are not extinguished with the body, mayest thou rest in peace, calling us thy family from weak longing and womanish grief to a contemplation of thy virtues, which it is wicked to bewail or mourn. Let us rather adore thee with admiration and immortal praise, and with imitation, if nature will afford the support. That is true family honour and loyalty. And I would enjoin upon his daughter and wife, so to revere the memory of a father and husband that they turn over in their hearts all his doings and sayings, cherishing the form and figure of mind rather than body. Not because I would think to do away with statues fashioned in marble or bronze: but, just as human countenances are insubstantial and mortal, so are their images; while the mind's form is everlasting and thou canst thyself preserve and express it by no other material or skill except thine own standard of behaviour. Whatever we loved or admired in Agricola endures and will endure in the souls of men forever, the fame of his deeds. For oblivion has overwhelmed many of old as if they had been neither glorious nor noble. Agricola will survive, described and handed down to posterity.'[1]

This noble and passionate declaration of belief is the very counterblast to the *damnatio memoriae* just then in everyone's

---

[1] Tacitus, *Agr.*, 46.

mind, which had condemned Domitian to eternal oblivion. Even if it had stood alone, it would be a remarkable statement of the relationship between fame and immortality. But another equally interesting statement of coeval thought made by a slightly earlier contemporary, is put into the mouth of Titus by the historian Josephus. This statement concerns a warrior's death, and comes from a speech to the army of Jerusalem, at a critical period of the famous siege.

'Leaving on one side just now an encomium of death in battle and the immortality destined for those who fall in its heat, the worst I could wish for those who think otherwise is a peace-time death from disease, in which soul as well as body is condemned to the grave. For what brave man does not know that the purest of elements, the upper air, receives souls released from the flesh by the steel in combat and settles them among the stars; and that these souls appear to the descendants as good spirits and kindly disposed heroes: whereas darkness below and deep oblivion blot out and receive souls, however spotless, that waste away with the body, cancelling simultaneously life, body and even memory?'[1]

These are highly interesting sentiments with which to inspire reckless bravery, and it is still more interesting that they did in fact succeed, as Josephus goes on to narrate, though that side of the story is not our concern here. They introduce us, on the one hand, to the fact that no common belief existed as to the fate of the soul. On the other hand, they affirm in a new form the beliefs expressed in the Ciceronian *Somnium Scipionis*; firstly, that 'all who have saved, succoured or glorified their country have a sure allotted place in heaven, where such blessed souls will enjoy everlasting life';[2] and, secondly, that such souls could appear to the living in an individual form, recognizable by those who had known them on earth, yet remote like a statue and agleam with heavenly brightness.[3] For, whereas Cicero, and Vergil after him, applied the conception only to the august figures of the Roman world, Josephus, who intended to win the approval of Titus,

---

[1] Josephus, *Bell. Jud.*, vi, 46–8.   [2] Cicero, *Rep.*, vi, 13.
[3] Perhaps Cicero, *Rep.*, vi, 10, but the reference is not clear.

represents him as extending the notion to soldiers who die a hero's death in battle. In other words, dedicated service is the criterion of the reward. It is in fact, the extension to the common man, in special circumstances of exalted bravery, of the view taken by Tiberius concerning the conferment of divine honours upon Augustus, that he had earned them 'by the magnitude of his benefactions to the whole world.'[1] Even tipsy Trimalchio is made by Petronius to include this notion in his crude mixture of ideas upon survival. In his first spate of enthusiasm, he conceives of life being actually conferred upon the dead by carving upon their monument the things they enjoyed upon earth, and by associating their ashes with a rich planting of fruits and vines. 'I beg you earnestly to do it', he is made to say, 'that by your kindness I may have the good fortune to live after death.'[2] But his next and most emphatic fancy seizes upon the representation of those achievements and activities of life in which he had taken most pride – his ships in full sail, himself in official robes distributing largess, his dinner to the public, with the people at table doing themselves nicely (*populum sibi suaviter facientem*).[3] This takes us back to the Tacitean conception that the truest and best service to be conferred upon the dead is the perpetuation of their deeds and actions, the *fama rerum*. This is not indeed itself immortality, but it is the way they survive, 'described and handed down to posterity.' Of those in oblivion Horace could say, '*carent quia vate sacro*'.[4] But the dumb narration, sometimes a virtual pantomime in stone, could take the place of the written word.

Fame is thus seen to have a double meaning, but only in virtue of a transference of ideas. First and foremost connected with *fari*, 'to utter speech', it means what is said. The proud statement of Ennius on his fame exploits this notion; ' "*nemo me lacrimis decoret nec funera fletu*", Faxit, "*cur? Volito vivu' per ora virum.*" '[5]

---

[1] *SEG* xi, 923 (V. Ehrenburg and A. H. M. Jones, *Documents illustrating the Reigns of Augustus and Tiberius*, 1955, p. 87, no. 102): I owe this reference to D. Shotter and M. M. Willcock.

[2] Petronius, *Satyricon*, 71.   [3] *Ibid.*   [4] Horace, *Od.*, iv, 9, 28.

[5] Ennius, in Cicero, *Tusc.*, i, 15, 34.

Secondly it comes to mean 'good report' or 'glory'. While therefore *fama* in the sense of glory is conceived as conferring immortality upon a mortal, it must be earned by outstanding service or achievement. But it becomes clear that a title to such exaltation was considered to be conferred upon the dead by their *fama* in the sense of a statement of their achievements, either by literary description or by any other representational medium. Fame and immortality are thus curiously commingled and are almost inextricably interwoven in the Roman development of eschatological thought.

5

THE *ARA PACIS AUGUSTAE*

The monument now before us has long been identified as the *Ara Pacis Augustae*, formally constituted on 4 July 13 B.C., and dedicated three and a half years later, on 30 January, 9 B.C.[1] That altar was recorded by Augustus himself, in the *Res Gestae*, as having been commissioned by decree of the Senate as a thanksgiving for his homeward return in 13 B.C. after absence since 16 B.C. in the Western provinces.[2] Recently the identification has been impugned, with great learning and penetrating scepticism, by Dr. Weinstock,[3] who points out that there is no actual proof that it is the *Ara Pacis*, that fault can be found with an identification based upon numismatic representations of the monument, that the type of sacrifice depicted upon the altar is not appropriate to the personified goddess Peace, and that her particular attribute, the *caduceus*, nowhere appears among the symbolic decoration on the reliefs. This is an apparently formidable arraignment. But the points which seem cumulatively so formidable, are individually much less strong. Numismatic representations of ancient buildings are notoriously unreliable in detail, and it is solely upon detail that the argument depends. The sacrifice may have included other deities. If the *caduceus* is not seen, there are missing scenes, for example, that of the goddess *Roma*, in which [it] could well have appeared. Further the problem of identification, if that with the *Ara Pacis* is discarded, is difficult. Granted that there may have been great public occasions of which we have no record, so important a one as this, involving the whole

---

[1] See J. M .C. Toynbee, *Proc. Brit. Acad.*, xxxix, 67 ff.
[2] *Res Gestae*, 12.   [3] S. Weinstock, *JRS* l, 44 ff. (J.M.C.T.).

[205]

priesthood, magistrates and people and the entire Imperial family is not likely to have been missed out by Augustus from his catalogue of distinguished honours and achievements, and it may be expected that there will be a return to the identification, perhaps accompanied by new light upon it.

For the meantime, however, the monument must be regarded as what it is, a great Augustan monument commemorating a great occasion upon which Augustus and the Imperial family met the representatives, religious and secular, of the Roman Senate and People. In Imperial art the decoration, like the occasion, presented a new problem, requiring ornamentation not only for the altar itself, but for the great screen-wall which surrounded it, defining the *templum* or hallowed area within which sacrifices might take place.

The space enclosed was not a large one, and there was no room inside it for a large concourse of people. What was demanded was a group of functionaries very like those described in connexion with the *Ara Pacis*[1] namely 'the magistrates, priests and Vestal Virgins'. If all these participated in the rites there would be room for them but no more, and the great procession of the Imperial family and notables which is portrayed on the southern and northern external faces of the screen-wall would be gathered outside the precinct like a congregation grouped before an *iconostasis* or in front of a screened chancel. Most could only glimpse the ceremony through the west doorway. Similarly, the animal sacrifices, of heifer, steer and sheep, would take place outside the east door, the attendants, hidden by the altar itself, bringing in the portions for offering from behind it.

It has been suggested, on the basis of the history of the *Ara Pacis*, which was founded in 13 B.C. and dedicated in 9 B.C., that there were two phases in the creation of the monument. Nor can there in fact be much doubt that, as Pasqui observed,[2] the architecture of the screen-wall indeed reflects a temporary stage, particularly on the internal face, where the fluted lower dado seems to correspond to an original screen-wall of upright planks

[1] *Res Gestae*, 12.   [2] A. Pasqui, *Studi Romani*, i, 283 ff.; 296, fig. 6.

on end, while on the upper panels the swags set between the framing pilasters might represent original swags of real fruit and flowers swinging in open panels. The theory is attractive; but it should probably be modified in order to conform to the religious purpose of the screen, which was to cut off from the officiants any sight or sound of evil omen. It need not be supposed that the swags were originally real, any more that it would be seriously imagined that the conventional decoration of *bucrania* will have been, at this stage in Roman civilization, clean-picked real skulls. It would not be difficult rapidly to prepare any such decoration in either painting or stucco, and to erect very speedily a suitable and more seemly monument by using a temporary wooden framework. This type of decoration will explain the scroll-work of the external dado far better than, for example, the assumption that they repeat the pattern of a tapestry or carpet with which the temporary work was draped. It does not, on the other hand, at all easily explain the major compositions represented by the scenes in the external upper panels. Of these, the long panels are, as we shall see, undoubtedly the actual procession at the time of the altar's inauguration and cannot have been inspired except by the ceremony itself. They belong therefore to the decorative scheme of the permanent altar, and the designers of the temporary work may well have been content to repeat on these surfaces the orna-mental swags and *bucrania* which were permanently retained for the internal walls. The same immediacy, however, cannot be attached to the panels flanking the doors. Without for the moment considering these in detail it may be remarked that all are of themes which had been fashionable for some time. Those on the main west side refer to the *Aeneid*, those on the east side to personifications of Rome and *Tellus*.[1] It is thus a possible though not a necessary supposition that these in an original temporary form were paintings, and the possibility carries with it the corollary that other paintings (four would fit the space) might have graced each long side, portraying, whether in panels or in

---

[1] Toynbee, *op. cit.*, 81, modified her earlier view and thought that the figure was at least predominantly a personification of Italy.

continuous scenes, the legends of early Rome. This, however, cannot now be known, and further conjecture would be unprofitable. The easiest assumption of all would be that the temporary screen carried conventional decoration only, in stucco or painting throughout.

When, however, a permanent form for the altar was sought, the upper external panels assumed an importance which almost transcended the ceremonies, original or annual, and their intention. For they were now designed to display day in day out both the original occasion of the foundation and the associated ideas in the form of religious scenes or personifications dear to the Roman mind. Adorning the outside of the building, whose gates or doors were normally closed, they were to proclaim its purpose and the achievements and hopes which had brought it into being. For the historian of today, as for the general public of ancient Rome, they become, the most expressive part of the monument.

In relation to the *Via Flaminia*, in ancient times and still today the arterial route through the *Campus Martius*, the altar was approached from the east. This doorway, the back door from the point of view of the celebrants at the altar, is flanked by two great panels containing personifications. On the right, or north, side was *Roma*, seated upon a pile of arms. Unfortunately only the knees of this figure remain and it is highly doubtful how the rest of the panel was composed. In most general and schematic detail the type is given by the view of the *Ara Pacis* on a *sestertius* of Nero, showing Rome as a helmeted figure, seated as described. But subordinate figures are omitted, and there must have been two, probably designed as a pair. If Studniczka[1] and Professor Toynbee[2] are right, the male head from a right-hand standing figure, by others assigned to the Aeneas panel, may belong here and represent a minor deity standing behind *Roma*. This would imply a main scene of action in front of *Roma*, who might be thought of as receiving *Pax*. As for the figure itself, Professor Toynbee is surely right in recognizing the object

[1] F. Studniczka, *Abhandl. d. Phil. Gesell.*, xxvi, 901 ff.
[2] Toynbee, *op. cit.*, 80.

III. Aosta: '*Porta Praetoria*': note the enormous size of the central arch and the well-preserved fragments of the facing.

against its left shoulder as a *cornucopiae*, so that we are to think of a personification. Professor Toynbee suggests *Honos* or *Bonus Eventus* or the *Genius Populi Romani*, and it would be difficult to narrow the choice. What it was not was the *Roma* of the Carthage *Ara Gentis Iuliae*.

The south side of the door was graced by a famous panel, the wonderful personification believed by a majority of scholars to be *Tellus*. A powerful minority would recognize the piece as *Italia*.[1] But the whole conception so vividly, if not exactly, echoes the description of *Tellus* in the *Carmen Saeculare*[2] that it is difficult to dismiss the correspondence as fortuitous, since the *Carmen*, published in 17 B.C., had by then become a classic. The words are still worth quoting with the piece in view:

> *Fertilis frugum pecorisque Tellus*
> *spicea donet Cererem corona;*
> *nutriant fetus et aquae salubres*
> *et Iovis aurae.*

But if the subject recalled a poem, it might also recall to some of its viewers the no less famous line of the Georgics: *Salue, magna parens frugum, Saturnia tellus*.[3] In other words, the secondary allusion to Italy would strike all who saw it, through the very familiarity of the primary reference to *Tellus*.

The western doorway is flanked by scenes more closely connected with Rome and its foundation legends. On its south side is the well known panel of Aeneas sacrificing a sow to Juno at the Tiber mouth: *Quam pius Aeneas tibi enim, tibi, maxima Juno, mactat sacra ferens et cum grege sistit ad aram*.[4] This portent was to be the sign of the place where *Lavinium* was to be built[5] and it is in this very literal sense that Moretti,[6] who has published the complete monument, interprets the reliefs of the southern side of the monument, as a procession from the temple of *Tellus*, indicated by the *Tellus* relief, to *Lavinium*, represented by the

---

[1] See Toynbee, *op. cit.*, 81.
[2] Horace, *Carmen Saeculare*, 29–32 (I.A.R.).
[3] Vergil, *Georg.*, ii, 173 (I.A.R.).
[4] Vergil, *Aen.*, viii, 84–5 (I.A.R.).
[5] *Aen.*, iii, 390–3 (I.A.R.).
[6] G. Moretti, *Ara Pacis Augustae*, 1948.

sacrifice. The northern scene was that of the *Lupercal*, and of this, as of its counterpart at the east end, little remains. Mars, the father of Romulus and Remus, and Faustulus, who rescued them, survive in fragments. Here Moretti would recognize the goal of a different procession, from Rome, or in Rome, to the *Lupercal*. But although both acts might conceivably be brought into connexion with the religious policy of Augustus, they remain devoid of immediate reference to the altar and they lack unity of theme. The artistic dichotomy postulated is both unwelcome and illogical. It is, then, more rational to link the two processions, as their complementary composition demands, and to regard the legendary scenes as poetic expressions of the same theme. The subjects are indeed themselves complementary. On the east side, Rome at rest and *Tellus* in tranquillity are different aspects of the same thing: and their intimate connexion as corollaries of peace cannot escape notice. On the west side, the sacrifice of Aeneas, and the scene of the twins in the *Lupercal*, would typify the beginning of a new age of rest for Augustus, who, like his ancestor Aeneas, was the *dux bonus*, a leader of his people; it would mean also security for the *gens Romula* and Rome as represented by the twins and the *Lupercal*. The theme of the front facing the main line of approach is thus the beginning of a new age for Augustus and his people. The historian may find food for thought in the nature of the compliment here paid to Augustus. It is acknowledgment without adulation. To compare Augustus with Aeneas was to liken him neither to a god nor even to a mortal who, like Romulus, had won divine honours. It reflects a positively late-Republican or Ciceronian view of the leader of the State; leader and commander, dutiful to gods and men, even avenger (if we recall the final act of the *Aeneid*) but no second Romulus, no Hercules, no Bacchus, no Apollo: this is to confer upon the *princeps* proper human stature.

This respectful and restrained outlook may prepare us for the tone of the processional friezes. First there are those on the altar itself. This table of sacrific was raised upon a platform with four steps, and consisted of a great flat-topped bench planned like an E without central bar, the middle void occupied by four more steps, leading to its top. The back and sides were bordered by a low screen, its panels decorated externally with scroll-work and crowned on the ends or sides by elaborate terminals of opposed scrolls carried by winged lions. These bold subsidiary creatures have all the vigour and vitality which characterizes such ornaments, and may be compared, for example, with those on the beam-ends of Caligula's Nemi ships. The top of the screen carries everywhere a narrow frieze which portrays the sacrifice and its participants, the Vestal Virgins, with their apparitors, so far as it survives. This is of great interest as being one of the few surviving reliefs that illustrate the Vestals in attendance at worship: in its rather hard and dry execution it compares, as Professor Toynbee has observed,[1] with the sacrificial frieze from the temple of Apollo *in Campo*; but it might be claimed that here the standard of execution was better.

It would seem, then, that the participants in the sacrifice were portrayed round the altar, not as they stood at the ceremony, unless the beasts were there paraded before slaughter, but rather as they walked in procession towards it. This is manifestly the treatment accorded to the principal external panels, which figure on the south side the consuls and Augustus, followed by *pontifices*, and the Imperial family and upon the north side senators, *sacerdotes* and citizens with their wives and children. There is no doubt about the meaning of this grouping: and, while Moretti has thought to see in them two independent processions, the complementary character of the two groups, which, taken together, form a gathering wholly representative of the Roman State, is a powerful and, it may be thought, a completely convincing argument in favour of the unity of the two scenes. Further, the topographical interpretation of the religious reliefs, to which reference has already been made and which is a necessary step in Moretti's argument, stretches belief to breaking-point. It is far easier, more logical and in every way more attractive to regard the two processions as complementary parts of a unitary act.

[1] Toynbee, *op. cit.*, 75.

Both processions proceed westwards towards the main doorway
of the precinct as they must have done on the day of the altar's
inauguration. But there is a significant difference in composition
between them. The northern procession, comprising senators and
distinguished Roman notables, wends its way steadily forwards,
linked only by a subtle rhythm of conversational attitudes and
gestures between this and that member of the throng. The
southern procession builds up very similarly from the back, but
at a point rather more than one-third of its length from the front
it comes to a firm stop. Here stands Augustus himself, flanked by
two consuls. One of these has been reasonably identified with
Tiberius and the other would then be Varus, of whose iconography nothing is known. If the Tiberian identification is certain
the case for the dedication as that of the *Ara Pacis* would be very
strong. Augustus is reaching out to use a ritual object, now lost.
The attitude closely, and no doubt deliberately, echoes that of
pius Aeneas himself on the adjacent panel. What then followed
to the left is not clear. Augustus himself is hedged about by the
two consuls and their lictors, while a *camillus* with fringed cloak
and incense box appears beyond them. He is, however, moving
away from Augustus, and the presence of further lictors beyond,
moving in both directions, would indicate that another figure of
prime importance occupied this end of the frieze. This personage,
as Poulsen[1] and Professor Toynbee[2] suggest, may well have been
Livia. But it may be suggested, without prejudice to the question
of identity, that this important actor in the scene does not head
the procession of Augustus: no one could do that except a god, as
a matter of protocol: this major figure must head the procession
of the northern frieze, whose members are pressing forward to a
conclusion which on that side never appears: and the end is, then,
not, as Moretti thought, in the *Lupercal* but lies in the continuation of the procession, whereof the real head and focus is Augustus
himself.

Little attention has been paid to the identification of figures in
the northern frieze, though it contains some highly individual

[1] *Acta Archaeologica*, xvii, 6.   [2] Toynbee, *op. cit.*, 85.

personalities. Their rank emerges here and there. Three *sacerdotes* are seen, *capite velati*, each with an attendant *camillus*; one thinks of figures like Statilius Taurus, the *curio maximus*: and the rearmost *camillus*, who is accorded more prominence than the priest whom he attends, is no doubt a youth of especial distinction. At least two priestesses, with fringed cloaks, also appear.

But these venerable figures, many of them no doubt *novi homines*, like Statilius Taurus, are not the greatest religious personages of the Roman state. These are seen on the south side, where, behind Augustus and the consuls, proceed four *flamines*, first the *flamen Dialis* and *flamen Martialis*, then the *flamen Iulialis* and *flamen Quirinalis*. It will be observed that, while the old-established *flamines maiores* are shown full-figure, the recently created *flamen Iulialis* occupies the background, with only head and shoulders in sight. This man has been identified as Sextus Appuleius, husband of Octavia Maior. Next should follow, in the *ordo sacerdotum*, the *pontifex maximus*. But this august figure was not available at the time of the constitution of the Altar, when the office was held by Lepidus, long in exile, After the death of Lepidus, in 12 B.C., the coveted position came to Augustus. Thus, in either case, a deputy was required, and the man in question, to emphasize his position, is preceded by an attendant with the ritual axe or *sacena* of the pontiffs. The prominent and imposing figure is best identified as Agrippa. Unfortunately the nose of his face is restored, and this hinders identification, for Agrippa's nose was markedly individual. But the age of the figure, the high cheekbones and sunken cheeks, the hair pattern and the short line at the corner of a small mouth, so far as they go, support the identification. Lepidus it cannot be, both on grounds of physiognomy and because of the complete unlikelihood that he should have been recalled to take part in a ceremony, so intimately concerned with the Imperial House, where the irony and political illogicality of his position would have been glaring.

There is no doubt that Agrippa is here not only *pontifex* but *paterfamilias*, since the child clinging to his *toga* and looking towards his mother forms the link which connects the family unit.

[213]

This indubitable connexion would make the lady Julia, the daughter of Augustus; and it is unfortunate that here the restored nose and mouth again render an iconographic identification precarious. For the identity of this lady has been no less discussed than that of the figure now classed as Agrippa. Moretti and Mrs. Ryberg[1] claim her for Livia. But this, as Professor Toynbee[2] has pointed out, would relegate Julia, the daughter of Augustus, to a secondary place in the background, which is most unlikely in view of the prominence accorded to the adjacent nieces of Augustus, on whose identity all are agreed. It is more likely that Livia is to be found in still more prominent position at the west end of the south side and with her Gaius, Agrippa's elder son by Julia. The next figure is claimed for Tiberius by Mrs. Ryberg and Moretti. But this would imply that there are repetitions of principal figures in the scene, if Tiberius has been shown already as *consul* attendant upon Augustus.[3] The fact that one seeks in vain for any other instance of repetition among the thirty-three surviving foreground figures is enough to rule this notion out of court. Poulsen's attractive suggestion, that the young man is Iullus Antonius, *praetor urbanus* in 13 B.C., and nephew of Augustus by marriage, carries conviction.[4] From this point backwards the foreground figures are universally accepted as representing two family groups. First, the family of Drusus, the beloved brother of Tiberius, whose wife, Antonia Minor, comes first as the Emperor's niece. Between them and clutching his mother's forefinger, as babes do, comes two-year-old Germanicus, as 'old-fashioned' as a child in a seventeeth-century painting. Though the Imperial lady comes first she is placed before her elder sister in order to secure priority for Drusus over the father of the next family group, headed by Antonia Maior. This comprises Antonia herself, the children Gnaeus Domitius and Domitia, and Lucius Domitius Ahenobarbus. The secondary figures are of considerable interest. The veiled lady, who is admonishing quiet upon Antonia

[1] I. S. Ryberg, *Mem. Amer. Acad. Rome*, xix, 83.
[2] Toynbee, *op. cit.*, 87.   [3] Ryberg, *op. cit.* 85.
[4] *Acta Archaeologica*, xvii, 4 f.

and Drusus, is ingeniously identified by Riemann[1] and Moretti as Octavia Minor. The handsome young woman behind Drusus, who unobtrusively yet decisively elbows Antonia Maior back into the third place, is identified – again by Moretti – as Vipsania Agrippina, the wife of Tiberius; and if Tiberius was acting as *consul* she would belong appropriately to his brother's family group, since she could not accompany her husband in his official duties. Moretti further suggests that the highly distinctive elderly man between Antonia Maior and Ahenobarbus may be Maecenas. This seems on the whole unlikely, for by 13 B.C. Maecenas was in eclipse, although his death did not occur until five years later, and his inclusion with the Imperial family would be a signal mark of favour. If he was accorded a place on the reliefs at all, he might rather be expected on the north side. This runs the gamut of possible identifications, and it is now proper to return to the historical and artistic questions prompted by the reliefs.

It has already been observed, in discussing the choice of Aeneas for the religious scenes, that this choice presumably emanated from a senatorial commission, and may be said to reflect a sober and aristocratic view of the *princeps*. It fits the Vergilian conception *'tantae molis erat Romanam condere gentem'*,[2] but at the same time is not far from the Tiberian notion *'miseram et onerosam servitutem'*.[3] Nor is this the only reflection of a Tiberian point of view to be detected. In the procession of the Imperial family the senior Domitius Ahenobarbus, already a consular and his wife, the elder Antonia, yield place to the younger Antonia and her praetorian husband, Nero Claudius Drusus, Tiberius' brother: while Vipsania the wife of Tiberius and sister-in-law of Drusus, positively elbows Antonia Maior into the background. Ahenobarbus himself had a reputation for rudeness of the kind, which is here repaid. There is yet another touch. The elderly veiled lady, who admonishes Drusus and Antonia for talking, might be acclaimed for piety, but she is also decisively stamped for all time as the

[1] Pauly-Wissowa, *Realencyclopädie*, xviii, 1, col. 2100.
[2] Vergil, *Aen.*, i, 33.   [3] Suetonius, *Tib.*, 24.

[215]

interfering aunt: in fact the apparent compliment to her piety has that double edge which the Latin wit knows so well how to exploit. But who would represent the Emperor's sister in this guise except the powerful and dominant Claudii, who with Agrippa had outwitted the schemes of Augustus in favour of Marcellus, Octavia's first-born. In other words, the surviving portions of the relief furnish a vivid record of the Claudian ascendancy, and this alone demands that Livia, whose marriage with Augustus brought it about, should be accorded a prominent place in the procession, in no sense subordinate to Agrippa, as has sometimes been suggested. This is perhaps the best reason why Maecenas, whose political activities were not those of this family group, would be most unlikely to figure with them, even in the background. The record too has its irony. Two of the chiefest actors were walking in the shadow of death. Agrippa was dead in 12 B.C., Drusus three years later, 9 B.C., and the ensuing dynastic schemes of Augustus for Agrippa's children for a season almost eclipsed the Claudian House. Tiberius and Antonia Minor were in the end to live longer, Antonia never forgetting, and when both were old dramatically fulfilling, her obligations towards him. Thus, if the altar is the *Ara Pacis*, and the concatenation of personalities and offices makes this difficult to deny, fate had rendered its political setting out of date by the time it was dedicated; but it remained, an outstanding picture of the cabal which, assisted and presently wrecked by *atrox fortuna*, moulded the actions of Augustus to their own shape as much as his.

Artistically, the altar remains a highly individual creation. Its architectural ancestry has recently been traced to the Athenian Altar of Pity, as erected in the Athenian Agora in the penultimate decade of the fifth century B.C., to much the same scale, but with much lower screen-wall.[1] The pattern of the elaborate dado and of the swags may be matched in the Eastern Mediterranean at Pergamon and Eleusis, just as in stucco and painting they have already arrived on the Palatine, in the Republican Casa dei Grifi and in the so-called House of Livia. But the processional friezes

---

[1] Homer Thompson, *Hesperia*, xxi, 47 ff.

remain the real enigma. No sculptural ancestor for them exists in Roman Art, and to that extent they are as much a new creation as the *Odes* of Horace or the *Aeneid*. But in painting and its history there is already a long tradition, going back to the third century B.C., of the rendering of historical events, principally victories. They differed from the Greek conception of such subjects, portrayed in religious or legendary allegories, in their demand for actuality: and while the Hellenistic world was well prepared, in individual studies of Persians or barbarians, or in the Alexander battle, to meet such a demand, the demand itself was stimulated by the emphasis upon contemporary *acta* required for the Roman triumph and the glorification of the *vir triumphalis*. If the public could be entertained by large-scale compositions it need not be doubted that the great personages themselves had their own records in painted rolls and their own artist to make them. It is such a record, carefully manipulated and adjusted to political ends, that lies behind the composition of the reliefs: and it is this contact with actuality, rapidly captured in sketches at the actual time of the procession, which gives the compositions their lively immediacy and lasting appeal. The talent to translate such sketches or paintings into stone is not so much the problem, for it had long existed. Yet it could neither flourish nor blossom amid the intensities and rivalries of the Republican nobility; and until that society was curbed and dominated by an Emperor no such procession was possible. The work is of its time: no mere panegyric, still less the product of adulation. The rivalries of the nobility peep out in the detail and have affected the entire composition, unified by Augustus in an uneasy peace.

6

TWO FLAVIAN MONUMENTS

The Arch of Titus, commemorating in its main sculptured panels the subjugation of Judaea and the capture of Jerusalem by Titus, in A.D. 71, is proclaimed by its inscription to be a memorial to Titus after his death ten years later and his deification commemorated by its apotheosis relief. To-day the Arch stands powerful and dominant at the point where the *Velia* divides the valley of the Forum from the basin now marked by the Colosseum. In antiquity the monument was much less conspicuous: for on the Forum side the approach was marked by the Porticus of Nero which flanked and Hausmannized the *Via Sacra*, while on the east it was hemmed in by the Temple of *Iuppiter Stator* and by whatever was left in A.D. 81 of the vestibule of Nero's palace. It nevertheless formed a splendid monument, upon the principal approach to the Flavian Palace, to the most distinguished general of the Flavian dynasty: and its principal reliefs are concerned entirely with the earthly triumphs of Titus and in particular with his famous siege and capture of Jerusalem, in A.D. 71. Indeed, the wholly minor position, on the crown of the vault of the passageway, accorded to the apotheosis in the decorative scheme, has lent support to the suggestion that the work began as a monument to the Jewish war and only ended as a monument to a deceased Emperor. It is, however, very difficult to square this idea with the sole and exclusive appearance of Titus on the Arch. Nor is the notion helped by the illustration of the *Arcus in Sacra Via Summa* upon the Monument of the Haterii, where the entire detail and even much of the main configuration is free in the extreme and cannot serve as a basis for a serious study of the

[218]

monument[1] even if it in fact portrays it. It is easier to accept the work at its face value and date it to the early 80's.

The design of the work originally made a more gorgeous impression than now, since the restoration by Valadier, carried out when the remains of the mediaeval fortress of the Frangipani were stripped from it, deliberately refrained from all but a schematic reproduction of the ancient detail. We miss, except in scraps, the rich frame of fluted columns and the fastidious composite capitals, the first of their kind in monumental architecture. The archway itself is a single passage-way, flanked by remarkably simple narrow bays carried right up through the main entablature to the attic, where they frame the great dedicatory inscription. The entablature serves to hold the composition firmly down to earth, while its rich heavy cornice and crowded frieze are carried across the arch and are united with it by an elaborate console keystone decorated on the west by *Honos* and on the east by *Virtus*, both military qualities appropriate to the main theme. Within this carefully designed framework the large-scale decorative treatment of the Arch begins. The spandrels are occupied by flying Victories bearing *vexilla*, in somewhat different attitudes and by different hands on either side: those on the east front rest one foot upon globes and their carrying arms are in one case fully extended, in the other flexed. The western Victories fly without globes and the *vexillum* is most conveniently arranged in relation to the shape of the spandrel. There is a rich archivolt mould and the vault is decorated with small coffers, each containing a rosette except in the centre of the crown, where a larger compartment displays the apotheosis of Titus. An eagle is seen from below, bearing the figure heavenwards the head of Titus appears over the eagle's right shoulder.[2] The subject is a most difficult artistic problem and it cannot be said that the solution is a complete success: in particular, the principle of the perspective is not understood. The main reliefs for which the Arch is famous occur in the covered passage-way, and their theme is the triumph of

[1] See F. Castagnoli, *Bull. Comm. Arch.*, lxix, 59 ff., pl. I (I.A.R.).
[2] E. Strong, *La Scultura Romana*, 1923, 115, fig. 74 (I.A.R.).

Titus. But the triumphal procession is also depicted in minor scale, like the sacrificial procession on the *Ara Pacis*. The little friezes which decorate the sides of the altar within the great screen-wall of the *Ara Pacis* are closely matched by the frieze of the Arch, which is preserved in fragmentary form on the east side. There is a fine procession of animals for sacrifice and soldiers moving towards the north, followed by the personification of a river, presumably the Jordan, carried shoulder-high on poles. The figures come in *staccato* groups, and many features in the great procession which are not otherwise depicted must have occurred in this frieze. The two main reliefs concentrate entirely upon two principal themes, the *triumphator* and the most famous spoils.

Their position is, in comparison with later works, a curious one. Only to be viewed by the passer-by, never by the distant beholder, their placing contrasts sharply with that of reliefs on, many later arches whose main façades were, as might be said, frameworks for pictures. Here the spectator is required not to stand and gaze but to move through the Arch alongside the reliefs, so that he is for a moment accompanying, even taking part in, an eternal procession, which on each side of the Arch wends its way towards the Capitol. However briefly, in sharing this *memoria* of the dead, he becomes virtually a partner in the activities of the deceased, which live again and perpetuate his memory the more vividly.

It could have been said of Titus, as of Agricola, '*posteritati narratus et traditus superstes erit*'.[1] The reliefs thus reflect contemporary thought concerning survival.

The north side of the passage, on the right of the main approach, is occupied by the culminating scene of the triumphal procession.[2] The four-horse chariot, driven by Titus as *triumphator*, is guided towards the Capitol by the goddess *Roma* herself. The motif is repeated with greater freedom and imagination in the contemporary relief of the Vatican Belvedere. Here Rome stands to the

[1] Tacitus, *Agr.*, 46.
[2] See *e.g.* D. E. Strong, *Roman Imperial Sculpture*, 1961, pl. 59.

right of the horses, leading the offside animal and giving the team pride of place. Background is provided and ingeniously suggested by thirteen *fasces* held aloft by lictors, who are themselves visible only at the front of the procession and in the gaps which occur between the horses' heads and the front of the chariot. The men in the group at the horses' heads confront one another in conversation, as at one moment on the *Ara Pacis*, and introduce a static note which forms a caesura in the composition, helps to emphasize the sense of movement in the other figures and unites the spectators graven on the relief with the living spectator in the archway. The device is a good example of the Roman method of obtaining a kaleidoscopic effect by a series of compositions related to one another by no law of perspective but through the successive perceptions of a moving onlooker. The depth of relief and the complicated number of planes – no less than seven are exploited between the nearest horse and the *fasces* behind the furthest horse – give these reliefs a new sense of depth and movement, aided by the rich interplay of light and shade, which marks a substantial advance upon the *Ara Pacis*. The general composition is also more ingenious: Titus in his triumphal car approaches from the right out of the background and allows room for the group of four figures which so well give the effect of a procession between crowds. The horses are swinging right and this tendency is checked and directed once again towards the front by the figure of *Dea Roma* guiding them. The result is a gentle sinuosity which helps the sense of movement. *Dea Roma*, though prominent, is not the sole divine or semi-divine figure in the scene. The half-naked figure, who masks the chariot and once carried a *cornucopiae*, is the *Genius Populi Romani*, while the headless figure on the extreme right may be identified as the *Genius Senatus*, on the basis of the head of the senator's official staff (*scipio eburneus*) seen in his left hand. The bearded figure next to *Dea Roma* remains unidentified. But his beard distinguishes him from the human members of the cortege, two of whom appear in the background between the two *genii*. Above them all the magnificent Victory who flits

[221]

behind the triumphal car and crowns Titus with a wreath emphasizes the number and variety of divinities who accompany and welcome him in his greatest hour.

The opposite scene, on the south side of the passage-way, is of markedly different type.[1] It depicts not the *triumphator* but the procession itself, with its principal spoils, which is passing under a triumphal arch, probably that of Tiberius at the foot of the *Clivus Capitolinus*. The figure of a *camillus*, emphasizing the dedicated nature of the spoils, carries first a pole with a *tabula ansata*, or placard, proclaiming the nature of the booty. Then follows a feretory or *ferculum*, carried by bearers, four at the front and three visible at the back, upon which are displayed the gold-plated Table of Shewbread, carrying two sacred vessels and flanked by two golden trumpets blown at sacrifices. The exhibit is attended by a robed figure, mutilated beyond recognition, who screens the fourth rear bearer. Hard upon the heels of the first *ferculum*, with a real sense of crowded profusion, comes the second – 'it was like a rushing river of spoils' wrote Josephus the eye-witness.[2] Again there is a placard telling the nature of the booty; and once more the eight bearers, the rearward group screened by another robed figure, whose breast is covered by a curious arrangement of straps. Neither personage wears Roman costume and the two figures may be regarded as important captives, who, as Josephus noted,[3] were exhibited in the procession in finest captured raiment. The spoil here displayed is the golden seven-branched candlestick, which formed with the Table of Shewbread the conspicuous furnishings of the Holy Place. The fact that these were the holiest possessions of Jewry, accessible in their sanctuary to priests alone, made them the foremost exhibits, apart from their immense bullion value. But they were only outstanding examples of the stream of precious things in the procession and a hint of more to come is conveyed by a third poster-bearing *camillus*, who brings up the rear. As on the north external frieze of the *Ara Pacis* screen-wall the proces-

[1] *e.g.* D. E. Strong, *op. cit.*, pl. 60.   [2] Josephus, *Bell. Jud.*, vii, 134.
[3] *Bell. Jud.*, vii, 138 (*cf.* 118).

sion is here abruptly cut off. There are, however, some important differences in treatment, which deserve careful note. The richer elaboration of planes has already been observed. But in the disposition of figures the relegation of the principal actors to the middle ground upon a higher plane is noteworthy, for it enables them to be enclosed in a crowd of foreground figures in quite a new manner. The background figures also begin to rise above those of the middle ground, as if a bird's-eye view of the scene were being obtained. This very soon becomes a cardinal feature in the design of Roman reliefs, and a generation later, under Trajan, the treatment is not longer tentative but bold, and even more effective. The conception of subject has also changed. On the *Ara Pacis* the actual and the legendary are kept strictly apart: only the legendary and the divine commingle. But on the Arch of Titus minor deities or personifications form part of the human crowd and take charge of the action when the Emperor is present, while the minor human figures continue their particular action independently, oblivious of the abstractions in their midst. But the composition varies, avoiding over-stress or monotony. Action and the ideological reaction to it are combined in the representation of the *triumphator*: action alone, leaving the terms of judgment completely free, is the theme of the procession of spoils.

The Arch of Titus is an old favourite of the student of Roman art. Two panels, now to be considered and with which its main friezes may be closely compared, are new, or relatively so, having been found in 1938 below the Palazzo della Cancelleria at the south end of the *Campus Martius*.[1] Unlike the frieze of the *Ara Pacis*, the slabs were not in their original position and perhaps not very near it. In Roman times they had been carefully piled, with regard for the sculptured surfaces, against the disused tomb of Aulus Hirtius, together with other marble-mason's scrap. But

[1] F. Magi, *I rilievi flavi del palazzo della Cancelleria*, 1945; J. M. C. Toynbee, *The Flavian Reliefs from the Palazzo della Cancelleria in Rome* (Charlton Lecture), 1957 (which also deals with the theories of Magi, Bendinelli, Thimme and Rumpf): I.A.R. and Toynbee largely agree.

their correspondence in size and, very generally, in style, combined with the fact that both were designed to face in the same direction on opposite sides, leaves no doubt that they came from the same monument. What that monument was is more doubtful. The site cannot have been far away: and since one relief celebrates an *adventus* and the other a *profectio*, their connexion with the Temple of *Fortuna Redux* or an associated monument, for example, the *Porta Triumphalis*, is highly probable.

The first relief is in general a simple composition.[1] Vespasian advances from the right with a *lictor* and another figure, perhaps a *speculator*, behind him. Over his head is borne an oak wreath, the *corona civica*, carried by a flying Victory whose legs are seen in what remains of the background. Domitian accompanied and supported by the *Genius Populi Romani* and the *Genius Senatus*, meets his father and is greeted by him. He is attended by a *lictor*, while another attendant, probably a *lictor* also, turns his back upon the spectator in order to make contact with a third figure. This man, probably also a *lictor*, is ushering in a stately group of Vestal Virgins accompanied by an *apparitor*, while *Dea Roma*, enthroned in the background, watches over them and the scene in general. In spite of the lost fragments, little is missing from the scene, and enough remains of the Vestals to reconstitute their number as five.[2]

The confrontation is a remarkable scene, reverting to the earliest days of Vespasian's rule, when he had come late to Rome, captured in A.D. 70 from the Vitellians and now policed by Domitian and Mucianus. Many rumours had circulated as to Domitian's conduct, many concerning his relationship with his father. A story of rebukes at *Beneventum* lasted among historians.[3] This relief is intended to kill such stories and to indicate that there was mutual trust between Vespasian and his younger son from the beginning. Titus, who was still at war in Judaea, does not appear and this was the one occasion which Domitian could take to

---

[1] See *e.g.* D. E. Strong, *op. cit.*, pl. 61.

[2] Toynbee, *op. cit.*, 5, points out that the sixth Virgin would have been left behind to tend the sacred and undying fire.   [3] Dio, lxvi, 9, 3–10, 1.

IV. Aosta: amphitheatre: outer arcading of the substructure, built into the convent of St Catherine.

himself as an important political triumph without sharing it with Titus until death parted them eleven years later. In view of the relationship between the two brothers there can be little doubt how gladly it was seized. And the intention here is to show Domitian the radiant receiving with Senate and People the new *princeps*, who is here represented as a dignified first citizen, solemn, shrewd and wide-awake.

The greeting between father and son, watched with interest by the adjacent *lictor*, is kept intimate. The two *genii* look past the scene and above it, into the heavens where Victory is hovering, holding not the victor's laurel, but the oak-wreath which it was the special concern of Senate and People to award, *ob cives servatos*. It is this upon which *Dea Roma* and the Vestal Virgins also have their eyes. It is noteworthy how while the humans, both Imperial family and *lictor*, are treated with a free and vividly realistic touch, the divine figures, *Dea Roma* and the *genii*, are cast in severely classic mould: while the Vestal Virgins, whose cloistered chastity and high religious office set them apart from ordinary mankind in a holy caste of their own, are shown in the same heroic and almost inhuman guise. The pre-occupation of Domitian with the discipline and reputation of the Vestals is too well known to require emphasis.[1] Their presence here typifies the virtue and strength of Rome as he saw it in their holy sisterhood, and their appearance is to give him moral support as they often gave it, in good cause or sometimes bad. The classic tradition also affects the general design. The elaborate crowding of the Arch of Titus is absent, and this relief compares much more closely with the *Ara Pacis* in relative simplicity of composition, though its treatment of drapery is much more statuesque and sets off the human form rather than sits upon it.

The second scene, which is a counterpart to the other in size and intended to face either it or one like it in position, is not so immediately clear. The focus of interest lies at the very end of the scene and that is lost to us. The only hint of what filled it is afforded by a great wing of a Victory, masked by a *lictor*, now

[1] Suetonius, *Dom.*, 8; Pliny, *Epp.*, iv, 11.

represented only by his *fasces*. Domitian, who is in travelling dress, is pointing ahead, while his patron goddess, Minerva, and Mars prepare to accompany him forward and *Dea Roma*¹ supports him. Mars has unsheathed his sword, while Minerva has just donned her helmet. Victory, it might be thought, flies ahead. The scene is interpreted by F. Magi, the first publisher, as an *adventus*. But it is difficult to see why in that case Domitian turns his back upon *Dea Roma* and the *Genii Senatus et Populi*; and these might be expected to be receiving him, whereas in fact they are plainly ushering him out. A *profectio* is thus much more acceptable than an *adventus*,² for this explains not only the attitude of the crowd behind him but the urgency of mood so evident in Mars and Minerva, not to mention the *lictor* beyond them. The truth appears to be that Domitian was being called to victory by a crisis; and the most suitable occasion for such a commemoration would be either the Chattan war of 83 or the Suebo-Sarmatian war of 92. The Dacian war of 86, followed by the catastrophic defeat of Cornelius Fuscus, is less likely.³ If, however, the one piece is a *profectio* and the other an *adventus*, these events, however interpreted, lie so far apart in the life of Domitian, and are not only so far separate in time but so markedly contrasted in subject, that it may be thought difficult to see them as the sole decoration of a single monument. It would be far easier to suppose that they formed part of a series of such pieces, in which for example the *adventus Augusti* after the Chattan war might have figured, and perhaps another *profectio*. It would be wrong to dwell upon hypotheses which we cannot test, since it remains obvious that the reliefs need not have stood alone and it would be foolish to conclude that so strange a chance as preserved the reliefs has extended to giving us all the decorative panels of the lost monument.

Turning then to the style of the second relief, it may at once be

¹ This is Magi's identification: Toynbee, *op. cit.*, 10, argues for *Virtus*.
² D. E. Strong, *op. cit.*, 32 f. takes the same view.
³ This war, however, continued till 89 and there was in a later stage the success in battle of Tettius Iulianus.

observed that it is executed with less restraint and richer feeling than the first. It also passed through a change not reflected upon its companion. The features of the young Domitian, still Caesar, *ignotis adhuc moribus* as Tacitus grimly remarks,[1] have survived unchanged and the head unmolested at the time of the *damnatio memoriae*. The head of the *Emperor* Domitian suffered a very different fate. It was not removed and substituted by another, as was that of Marcus on the reliefs re-used for the Arch of Constantine, but was trimmed down and re-shaped in order to resemble Nerva. The re-cutting, producing a wig-like effect above the forehead, is clearly in contrast with the old surface, from which the hair springs appropriately and realistically, as on the neck. The bony structure of the cheek and the setting of the ear and side whisker have also been remodelled in order to resemble Nerva. The monument was thus not demolished but considered important enough to retain. Domitian's doings as Caesar were unmolested, primarily, no doubt, out of respect for Vespasian, who is, after all, the principal actor on the first relief. The Imperial *profectio* was re-cast and this at least would be appropriate to the first year of Nerva's reign, when a *profectio* might be called for and no one knew what the new military policy was to be.

Further than this it is impossible to go. The circumstances in which the reliefs were dismantled must remain unknown. Their careful stacking in a marble-mason's store, uninjured, at least means that they were not violently defaced or cast down. As the structure, modified to suit Nerva, was certainly not demolished as an act of spite against Domitian, it may just as easily have been dismantled by a later Emperor with reference only to contemporary needs or desires. It would be equally idle to speculate upon the nature of the monument, but this point must be observed. Doctor Magi, who publishes the reliefs, excludes them from an arch because of the overhang of their tops. This will not do. Flat panels are not necessarily characteristic of arches. The coming and going which is the subject of the reliefs suits an arch better than most settings. But the position of the pieces in any

[1] Tacitus, *Hist.*, iv, 40 (I.A.R.).

monument, arch or not, must remain problematic, since, in particular, the two surviving probably belong to a larger set, of unknown number.

The contrast between the reliefs of Titus and Domitian could hardly be greater. Artistically, they represent opposites in a marked degree. The composition and grouping of the Arch of Titus looks forward and can be seen as the precursor of the Trajanic style in Imperial monumental sculpture. The arrangement of crowds, the exploitation of planes, the treatment of foreground and background are the beginning of a tradition which breaks away from the *Ara Pacis* and leads on to the age of Marcus Aurelius. The Cancelleria reliefs, on the contrary, look back to the classical tradition of grouping seen in the *Ara Pacis*. Their treatment of background is no less simple. Their Greekish divinities are the only feature which might claim to look forward, since they belong to the same current of taste as that which sets in strong under Hadrian and Antoninus Pius. In other words, they are not consciously reactionary but represent a completely different taste, no less alive and no less of its age than the reliefs of the Arch of Titus, which have so long been employed as the sole yard-stick for Flavian monumental reliefs.

Finally, it should be emphasized that, while the panel on the Arch of Titus portraying the procession of spoils may well go back to a very close copy of the actual procession and its details, the panel of Titus in triumph certainly does not. Josephus, who gives an eye-witness account of the great event, indicates clearly that on the actual day of triumph Vespasian and Titus drove in their chariots, while Domitian accompanied them on horseback.[1] Here Titus alone appears, and alone is attended by divinities, in a manner which could have no close relationship to the events of the day itself, whether they are viewed actually or ideologically. This panel is an abstraction, based upon reality, but designed so as to give to Titus the sole glory, as the representation of his supreme achievement. Its immediate purpose, well fulfilled, is to constitute such a *memoria* as shall give him immortality in the minds of men.

[1] Josephus, *Bell. Jud.*, vii, 152.

7

THE ARCH OF *BENEVENTUM*

Trajan's Arch at *Beneventum*[1] was voted between Dec. 10 A.D.
113 and Dec. 9 A.D. 114 by the Senate and People to Trajan as
Optimus Princeps, on his departure for the Parthian War. It is well
known that from these campaigns Trajan never returned, and
that Hadrian succeeded him in A.D. 117 in circumstances regarded
by many as equivocal. The Arch exhibits in its reliefs, as von
Domaszewski long ago observed,[2] undoubted traces of Hadrianic
political influence. It is therefore clear that the reliefs were by no
means finished when the succession took place, and it may be
thought that a three-year interval is not impossible, having
regard to the letting of the Senatorial contract, the quarrying and
transport of stone and the shaping of the new structure.

In general design the Arch is so like that of Titus that it must be
judged either to have come from the same contractors' *atelier*, or to
have been built to the same specification. The architectural framework is strikingly similar, resemblances extending not only to
the general scheme but to details, such as the treatment of the
capitals and entablature in the composite order. Yet the differences
deserve no less emphasis. While the Arch of Titus was erected in
one of the most prominent positions in the Capital, the Arch of
Trajan was set up on the northern outskirts or boundary of
Beneventum, at the point where the new version of the *Via
Appia* left the town for *Brundisium*. The new road, the *Via Traiana*, was Trajan's creation and the Arch, marking its beginning,

[1] See K. J. Hassel, *Der Trajansbogen in Benevent*, 1966; C. Pietrangeli, *L'Arco di
Traiano a Benevento*, 1943.
[2] A. v. Domaszewski, *Österr. Jh.*, ii, 173 ff.

is not only the commemoration of Trajan's work for the Empire, but a thank-offering for the road. In that respect the work has a double purpose. The greatest difference between the Arches of Titus and Trajan is, however, the decoration of their main façades. Whereas those of the Arch of Titus are almost plain, those of the Arch of Trajan are everywhere decorated with historical reliefs. While in the Arch of Titus the sculptured panels, confined to the passage-way only, form the chief attraction, in the Arch of Trajan the reliefs of the passage-way, splendid though they be, are of local interest only. It is the reliefs of the main façades that arrest attention and proclaim two distinct themes. The inhabitant of *Beneventum*, or the traveller from Rome saw the glorification of Trajan's home policy, for Rome and Italy: the traveller approaching from Brindisi and overseas was confronted by a façade proclaiming provincial policy and benefits. In the passage the scenes illustrate the local effect of both policies, one commemorating the inaugural sacrifice, when Trajan dedicated the new road to the East, the other the relief of the poor in the district organized through the *alimenta*. Both façades carry the same inscription. Trajan receives the title *Optimus Augustus,* and *Fortissimus Princeps*: but he is not yet *Parthicus,* as he became in A.D. 116. The façade of external policy, however, goes later into history, for it contains a record not only of the Parthian embassy which followed the invasion but the actual subjugation of *Mesopotamia*. It is the latter relief which contains a clear allusion to Hadrian's renunciation of these Trajanic schemes of expansion, and which makes it impossible to date the series until after A.D. 117. And, since the reliefs in fact form an epitome of Trajan's achievements seen through Hadrianic eyes, it might well be considered that they were a first act of Hadrianic *pietas* combined with propaganda, rather than a last proclamation of Trajan's Imperial achievement. For it quickly becomes apparent how little stress is laid upon expansionist policy and how much upon other aspects. It may be well, then, to consider this aspect of the Arch first.

On both sides of the Arch the bays of the attic flanking the inscription are occupied by impressive reliefs of positively lowering proportions, intended to catch the eye of the spectator far below. To left, the group on the north side is imperfect. Trajan and his companions are missing. But the deities grouped with them are all there. These are the tutelary deities of the Danube provinces. *Liber* and *Libera*, the patrons of *Dacia*, Diana, patroness of *Moesia*, and *Silvanus*, guardian of *Illyricum*. They are exquisitely dignified figures, though the distinguishing emblems which they once carried are much damaged. Nevertheless, the *thyrsus* of *Liber*, the burning torch of *Libera* can be recognized in the background, while Diana's quiver and *Silvanus's* blossoming branch are also seen. It is clear that the scene is not one of conquest or submission, but welcome and acceptance: Trajan was welcomed by the concourse of gods for what he brought as a civilizer. The other flank exhibits a profoundly different scene. Trajan is besought in submission by a female figure representing *Mesopotamia*,[1] who kneels between two river deities, male and female. The female, supporting the suppliant and emerging from below a bridge, which the Romans have crossed or are crossing, is the Euphrates; the youth, who appealingly touches Trajan's left thigh, is the Tigris. Trajan stands aloof and preoccupied. He is being counselled, in an attitude of dissuasion, by a figure who is not wearing Roman dress, but a long fringed cloak and tunic, and is commendably identified by Petersen[2] with the Moorish chief Lusius Quietus. Hadrian, who next appears in the background, is himself being even more strongly restrained by

[1] As M. H. Braüde points out to me there has been considerable dispute as to whether the scene really is *Mesopotamia*: E. Groag, *Röm Mitt.*, xiv., 269 ff.; E. T. Merrill, *Trans. and Proc. Amer. Phil. Ass.*, 51; Hassel, *op. cit.*, 18. Braüde himself thinks that it is *Dacia*.

[2] Probably E. Petersen, *Röm. Mitt.*, vii, 242 – but he does *not* identify as Lusius Quietus, a point made to me by M. H. Braüde. Lusius Quietus was, remarkably, raised to the consulship – and executed after the 'revolt of the four consulars': for the latter reason it would perhaps be surprising to find him on a monument of Hadrianic date, unless perhaps as a sign of respect and rehabilitation by the Senate which had ordered the executions. The identification was in fact, as Braüde points out to me, made by Domaszewski, *op. cit.*, 185 f.: *cf.* and contrast E. Groag, *op. cit.*, 244 f. Hassel, *op. cit.*, 18, identifies as L. Licinius Sura.

another soldierly figure, surely one of the great marshals. The intention of the scene is thus to represent the fact of submission but to suggest that the renunciation which followed was pressed upon and was acceptable to Trajan himself, whose averted glance can have no other meaning. Contemporary historians, however, thought much otherwise, and discredited Hadrian as responsible for the decision.[1] The two more important lower scenes are those nearest the ground and eye-level. The left-hand panel shows the conclusion of a treaty with foreign chiefs. Trajan's head is missing and his expression unascertainable. But he is clasping hands with the chieftain in gesture of good faith and the action is witnessed by Jupiter *Feretrius*, the god of treaties. The identity of the foreign chieftains is not strikingly evident. They do not wear the trousers of either Dacians or north Germans, but compare well with the *Suebi* of the Aurelian panels and Trajan's earliest triumphal appellation, *Germanicus*, was based upon the settlement of this frontier, an act which secured peace in the Danube regions represented above. The right-hand panel is a different scene, acutely linked by Petersen with an episode described by Cassius Dio.[2] When the Parthian War had broken out an embassy sought peace, bringing among other gifts a remarkable horse taught to kneel at command. The horse, together with a great mastiff dog, is here shown and their conductors, with eastern haircrop, are introduced by Hercules, the patron god of Parthia. The emphasis upon good relations with Parthia is here deliberate and unmistakable, and is not part of Trajan's policy, but Hadrian's.

The two intermediate panels illustrate two aspects of Trajan's policy for the provinces. In the left-hand panel Trajan, wearing soldier's undress uniform, is receiving a recruit. The young and beardless *Mars Ultor*, forms a gracious intermediary between the stern Emperor and the young man, who stands stiffly to attention, though Trajan would have called him a fellow soldier (*commilito*). The recruit is presented by a centurion and both are overshadowed

[1] Fronto, *Principia Historiae*, 10 (Loeb, p. 206): *cf.* Augustine, *Civ. Dei*, iv, 29; S.H.A., *Hadr.*, 5.
[2] Dio, lxviii, 18, 2.

by the figure of *Virtus Militaris*, wearing an oak-wreathed *corona vallaris* and carrying a *vexillum*. The meaning of the relief is recruitment for the legions, and its intention is to indicate the wider extension of that recruitment to the provincial world, in the raising of new legions. The right-hand relief represents another aspect of the same policy. Trajan and *Mars Pater* are presenting to *Roma*, who in the guise of a city goddess yet carries a plough, the symbol of founding new colonies, two children, a little girl and her infant brother; these represent the *proles Romana* which the Roman colonies, or citizen land-settlements, will rear. And the goddess *Abundantia*, with her horn of plenty, is there to indicate the good conditions amid which they will flourish. Together these two reliefs symbolize the bringing of the provinces into the orbit of Roman duties and Roman responsibilities by means of extended reliance upon the growing number of Roman citizens within them.

The whole theme of the provincial side of the Arch is thus the settlement of the provinces, the conclusion of firm treaty relations with the frontier folk, and the extension of Roman stock to people and defend the Empire. While this in part looks back to Trajanic policy, it emphasizes much that was essentially Hadrianic. Finally, the figure in the spandrels of the Arch should be noted. To left reclines the Euphrates, to right the Danube, the two frontier rivers beyond which Trajan had operated, with such contrasting results.

The Roman side of the Arch may now be described. The attic presents a famous scene in which Trajan, with Hadrian close at his side and, except for lictors, his sole attendant, is received by the two consuls who are extending their arms in welcome or offering. Behind them *Roma* greets the Emperor, and she is followed not by lictors but by two *di penates*. This panel, in which the consuls, though most prominent, are overshadowed by divine beings, is the complement to a scene completely filled with deities. The Capitoline triad, glorious and gracious, occupies the foreground and Jupiter is offering his thunderbolt to Trajan, whose somewhat deprecating attitude is thus explained, as is also the gesture of offering by the consuls, who are surely here viewed as Jupiter's agents or spokesmen. In the background stand the minor tutelary deities of Rome, Mercury, Ceres, *Liber* and Hercules.

The meaning of this scene has been much discussed. The gesture of Jupiter indubitably associates Trajan in some way with his power; but how? It has been suggested that this might dub him Jupiter's vice-gerent on earth: and there are climates of thought in which this view has won much favour. But the consuls, who represent the dyarchy of Senate and Emperor, have no part in such a theory, which is the very negation of the current political notion of the dyarchy of Emperor and Senate, with the Senate in the delegating role. It is more natural, therefore, to suppose that the scene is simply the conferment, upon Trajan, under the auspices of the Gods of the Roman State, of the title *Optimus Princeps* which was in fact half the title of *Iuppiter Optimus Maximus*. If it were the conferment of Jupiter's power to fight, it should have come in the provincial series, yet would these have been totally out of tune with the programme suggested by the reliefs which are explicitly not a glorification of conquest but a proclamation of settlement. The power of *Optimus* is not Jupiter's might, which is covered by *Maximus*, but the divine power for good.

This mild and gracious interpretation is borne out by the theme of the two more important lower reliefs, where Trajan is being solemnly received by the people of Rome. Heading a wonderful procession of lictors, which wheels through a complete and stately semicircle behind him, Trajan is received on one panel by the *praefectus urbi*, and on its counterpart, with the *Curia* as background, by the *Genius Populi Romani* and two figures representing the senatorial and equestrian orders. The intention is to indicate the new *concordia ordinum* achieved under Trajan, in contrast with the disrupting effect of the Domitianic tyranny which had preceded it.

As on the other side of the Arch, the middle scenes represent benefits associated with the Roman citizen body for which

[234]

Trajan had been responsible. The subject of the lefthand panel is the conferment of lands upon veterans, two of whom approach Trajan under the auspices of the appropriate deities. That five *coloniae* are intended, each connected with legionaries, is shown by the *vexillum* carrying five eagles and held by *Virtus*. In the background stand Diana and *Silvanus*, the propitiated deities of the wild out of whose territory the newly developed acres were carved. The names of the colonies founded by Trajan are known, and these were in fact five of them: the *colonia Ulpia Traiana* at Xanten, where the Lippe meets the Rhine; the *colonia Ulpia* at Poetovio in *Pannonia*: the *coloniae Ulpiae* at *Ratiaria* and *Oescus* in *Moesia*; and the *colonia Ulpia* at *Sarmizegethusa* in *Dacia*. This meant a substantial increase in the great urban trading communities of the Empire.

Trade improvement is the theme of the complementary panel, in which Trajan receives a deputation of merchants and hands them rights. In the background are the three trading deities of Rome, *Portumnus*, Hercules and Apollo. Here will be recalled the immense harbour works of Trajan at *Ostia* and *Centumcellae*, which so greatly improved the port facilities of the west coast of Italy and in consequence the Tiber trade. On this side of the Arch the spandrels contain Victories, for it was the spoils of the Dacian victory which had provided the capital sums for such improvements, whether the founding of colonies or the creation of new harbours and docks.

The Roman theme, like the provincial, is thus one of peaceful achievement, the rewards of victory as opposed to the conquests themselves. The *Beneventum* theme, as it may appropriately be called, for the *Beneventani* must have especially treasured these scenes of local reference, is half way between the two. On the west side of the passage-way Trajan is sacrificing to inaugurate his new road. On its east side, local benefactions by Imperial favour are vividly and movingly commemorated.

The sacrificial scene is a bold one. Trajan, wreathed and veiled, is sacrificing by sprinking incense or, more probably, *mola salsa* on a metal portable stand loaded with *exta*. Two *camilli*, one holding the box, are in attendance, while a flute-player or *tibicen*, stands behind them. Facing Trajan beyond them is an important figure, probably Hadrian. Lictors fill the background. Further to the left two *popae* are poleaxing a bull, one swinging the axe aloft, the other holding the bull's horn and snout. A third burly *popa* stands firm in the background, while a bull looms up behind him. The whole scene has the vivid immediate interest of the procession on the *Ara Pacis* and must have been long talked of and shown with pride in the country town.

The second scene is perhaps the more remarkable. Trajan, followed by his suite, is presiding at a table piled with *congiaria* which are being distributed to needy families and children. A father, carrying a little girl pick-a-back, strides off leading a boy with well-filled cap. Another father, this time with a boy on his back, stands stiff with excitement and hope in front of the table. But communities also take their part. A veiled city-goddess, with her lap well filled, and three goddesses wearing mural crowns, cities or district communities, move onwards in the queue of suppliants. The veiled goddess carried something now vanished: and two of the three behind her have protegés. The nearest to the table pushes forward a little boy, who stands with his toga held like an open apron, eager to catch what comes. Her neighbour carries a whimpering baby in arms. The whole scene is a pathetic reminder of the fact that benefactions or charities entered little into the lives of the Roman poor and were seized with both hands when they came; here the recipients are poor *patres familiarum* with children and communities with orphans. In this very district Trajan was the founder of *alimenta* or charity funds for the poor and needy, paid for by the interest from loans secured upon the great estates.[1] The panel gives a vivid glimpse of the working of the system, through public distribution of staple commodities, comparable with the *frumentum dandum* in Rome.

Like the Arch of Titus, the frieze of the Arch of Trajan carries the scenes of a triumphal procession, and enough is preserved to

---

[1] *ILS* 6509.

show it from start to finish, with Trajan in his *quadriga*, the sacrificial beasts and their attendants, and the long procession of spoils and captives. The captives are handcuffed and either walk or ride, in various types of their own native ox-cars or horse-chariots. Their physical type identifies them as Dacians. The portable stands (*fercula*) for booty appear many times, and some special items can be recognized, like the treasure of Decebalus, comprising gold and silver vessels heaped high, or a large cauldron or special dishes and drinking-horns. But, unlike the Arch of Titus, that of Trajan makes no large feature of the triumph, and the only point where Trajan is wreathed as victor is in the central plaque on the underside of the passage-vault, where Victory herself crowns him as *imperator*, distinguished by his cuirass and *paludamentum*. This can have been seen by few. Everyone knew, however, that the Dacian spoils had paid for the great benefactions and many might think that it was in virtue of that fact rather than in its own right that the triumphal procession appears.

Here is the greatest possible contrast with the great monuments of Trajan's Forum, where the victorious conquest of *Dacia* is the prominent theme, expressed in so many rich variations, throughout all the buildings. There the expansionist theory of Empire receives its most glorious and most trenchant expression, not merely on Trajan's Column but on the famous panels which decorated the main buildings. The Arch of *Beneventum*, on the contrary, in offering an epitome of Trajanic policy, not only selects completely different themes but curiously and specifically excludes the conquests. As was observed previously, the emphasis is upon *optimus* not *maximus*. It is an odd choice: as if, in commemorating Napoleon, all stress had been laid upon the *Code Napoléon* and virtually none upon the achievements of the *Grande Armée*. Recollecting that the work is voted by the Senate and powerfully influenced by Hadrian, two questions may properly be asked. Did the Senate vote an Arch, modelled upon that of Titus, which was to be solely of local reference, with triumphal frieze, and passage-way reliefs referable to *Beneventum*? Were the sculptured façades an addition to the original design, commissioned by or through Hadrian to forestall or to answer criticism, and to advertize a continuity in policy with those aspects of Trajanic *acta* which best suited his own? For there can be no doubt that the reliefs evince the strongest bias in favour of Hadrian as Trajan's destined successor and that they refer to the Hadrianic reversal of Trajan's eastern policy, and so must in fact postdate the title *Parthicus*, which the inscribed dedication of the Arch does not contain. The difference in the dates of the two designs is a demonstrable reality and is difficult otherwise to explain.

But apart from political or historical explanations the Arch holds a special position as a work of art. It is the sole example now surviving of a triumphal Arch which carries a complete scheme of decoration in the grand manner and which is intended to proclaim the relationship between an Emperor and his people, as opposed to a victory in war, external or internal. In that respect it echoes a note in propaganda apparent in the *Ara Pacis* or the *Res Gestae*, on the *plutei* of the Forum or on coins proclaiming civil acts. No monument gives a finer sense of the spiritual sanctions held to underlie the actions of the Roman State, or nobler representations of the gods and personifications involved. Aesthetically, the surety of touch which shapes the individual figures and arranges them in groups places the Arch in a class by itself. The abundance of personifications connected with every part of the Empire heralds the cosmopolitanism of Hadrian; the treatment, going behind the prim simplicity of the Cancelleria reliefs to the complicated action of the Arch of Titus, can be recognized as a reaction. But it is also an advance in its power of composition and its treatment of planes in the relief. It will in its own turn inspire a reaction, that will result in the tense restriction and verticality of the great scenes on the major reliefs of Marcus Aurelius.

8

THE AURELIAN PANELS[1]

The Anonymous pilgrim from Einsiedeln, visiting Rome in the eighth or ninth century, copied '*in Capitolio*' an inscription of a triumphal Arch of Marcus Aurelius dated to his thirtieth tribunician power, that is, to A.D. 175–6. The inscription[2] was long and grandiloquent: but it recorded the recovery from the great invasions of Northerners which had struck Italy itself ten years before; and, when the text speaks of Aurelius as *omnes omnium ante se maximorum imperatorum glorias supergressus, bellicosissimis gentibus deletis aut subactis*, it reflects the sense of relief from dangers brought across the Alps so uncomfortably near to Rome. The existence of an Arch here is attested by mediaeval topographers, while close by, in the church of Santa Martina, three reliefs of appropriate scale and character were preserved until they were removed to the Palazzo dei Conservatori in 1525.

The three panels from Sta. Martina, which occupied the site of the ancient *Secretarium Senatus*, exactly match in style[3] and size the eight panels from the Arch of Constantine. They also retain the head of Marcus Aurelius, which on the Arch of Constantine has been removed, after recutting or substitution in antiquity, and replaced by modern heads of Constantine in 1732. And it has been shown by Stuart Jones that the whole eleven pieces fall into two series;[4] the war-scenes are related to the German and

---

[1] See now I. S. Ryberg, *Panel Reliefs of Marcus Aurelius*, 1967 (J.M.C.T.), especially her arguments for the arrangement of the panels.

[2] *CIL* vi, 1014 (I.A.R.).   [3] This is not generally accepted.

[4] *Pap. Brit. Sch. Rome*, iii, 251 ff., esp. 258 (for illustrations see pl. xxii–xxvii, and H. Stuart Jones (ed.), *The Sculptures of the Palazzo dei Conservatori*, 1926,

Sarmatian wars of Marcus, the civil scenes are set in Rome itself, and illustrate the emperor's arrival and departure, his triumph and a *congiarium*; while field-scenes, including an *adlocutio*, an investiture and a *lustratio exercitus*, also appear; and the investiture at least is Germanic as opposed to Sarmatian. Their distribution on the Arch of Constantine, to which they were transferred, is in pairs, like the *tondi* that were also pillaged for the Arch from another source. But it is on many counts unlikely that this reflects their original arrangement, even though some are clearly connected in subject. It is plain that they were designed as isolated panels, like pages in a book, and their scale and deep-set panelling suits best the façade of a single arch, in the manner of the Arch of Titus or Trajan's Arch at *Beneventum*.

The first impression conveyed by these reliefs is of innovation in design. The human elements in the background are reduced in favour of schematized landscape or buildings, while the principal figures occupy relatively more space in their panels. Each figure, principal or subordinate, has therefore to play a greater part not merely in the composition but in its meaning and symbolism. The same simplification, not of theme or symbolism, but of staging, is seen on the Column of Marcus. If its scenes are compared with the crowded settings of the Column of Trajan there is quickly perceived a new concentration upon principal actors and an isolation of the individual scene which tends to abandon any attempt at flow or kaleidoscopic effect and concentrates attention upon the most important figure. The effect is thus at once more static and, when the person of the Emperor is, as usually, concerned, more hieratic.

The two first scenes concern two aspects of the German campaign. Under the shadow of two great oak-trees, whose tufted tassels are contrasted with two richly tasselled *vexilla*, Marcus

pl. 12). Others divide them rather into the re-used group and the Conservatori group and there have been attempts to allocate these to different monuments. Ryberg (*op. cit.*, 77 ff.) argues that the second group came from the arch celebrating the triumph of A.D. 176 and the first from another, posthumous, arch in honour of the deified Marcus, a reconstruction of which she offers.

and his praetorian prefect, probably M. Bassaeus Rufus,[1] ride to a halt in front of an officer in scale-armoured jerkin with double kilt, who presents two German chiefs on their knees with outstretched hands. The Germans are making a *deditio*, and Mars,[2] who stands beside the Emperor, has already sheathed his sword. The fate of the petitioners is not yet disclosed, and the intention of the piece is to indicate a surrender in the field.[3] Contrasted with the *deditio* on Trajan's Column, this is an abbreviation; but the effect is to isolate and to freeze the act into something more symbolic. It is now becoming a subjective rather than an objective treatment of the theme *deditio*. The depth of the relief is striking; seven planes are handled so dexterously that their intermingling gives an effect of rich crowding without in any way destroying the emphasis upon the principal figures.

The second German scene is very different. The Emperor is still in the field, but is placed upon a high *tribunal*, seated upon a *sella castrensis*, richly cushioned and embossed. The *praefectus praetorio* stands by his side, stiff and rather grim. In front of the *tribunal* a trousered German chief, in a long belted tunic and fringed cloak, is supported in half fainting condition by a young boy, who is bracing himself to carry the weight of the old man.[4] His right hand touches the Emperor's knee in supplication, and the Emperor's hand is extended, as if in mercy. Further into the background, behind the Emperor's knee, a second German chief[5] looks on in sympathy. But the background itself is supplied by the Roman army, typified by four standards, three standard-bearers in bear-skins and two soldiers in crested helmets. The standards comprize a legionary eagle, a cavalry *vexillum* and two manipular standards. This time the scene is not a *deditio*, but rather an appeal for mercy and an opportunity for the exercise of *clementia*.

[1] Now generally here and on other panels identified as Ti. Claudius Pompeianus, not the praetorian prefect.
[2] Ryberg (*op. cit.*, 11) identifies this figure as an officer.
[3] Ryberg (*op. cit.*, 9 ff.) interprets as a representation of imperial *clementia*.
[4] It may rather be the boy who is in a state of despair and collapse.
[5] Identified by Ryberg (*op. cit.*, 63) as a bareheaded soldier.

In direct contrast are the next scenes, illustrating an *adventus* and a *profectio*. The background is this time both architectural and topographical, and so closely similar on both scenes as to link them in setting, contrasted though the subjects are. In the *adventus* a tetrastyle temple occupies one half of the background, shown large enough to place in the pediment two *cornuacopiae*, the globe and the wheel of Fortune, ranged on either side of a figure of the goddess herself. Next to the Arch come two sides of a tetrapylon or four-way Arch, decorated with swags, which are being affixed to the buildings by a flying Victory. The tetrapylon also occurs upon the *profectio* relief, though it is then seen from the other side, and its crowning statues are revealed as *quadrigae* drawn by elephants. These details make the topographical identification of the monuments certain. They are the Temple of *Fortuna Redux* and the triumphal Arch of Domitian, crowned by elephant-drawn *quadrigae*.[1] Both are mentioned in close topographical association by Martial[2] and the *quadrigae*-crowned Arch appears on coins of A.D. 90–1 and A.D. 95. Both buildings lay on the *Via Flaminia*, not far from the modern Piazza Venezia, and therefore suit exactly the scene required for the home-coming of Marcus from the North.

Below this stately background Marcus occupies the central position. Mars in full panoply walks behind him, while *Roma*, in the Amazonian costume already familiar from the Arch of Titus, receives him and prepares to lead him into the city. Between *Roma* and the Emperor stands the personification *Felicitas*, with *cornucopia* and *caduceus*, and between the Emperor and Mars a veiled and solemn figure, identified by Charlesworth[3] and Hamberg[4] as *Aeternitas*. The reduction of the figures to five only, the increase in their size and increasing formality of the background,

[1] The relief shows one *quadriga*: coin representations vary between one and two.
[2] Martial, viii, 65 (I.A.R.).
[3] M. P. Charlesworth, *Harvard Theol. Rev.*, xxix, no. 2, 122 ff., discusses *Aerernitas* but does not mention the Aurelian panels. Ryberg (*op. cit.*, 68) follows Aymard in identifying the figure as *Aeternitas* conflated with Diva Faustina the younger.
[4] P. G. Hamberg, *Studies in Roman Imperial Art*, 1945, 81.

endow the whole composition with a fine solemnity, and may be regarded as a preparation for later-Roman art. There is a growing acceptance of fixed conventional form in the deities which must owe something not merely to standardization of the type in sculpture but to the fixing of forms for figures and scenes upon coins.

The *profectio* scene,[1] however, which forms a doublet with the *adventus*, is more traditional.[2] The *quadriga*-crowned Arch in the background, with its trophies and prisoners, all schematically indicated in single units to economize space, whereas they must in reality have been a balanced composition, serves as a framework for the Emperor and his praetorian prefect, whose distinctive face is seen behind the renewed Imperial head of 1732. Behind them come a pair of stately figures, the *Genius Senatus*, wreathed and once carrying emblems, and a curious figure so faunlike in expression as to suggest *Faunus* himself.[3]

At the Emperor's feet reclines, with arm outstretched to receive him in attitude of welcome or homage, the personification of a great road, certainly the *Via Flaminia*. The conception owes much to Trajan's cointype of A.D. III, personifying *Via Traiana*, except that here the figure does not hold out her wheel but reclines upon it, as a water-goddess might upon her water-pot, and her extended and unburdened hand links her with the other actors in the scene. Beyond stand the soldiers. One *vexillifer*, whose flag is framed in the Arch and hangs symbolically above the Emperor's head, holds a horse ready for the Emperor. Another grips, close to the bit, the bridle of a whinnying second horse, impatient to be off, while his *vexillum* flutters in the breeze. The static scene is thus transformed into preparation for action and two soldiers in the background are alert to start. It will be observed that, however little is shown of the figures or forms of these men, they are all important to the *mise en scene* and that their

---

[1] Toynbee (*Cancelleria Reliefs*, 11 f.) agrees that this is a *profectio* and not, as Magi would have it, an *adventus*.

[2] Ryberg links the *profectio* relief with the *lustratio* (see p. 246) below.

[3] Ryberg thinks this the portrait of an unknown citizen (*op. cit.*, 34).

interest is focused upon the main action in a manner quite foreign to the older fashion of background treatment, in which the figures move indifferently and almost independently over the backcloth.

It is certain that the two scenes, of *adventus* and *profectio* are intimately connected, since care is taken to show in each the same kind of decoration. Stuart Jones is surely right in suggesting that they mark the interlude between the five-year Germanic war concluded in A.D. 174 and the Sarmatian wars which opened the following year. The latter phase is now represented by one relief only, in which prisoners are brought before the Emperor. Here, as in the German chieftain's submission, the Emperor is on a *tribunal*, but this time standing, with the praetorian prefect behind him, as if at a review. The background is made up of three *vexilla*, fluttering in the breeze, two spears, which emerge from the throng of prisoners and guards in front of the *tribunal*, and an ancient tree now too mutilated to make its species obvious. In the foreground two prisoners of Slavic type[1] are haled before the *tribunal*. A legionary, with back turned towards us and shield slightly more than half shown, is about to present a handcuffed captive, who looks hopelessly resigned to his fate. The captive in front of the Emperor has been pulled forward by a second guard, whose helmeted head alone is seen. But in order that the Emperor may see the prisoner properly, or the prisoner be compelled to look at the Emperor, his head is brutally pulled back and upwards by the hair. An Emperor's guard or *speculator* pushes forward to prevent too close an encroachment upon the *tribunal*, and looks up in expectation for an order, probably for execution. In the background four more soldiers' heads are seen, all in deeply interested attitude, but with greater depth and more crowding than in any scene so far described. The scene is a turbulent one, and if it echoed any words of the dedication, *bellicosissimis gentibus deletis* might be the theme: for here is neither submission nor hope of pardon.[2]

---

[1] Ryberg (*op. cit.*, 59) thinks the difference stylistic rather than racial.

[2] Ryberg, however, (*op. cit.*, 60 f.) interprets the Emperor's gesture as one of clemency.

V. Aosta: façade of the theatre.

The next two scenes again return from the field to the Capital, and represent the triumph of Marcus in A.D. 176. The triumphal procession is an astonishing contrast with those of Titus or Domitian. The subordinates are reduced to two. The first is a trumpeter, who marches through a triple arch, with a temple high on the left, assumed to be the Temple of *Iuppiter Custos*.[1] The Arch is presumably that of Tiberius, as in the procession of Titus. The second subordinate figure is a lictor, whose *fasces* merge with the architectural background and deliberately do not cut across it. These figures represent the entire attendant procession: the real interest of the scene is completely concentrated upon the four magnificently caparisoned horses and the triumphal chariot, whose elaborate wheels and Dionysiac[2] bronze body decoration form a wonderful setting for the standing Emperor upon whose head a small-sized Victory places a wreath. The *quadriga* and its occupant dominate and fill the picture, so that the Emperor in glory is the sole theme,[3] eclipsing all accessories and abstracted from the crowded festivity of the triumphal procession.

Older fashion, however, again dictates the matching panel, though the rich architectural background is in the new mode. This time the setting is nothing less than the Temple of *Iuppiter Capitolinus*, its front simplified, as often upon the coins, from hexastyle to tetrastyle, in order to emphasize the triple shrine with its three doors, and so to place the scene under the auspices of the Capitoline Triad. To right is a *porticus*, crowned by figures of hunters, presumably that which is known to have run just inside the wall of the *Area Capitolina*.

The composition is of two processions, which meet in the act of sacrifice. From the left proceeds Marcus, to sacrifice upon a portable tripod. He is accompanied by the *flamen Dialis*, and

[1] But see now Ryberg, *op. cit.*, 19 f.

[2] It is not clear why the decoration should be called Dionysiac: the upper panel depicts an unidentified seated goddess between Neptune and Minerva; the lower two Victories and a shield.

[3] There is some evidence for an erased second figure in the chariot—presumably Commodus as Caesar (Ryberg, *op. cit.*, 17 f.).

followed by the *Genius Senatus*, the praetorian prefect and an elderly figure, perhaps Pompeianus,[1] his son-in-law. Over against the tripod stand a *camillus* with incense-box and a *tibicen* with flutes. In the background is a large bull, accompanied by *popa* and by a *victimarius* who carries a dish on his head.

Two processions are also represented on the highly remarkable panel of the *lustratio exercitus*, which probably marked the commencement of one or other of the campaigns commemorated. But on this panel they diverge rather than converge. The Emperor stands once more at a tripod, with *tibicen* and *camillus* in attendance, while the sacrificial animals, boar, ram and bull, are guided on their way in front of him by attendants. Behind him stand the praetorian prefect and three standard bearers, *signifer* and *aquilifer* of the legions, and praetorian *vexillifer*. This procession has come to a halt. But the soldiers, who are to make a circuit round the spot due to be hallowed, and are to be followed by the sacrificial beasts, have only just started, headed by a *tubicen*, who is blowing with all his might and moving off to the right followed by a crowd of soldiers, whose *vexilla* and spears make a fine pattern. Overhead flutter garlands or swags, restored as large wreaths. But the upper portion of this panel has been entirely restored and it is not evident how it was originally composed, or whether the swags were held by personifications or hung from a tree.

The *lustratio* is not the only field scene to be reproduced. There is also an *adlocutio Augusti*, a subject familiar enough from Trajan's Column. Here, however, the treatment is in the new style. Emperor and praetorian prefect face left, standing upon a *tribunal*. Three *speculatores* stand in the foreground.[2] In the background are two standard-bearers and two soldiers, so spaced as to avoid a sense of crowding, but endowed with an intensity of interest which makes us feel that they are hanging upon the Emperor's words.

[1] In this case I.A.R. and Ryberg agree: but not over the other figure whom I.A.R. identifies as the praetorian prefect.

[2] Ryberg thinks they are a representative selection of troops (*op. cit.*, 53).

A no less remarkable scene[1] is that centred in the courtyard of a legionary headquarters. The background is formed by a great hall with large open bays and a clearstorey, in which the windows, hardly recognized by commentators, are carefully distinguished from the ashlar masonry of the lower part of the building. In front of the open arches, which, in order not to distract attention from the main scene, are treated without voussoirs or keystones, are grouped three *vexilla* and four *signa*, two crowned by figures of Victory, the third by Mars and the fourth perhaps by Hercules, and there is just the suggestion of an eagle on the extreme left. The heads of some of the standard-bearers are also seen.

The Emperor and praetorian prefect, facing right, occupy a *tribunal* and are faced by a front rank of four soldiers in undress uniform. At the foot of the *tribunal*, in the act of being invested by the Emperor stands a barbarian chief in German costume of fringed cloak, tunic, long sleeved vest, trousers and boots. The vassal's head, like the Emperor's, is a restoration of 1732, and this not only mars the effect but has led to some equivocations as to the significance of the relief.

One of the final scenes in the original arrangement must have been that of the *congiarium* which followed the celebration of the triumph of A.D. 176. This is a vivid picture. The Emperor sits upon a fine *sella curulis* and hands the gift which he is conferring to an attendant, who will in turn pass it to the citizens below. These are represented in two attitudes. The man on the left, who is yet to receive a gift, is clinging to the edge of the *tribunal* with one hand and is gazing intently upon the Emperor. His other hand, now broken away, must have been ready to grasp the gift the attendant was handing. To right, two classes of citizen move off: an elderly man leads away a small boy whose hands were uplifted to hold a gift. A younger married pair, the father carrying his child pick-a-back, walk away satisfied. Every generation of the populace, from the elderly to the younger adults, the

[1] Generally known as the '*rex datus*'. Ryberg (*op. cit.*, 48 f.) identifies the king as Furtius of the *Quadi*: however he was established (at *Aquileia*) by the *two* Augusti, Marcus and Verus, while only one is represented on the panel.

child and the child in arms is represented. There is a notable absence of personification as compared with the analogous Beneventan scene.[1] The concentration is upon the Emperor, and his attendants, among whom the praetorian praefect is again recognizable, are human beings; there is not even the characteristic figure of the *Genius Senatus*. High above the tribunal the garlanded building, a portico rather than a temple front, suggests the public place in which the scene is enacted.

[1] See above, p. 236.

9

AOSTA

The *colonia* of *Augusta Praetoria* was founded by Augustus in 25 B.C., following the final subjugation of the *Salassi*. This tribe, master of the extensive Alpine basin of the *Duria* (Dora Baltea), had long been vexatious to Roman settlers in Northern Italy for two reasons. They controlled the gold-washings of the lower valley; they also commanded the two important trans-Alpine traffic routes through the Little and Great St. Bernard passes, the former leading to Gaul by the Isère valley, the latter to Switzerland and the Rhine by the Drance. Already in 143 B.C. the Romans took control of the gold-mines. The problem of controlling the traffic lasted much longer. Even as late as 100 B.C. only the very mouth of the valley was sealed or secured by the *colonia* at *Eporedia*, now Ivrea, founded in 100 B.C. In truth no permanent military decision was possible until continuity of policy was achieved under Augustus, when the northern boundary of Italy could be settled and the wider question of European communications became an urgent reality. It speaks for his sense of reality that even as *triumvir* Octavian was already attacking the local problem of Alpine peace, in 35 or 34 B.C., through Antistius Vetus:[1] and as *princeps* he undertook further campaigns through Messalla Corvinus,[2] perhaps in 28–27 B.C., and lastly through Terentius Varro Murena in 25 B.C., who finally conquered the tribe. Two versions of the conqueror's actions are current. Strabo states that 'all were sold as booty, thirty-six thousand individuals and 8000 fighting men, Terentius Varro the victorious general vending them by public auction'.[3] Cassius Dio reports

[1] Appian, *Illyr.*, 17 (I.A.R.).   [2] Dio, xlix, 38, 3.
[3] Strabo, iv, 6, 7 (I.A.R.).

[249]

that 'under pretence of collecting a levy in cash, he arrested those of fighting age and sold them, on the condition that none should be manumitted for twenty years'.[1] Strabo's story cannot be an invention: and, if Dio's information is regarded as qualifying the sale of the 8000 fighting men, the two versions are not irreconcilable. This policy, plainly applied to the wilder side-valleys, was cold-blooded and savage, but it did not wipe out the tribe. There were those who from the first came into the new town as *incolae*, that is, colonists with inferior rights, and they could on occasion be vocal. The earliest dated inscription from the town, of 23 B.C., records them as *Salassi incol(ae) qui initio se in colon(iam) cont(ulerunt)*, and is itself a dedication to Augustus as their patron.[2] It is dated just after the conspiracy of Murena, since it mentions not only the eleventh consulate, but the new *tribunicia potestas* of Augustus; it is a discreet yet transparent reference by the *Salassi* to the fate of the man who had enslaved them, an expression of political feeling which deftly used an expression of loyalty for the future to convey unspoken comment upon a sorry past.

The new town, which Varro had founded, lay, according to Strabo, where Varro had pitched his camp.[3] The situation was indeed good. Aosta lies on the north bank of the river Dora Baltea, the ancient *Duria*, which debouches into Piedmont at Ivrea, the Roman colony of *Eporedia*. Five miles above Ivrea, the river valley narrows into a gorge, running northwards. It does not widen appreciably again until, having turned sharply westwards at St. Vincent, it broadens out for some 14 miles between Chambave and Aymaville. This mountain vale is the heart land of the *Salassi*, and Aosta occupies its key position, where the valley of the Dora Baltea is joined from the north by the gorge of the Buthier, the waters meet lying half a mile below the town. Both these natural gateways carry vitally important routes: that by the upper Dora Baltea leads westward to the Little St. Bernard pass and so to the Isère valley and the Rhône; that by the Buthier and its tributary the Artaravaz or Artereva, carries the road to the

[1] Dio, liii, 25 (I.A.R.).   [2] *ILS* 6753.

[3] Strabo, iv, 6, 7. Note the Arch of Augustus (pl. VI) in this connection.

Great St. Bernard and so by the Drance valley through Switzerland to the Rhine. By seizing this position Varro paralyzed and
blockaded the *Salassi*; by founding there a *colonia*, Augustus
controlled both the great Alpine passes and established the natural
centre for civil development of the area. When Dio records that
the *colonia* was the best of the land (ἡ ἀρίστη τῆς γῆς) he could
better have stated that it was the sole sizeable tract of good land
that the tribe possessed.[1]

Apart from the military use of the site of Aosta by Varro, Dio
records that the colonists were ex-praetorian guardsmen and
their families.[2] But this does not mean that the town-plan followed
a military pattern. The plan is indeed very regular (figure 1).
The town-wall encloses a strict rectangle, 2350 feet long by
1860 feet broad. Each side is divided into four lengths by a gate
and four interval towers, and these divisions are marked by main
streets, so that there were sixteen large building-plots within the
town, each some 540 by 440 feet in size, and planned so as to
mirror the proportions of the town itself. It is clear that all these
principal streets were furnished with large sewers, but there were
minor streets with smaller sewers as well; and the disposition of
these, together with the placing of the theatre and public baths,
suggests first that the building-plots were mostly halved along
their length and secondly that minor streets in the other direction
also occurred, though quite certainly at more irregular intervals.
The gates are situated on the long axis, and at three-quarter
position on the long side.

The town-wall is just over 6 feet thick, reduced by three offsets
to some 5 feet at the top. It stands 21 feet high to rampart-walk.
It is faced with squared masonry set in regular courses,[3] with a
core of mortared cobbles and rubble. The rampart-walk is
marked by a plain string course or oversailing course. All traces
of original parapet, not to speak of crenellations,[4] have now

[1] Dio, liii, 25 (I.A.R.).

[2] *Ibid.*, (the families are not specifically mentioned).

[3] Particularly visible on the outside face of the south wall.

[4] C. Promis, *Le Antichità di Aosta*, 1862, pl. 4, H, L, I, restores a parapet with
crenellations.

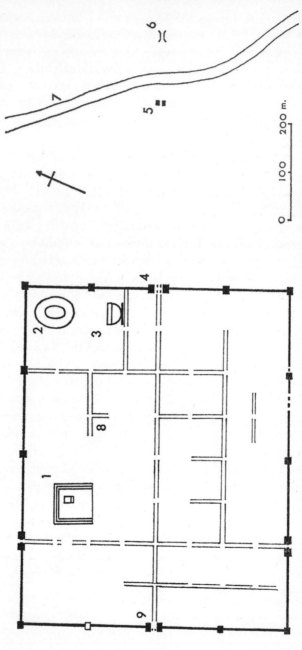

1. Aosta (after A. Boethius (*The Golden House of Nero*, 1960, 43, fig. 21), F. Castagnoli (*Ippodamo di Mileto e l'urbanistica a pianta ortogonale*, 1956, 96, fig. 50) and others): 1. 'Forum'. 2. Amphitheatre. 3. Theatre. 4. 'Porta Praetoria'. 5. Arch of Augustus. 6. Roman Bridge. 7. R. Buthier. 8. Baths. 9. 'Porta Decumana'.

VI. Aosta: Arch of Augustus (the roof is modern).

disappeared, though some attempt was made by D'Andrade to restore a parapet and may be based upon genuine original work. The wall had no earthen rampart behind it. Reinforcement against battering rams was provided by buttresses 6 to 4 feet wide and 10 feet deep, occurring at every 40 feet, a rare feature matched at Side and within other Pamphylian towns. The towers are rectangular, 30 Roman feet across the front and 33 Roman feet from front to back: they project from the wall at both front and back, but rather more towards the front, where the ground-floor wall is again thickened against battering rams to match the town walls. They are three storeys high, with three windows on each face on the second floor, and the same except that a door takes the place of a window at the first floor. The ground floor was hollow, and each floor was boarded. The top was presumably crenellated in the manner of conventional towers on contemporary mosaics or water-heaters.

The known gates were of two designs. Those on the north and south sides had single arches, the east gate, which was the chief entrance, reached from Rome, had a much larger single carriage-way flanked by footways $7\frac{1}{2}$ feet wide (plate III). It also possessed a very remarkable courtyard, $38\frac{1}{2}$ feet wide by 64 feet deep, and a huge central opening $22\frac{1}{2}$ feet wide, which, like the footways, was closed with a portcullis and could itself never have been closed with doors. The deep courtyard had no doors at the back, but the enemy could be enfiladed from rampart-walk level at its back and from the two upper storeys of the towers at its sides, if the portcullis were to admit them. Such a court also served for the levying of town customs or the examination of travellers. As already noted, both this large gate and the smaller gates were flanked by large and deep towers, projecting in the same fashion as the wall towers, but with twice as many windows at the side. No more remarkable example of the courtyard gate exists in the Roman Empire than this.[1]

The plan of the west gate, or so-called '*Porta Decumana*', is not

[1] The Roman bridge 500 m. to the east might also have been mentioned (see pl. VII).

certainly Roman. That of the north and south gates consisted of the usual two towers, flanking a single carriage-way, 16 feet wide, furnished with a portcullis. But here the portcullis was backed by a gateway-passage supplied with a double door. This gave room for a wide upper storey capable not only of containing the portcullis machinery but of housing defenders.

Within the walls three important public buildings are known in detail, a fourth in parts only. The most remarkable is the so-called 'Forum', a rectangular piazza 257 feet wide and 289 feet from back to front. This was surrounded by a double portico, $33\frac{1}{3}$ feet wide, carried upon a semi-basement or undercroft whose floor is nine feet below Roman ground-level. This structure consists of two parallel barrel-vaulted passages 12 feet wide and $14\frac{1}{2}$ feet high, separated by a low arcade and lighted by windows which lie almost at ground-level outside the building but reach inside it to the springing of the vault. The use of this remarkable basement has been much discussed, but there is no very clear evidence that it was intended for use at all. Doors into it are lacking, and it may well be that its principal function was structural, with the purpose of supporting an elevated portico, standing upon a podium over nine feet above the pavement. All traces of this superstructure are now gone, but fragments of some Tuscan and Doric columns suggest a simple treatment, of Republican tradition, such as is seen, for example, at *Minturnae*. Elevated platforms or podia of this kind are known to have surrounded the *fora* of Arles, Reims and Bavai, and there were no doubt others of the same kind.

The middle of the 'Forum' square was occupied by two great bays or platforms, one carrying a temple, the other probably an equestrian statue. The temple, 42 feet wide by 62 feet deep, was *in antis* with tetrastyle front, and stood upon a high podium, of which one side has been exposed, below the wall of a modern house, revealing the base mould and cornice of a structure $7\frac{1}{2}$ feet high. According to Promis[1] two small temples lay behind the front wall of the forum and looked into the square. But the

[1] C. Promis, *op. cit.*, pl. 8, A; 9, A.

remains as recorded hardly warrant so bold a restoration, despite the general acceptance by subsequent students. What is clear and indubitable is that the so-called '*Forum*' was not a commercial or legal centre, but a religious precinct containing what can only have been the *capitolium* of the colony. This will explain the presence of an altar to the Capitoline triad, now in the adjacent Cathedral. The site of the commercial *forum* yet remains to be discovered and it might be expected that this centre would lie nearer the main through street.

The next two important buildings are for entertainment. The most remarkable is the theatre, well-known for its lofty straight façade (plate V) which, unlike the straight façades at Orange and elsewhere, forms the back of the building and is tangential to the curved seating. It is immensely high and somewhat slight for its height, and comprises a ground-floor of arcaded bays separated by buttresses, each arcade being surmounted by three small square-headed windows, three round-headed windows, and a single very large round-headed window.

Within the narrow limits bordered by this bold architectonic composition lies the theatre itself, confined in size to two tiers of seats surrounded by an annular corridor, of which the central third is cut off by the straight external wall already noted. The orchestra is 60 feet in diameter, while the whole auditorium is 124 feet in diameter, but measures only 68 feet from back to front so that almost half is cut off at the back. Facing the *auditorium* stood a large and elaborate stage building. It is, however, clear that the whole of the stone-built *cavea*, or *auditorium*, is inserted within the monumental shell formed by the façade, of which the internal face exhibits many traces of offsets and corbels, intended not for the later vaulting, which frequently obliterates them, but for a wooden structure. Timber seating would both rise to greater height in less space and demand an altogether different arrangement of staircases, however achieved: again, unlike vaulting, it would exercise little or no thrust, thus explaining the extraordinary thin build of the façade and the lack of interlocked structure which so markedly differentiates it from the façade erected in relation to vaulting behind it. For, as the ruins today demonstrates, the tall and slender buttressed piers are not bonded with the walling between them, which is mere infilling. The date of the original theatre is in some doubt. It is stated that below the visible *auditorium* were found traces of earlier buildings identified as private houses. But in default of a plan and in recognition of the need for sill-walls to support the wooden seating their nature must be regarded as dubious. Arguments for style are equally perilous. All are agreed that the façade is unique, but none have recognized that the reason for its unusual character and build lies in its relation to timber construction. In this respect it is indeed rare, for no other example of a monumental stone façade belonging to a timber theatre is known to exist, though many must once have done so.

In contrast to the theatre, the amphitheatre is conventional. It occupies the north-east corner *insula* of the town, to north of the theatre, and its arrangement strongly suggests that the block was divided by a minor street running from north to south. The building measures approximately 300 by 245 feet, but little is known of its internal arrangements. Only the external façade of masonry and the vaulted underpinning of the seating survives, walled into the nunnery of St. Catherine (plate IV). The ground floor of the external arcade was a noble structure in the Tuscan order, exhibiting in building the peculiarity that in the attached columns framing the arcade the caps and a middle stone are bonded with the main structure, while the shaft and base of the column, in two portions, were simply applied to the main piers and tied by metal clamps. Once again the date of the building is doubtful: but there is no reason to suppose that it is not original, and the style of the masonry is strikingly like that of the so-called 'Forum'. That buildings of importance were still being erected 25 years after the first foundation is shown by a stray monumental inscription of 1 B.C. or A.D. 1 which has sometimes been associated with the monumental arch outside the town, but is in fact un-assignable to any specific building.[1]

[1] *CIL* v, 6834 (I.A.R.): *trib. pot. XXIII.*

VII. Aosta: Roman bridge.

Finally, the public baths have been identified,[1] in the street north of the axial street, below the Scuole Normali, under the courtyard of which many unexplored remains must still exist. The front of the building faced a side street 11 feet wide running from north to south. It was furnished with a colonnade and a balustrade of upright stone slabs. The north front, on the east-to-west street, appears to have been occupied by shops, surrounding, as often in Roman town-planning, the important building which formed the kernel of the block. Only the fringe of the principal building, however, has been examined, and exploration while revealing many heated rooms and three large apses, did not yield anything like a coherent plan. What is clear is that the whole building was not less than 140 feet square, exclusive of the shops surrounding it. There were manifest traces also of a late restoration, in which a cover-slab for one of the out-fall drains was cut from a dedication to Marcus Aurelius, belonging to A.D. 164–6, which must once have been paired with another to Lucius Verus, the co-ruler. Much marble facing also came from the building, and a tile with the stamp RPA for *Respublica Augustanorum*, indicative of building at public expense.[2]

The aqueduct which supplied the town and, as a second call, the baths was a relatively short one, as might be expected in Alpine valleys where good springs abound. The water selected for the purpose, and chosen for a second time by the municipality in 1922, came from the lowest tributary on the east bank of the Buthier, known as La Combe, below the hamlet of Porossan. It ran for about a mile and a half as an underground channel 1' 4" square, embedded in a mass of concrete, and appears to have crossed the Buthier valley at the bottom of the side-valley by means of an inverted siphon of lead pipes supported upon a masonry base. This is a minor example of the method employed on the grand scale for crossing the deep dry valleys west of Lyons (*Lugdunum*). The point at which it entered the town is unknown, but the north gate is the most likely point.

Private houses are little known in detail. But it is clear that they

[1] *Not. Scav.*, 1899, 107 ff. (I.A.R.)   [2] *CIL* v, 8100, 400.

existed in substantial architecture and large numbers. Pavements of *opus sectile*, or slabs of marble cut to pattern, point to wealth among the colonists: and this reminds us that the praetorian of the period seems to have been receiving 750 *denarii* a year and *praemia militaria* upon retirement of perhaps 3000 *sesterces*. There will have been some retired centurions also, men capable of attaining the equestrian census. Some of the more distinguished citizens are known from inscriptions. The family of the Petillii, whose cemetery lay at Villeneuve, up the valley from Aosta, numbered a *dunumvir*, Petillius Saturninus, amongst them.[1] The Avillii and Aimi of the Val Cogne were working and developing the iron ore there obtainable.[2] More interesting from the point of view of local history is L. Iulius Salassus, of St. Pierre, an *eques* and plainly one of the rich *incolae* of local origin. *Seviri Augustales* also, Salvius Myro[3] and L. Arruntius Augustanus[4] seem to attest wealthy folk of libertine origin. Of their works only the remarkable joint achievement of C. Avillius and C. Aimus Patavinus survives today and is even in actual use. This is the remarkable two-storey foot-bridge for pedestrians and pack-horses which spans the deep and narrow ravine of the Cogne at Pondel (plate VIII), the place-name itself derived from *ponticulus*.[5] The bridge itself is a little over 160 feet long, with an arch of 46′ 3″ in diameter. Above the arch is an inscription of 3 B.C.: *Imp. Caesari Augusto XIII cos designatus/C. Avillius C.F.C. Aimus Patavinus/ privatim*.[6] Then comes a covered passage-way, with small windows on each side regularly placed but staggered in relation to one another to avoid the violent winds which blow down the valley. The passage is 3′ 10″ wide and 8′ 2″ high, just large enough

[1] *CIL* v, 6896.

[2] *CIL* v, 6899 (I.A.R.): see G. E. F. Chilver, *Cisalpine Gaul*, 1941, 170 ff.

[3] *CIL* v, 6828.   [4] *CIL* v, 6837.

[5] C. Promis, *op. cit.*, pl. 14; I. Beretta, *La romanizzazione della valle d'Aosta* 1954, pp. 76–7, 92, 105, 111, 121; G. Lugli, *La technice edilizia romana*, 1957, ii, pl. clxxxvii, 2 and text opposite (I owe these references to J.M.C.T., who thinks the upper passage must have been an aqueduct).

[6] *CIL* v, 6899 (I.A.R.): which reads . . . *privatum*, following Promis (see Promis, *op. cit.*, pl. 14, D) who claimed to have inspected the inscription suspended over the gorge by ropes.

for pedestrians or a rider, but hardly big enough for a well-laden pack-mule. The animals must have taken the upper open walk, which is of the same width, but had a parapet 3′ 4″ high, over which packs might bulge. The rock-cut paths leading to the bridge at both levels are systematically embanked and underpinned. The lower path at the entrance to the bridge has at its side a niche for a shrine, from which the dedication has long been missing.

The purpose of the bridge is not declared upon the inscription, but so substantial a structure, erected as private property for pedestrians, horsemen and pack-horse traffic, is no ordinary phenomenon. The Cogne valley, however, which it spans is noted for its deposits of iron ore, and it is no doubt in connexion with the working of *ferrariae* that the bridge was built. It will be observed that Aimus Patavinus is of Patavian origin, from the wealthiest commercial city in northern Italy (over 500 knights); and his venture may be compared with the lucrative copper mine in the adjacent territory of the *Ceutrones*, developed by the knight Sallustius Crispus, friend of Augustus and grandnephew of the historian.[1] The copper mine was a short-lived venture, the iron mines lasted long and are worked today, and the name of the family of Aimus lies behind the village of Aymaville in the main valley, where the Cogne valley reaches it.

[1] Pliny, *N.H.*, xxxiv, 3 ; Tacitus, *Ann.*, iii, 30.

10

ROMAN PROVINCIAL PALACES

Those who would consider in a brief hour palaces of the Roman Imperial age are inevitably confronted by a difficult choice. If they seek to treat the palaces of Rome and its neighbourhood, then the highly intricate development of the Palatine, the far-flung and capricious oddities in planning and decoration of Nero's Golden House, the exciting and complicated design of Hadrian's summer palace or *villa*, or the Constantinian development of the Lateran would require some ingenuity of presentation to fit within an hour: and this consideration would exclude a substantial number of provincial structures which are less well known and which in their own right merit consideration. They are not always the Emperor's own palaces, though three will be found to win the title: they are the dwellings of the Emperor's representatives, legionary legates, provincial governors or frontier commanders;[1] and they are seldom collected, nor are they always available for study. The governor's *praetorium* at Gortyn in Crete, excavated in the twenties by the Italians, remains unpublished, except for the briefest of summaries and a singularly uninformative series of photographs;[2] the governor's residence at *Volubilis*, in *Mauretania Tingitana*, is completely uncommunicated by the French. This is greatly to be regretted since one represents the quarters of a senatorial governor, if of lower rank, the other those of a *procurator*

[1] The Flavian palace at London may now be added to those discussed in this paper: see *JRS* lvii, 191 f. and fig. 14; R. Merrifield, *The Roman City of London*, 1965, 273 f. no. 273. It is, however, remarkably difficult to make anything of the plan, as at present revealed: S.S.F. thinks there must be various periods. Traces of a possible slightly earlier palace have been found in Gracechurch Street.

[2] *Bolletino d'arte*, v, 418 ff.

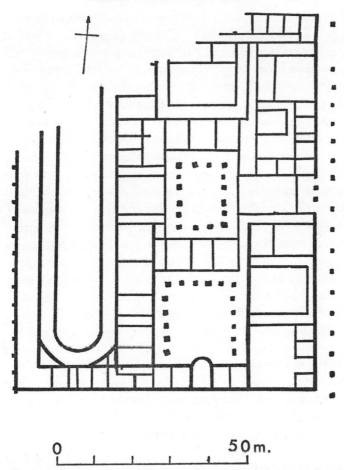

2. *Vetera* : first legate's palace (after H. Mylius, *Bonn. Jhb.*, cxxvi, pl. 6).

pro legato. But without these there is still much, and a beginning may be made with the two palaces or *praetoria* of the legionary legates in the Claudio-Neronian legionary fortress at *Vetera*, now Xanten,[1] on the Rhine, the most important strategic centre of Lower Germany, where the gateway of the Lippe valley leads into the heart of Westphalia.

[1] The legionary fortress (*Vetera I*) is in fact nearer to Birten: Xanten is the site of the *Colonia Traiana*.

[261]

The excavator's plan is largely one of foundations, or foundation trenches, for a palace built in masonry (figure 2).[1] There is an external portico, probably for sentries, a porch and vestibule, with porter's lodge or guardroom, opening into a large internal court and light-well, with surrounding colonnade. At the back of this is the great dining-room, the social centre of the house, mistakenly restored by the German architect Mylius[2] as a second and meaningless vestibule leading into a secluded formal garden. To left is a second and more private colonnaded court, no doubt containing bedrooms and the like; to right a court with veranda gives access to storerooms and servants' quarters, accessible from the the street; while it might be thought that the *officium* of the *legatus* was housed in the corner complex of rooms, also to be reached separately from the colonnade and street. Thus, what appears at first sight to be an extremely lavish allotment of rooms turns out upon analysis to be little more than what can have been required for reasonable comfort and for administrative needs. In particular, it must be borne in mind that only a single-storey building is in question. The sole extravagance would seem to be the formal garden, with its extensive portico. But when it is recollected that within the tightly packed plan of a legionary fortress there was no privacy and no place in which the commandant might rest or take exercise in peace and quiet the seeming extravagance becomes a concession to nature and a wise precaution against overstrain. In detail the plan of the garden carries a strong suggestion of a private door or wicket; and the secret comings and goings of Germanicus, investigating in semi-disguise the morale of his soldiery, will be recalled.[3] The second legate's house at *Vetera* is less completely known (figure 3). In general, its plan echoes that of its companion, and in particular the formal garden jumps to the eye. But in detail nothing is quite alike as between the two palaces.[4] The vestibule pretty clearly leads to a central court: yet there are in fact many more colonnaded courtyards, much more widely

[1] See H. Mylius, *Bonn. Jhb.*, cxxvi, pl. 6, facing p. 44.
[2] *Ibid.*   [3] Tacitus, *Ann.*, ii, 13.
[4] H. v. Petrikovits. *Das römische Rheinland*, 1960, 37, fig. 10.

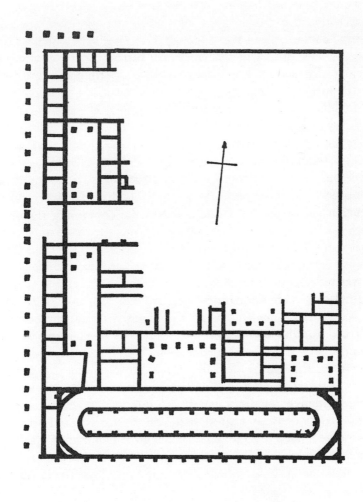

0   50 m.

3. *Vetera*: second legate's palace (after an original in the archives of the Rheinisches Landesmuseum, Bonn).

dispersed and much more diverse in plan. It becomes manifest that within the similar space allotted to the two houses a substantial choice of plan was possible. This recalls the differences in the tribunes' houses of the Agricolan fortress of Inchtuthil, and incidentally shows how these smaller dwellings, with their courtyards and great dining-rooms, are essentially the same type of building, scaled down to suit lower grades in the hierarchy of military rank and civilian society.[1] Just as the *principia* of auxiliary forts are legionary *principia in parvo*, so these *praetoria* are architectural statements in the same terms to differing scale. The gardens, which are such a feature of these interesting palaces, might be used for all kinds of social occasions.[2] The formal garden of the Severan palace on the Palatine shows the continuing vogue of such appurtenances, and in an earlier age the vivid record by Philo of Gaius administering scant and irritable justice to a Jewish delegation comes to mind.[3] But the next palace, which is as yet little known, involves the Emperor in the grip of a more formal court ceremonial, whether he liked it or not. This is the palace at *Carnuntum* (figure 4), the headquarters of the court of Marcus Aurelius and Faustina the Younger during the Marcomannic war of A.D. 171–3, and, as may well interest students of literature, the setting for the third book of the *Meditations*, with its rubric 'written in *Carnuntum*'.[4] Here indeed it is impossible to define the Imperial study, but the audience-room or *basilica* is evident, as a great hall with apsidal end.[5] It may be recognized as a deliberate echo of the great hall built by Rabirius for Domitian on the Palatine, though it does not form so majestic an ensemble. This is perhaps due to the fact that it belongs to a

[1] See *e.g. JRS* li, 158, fig. 9.

[2] For Flavian Fishbourne see *JRS* lvii, 199, fig. 19. (Reports: *Ant. J.*, xlii, 15 ff.; xliii, 1 ff.; xliv, 1 ff.; xlv, 1 ff.; xlvi, 26 ff.; xlvii, 51 ff.; xlviii, 32 ff.)

[3] Philo, *Leg. ad Gaium*, 351 ff. (cf. Suetonius, *Tib.* 15; *Cal.* 59; and *CIL* vi, 8668). There were the gardens of Lamia and of Maecenas on the Esquiline (see J.P.V.D. Balsdon, *The Emperor Gaius*, 1934 (1966 ed.), 140; S. B. Platner and T. Ashby, *A Topographical Dictionary of Ancient Rome*, 1929, 267 f., 269): they had become imperial property.

[4] Τὰ ἐν Καρνούντῳ (I.A.R.).

[5] E. Swoboda, *Carnuntum* (2nd ed.) 1953, 155, fig. 11.

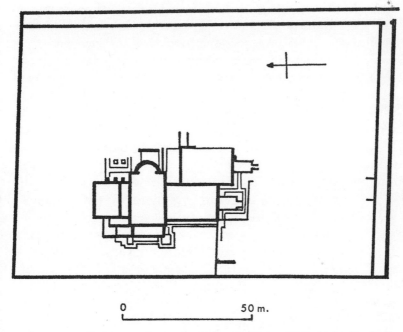

0   50 m.

4. *Carnuntum*: 'palace-type' complex (after D. Meyer-Plath, in E. Swoboda, *Carnuntum*, 2nd ed., 1953, 155, fig. 11).

series of heated rooms, a precaution against the vigours of an Austrian winter. It is much to be hoped, however, that excavation of the complex, whose limits are already known, will continue. For *Carnuntum* provides, as no other site in the Empire yet does, an idea of what sort of building might be erected for an Imperial residence when the Emperor planned a prolonged stay in a province. The *domus palatina* at York, mentioned in the *Life of Severus*,[1] which housed the Imperial court between 209 and 211 may be thought of as a comparable building, standing by itself on the fringe of the civilian settlement, with a good view of the

[1] S.H.A. *Severus*, 22, 7: however the Court might have used the legionary legate's house (which may already have become the governor's palace of *Britannia Inferior*), particularly if the legion, or part of it, was in the field or at Carpow.

river. In this matter of outlook may be detected an important difference between the legionary legate's palace and that of the civilian world. Within the tightly-packed military lines there was no possibility of a fine external prospect. Indeed, only the highest members of the officer class might enjoy the seclusion of a private view into their own garden or court. Privacy was something to be envied and a privilege rarely granted to the serving soldier. But the governor, whether military or civil, freed from the restrictions of garrison life, moved in a higher sphere, and might avail himself not only of privacy but of scenic opportunities as well. Recent Hungarian excavations at *Aquincum*[1] have uncovered substantial portions of the governor's palace on the Danube island with magnificent river views (figure 5). Here is immediately apparent the influence of the plan of the great country house, where an architectural façade, planned in specific relation to the enjoyment of a panorama, is the dominant feature. The great dining-room, flanked by side passages, as at *Vetera*, takes pride of place in this front block and is flanked by rooms of interesting plan, implying barrel vaults and domes, while the whole range ends in rotundas which quite literally round off the composition. The roof lines might have been as interesting as Brighton pavilion. Behind the façade is a great court, into which projects a large bath-suite, wherein can be recognized both the *caldarium* and the highly elaborate hot plunge-bath associated with the Turkish bath and the round *laconicum* or Swedish bath of dry heat. Both these hot bathing suites are planned in relation to the cold room or *frigidarium* with central douche and cold bath beyond. It is plain, however, that apart from the main façade, something more than half the principal block remains to be discovered, while subsidiary buildings, which none the less form an integral part of the complex, lie to south. Here resided the *legatus Augusti* of *Pannonia Inferior* during the second and third centuries, and the *dux Valeriae* during the fourth.

It is interesting to compare the plan of the *Aquincum* palace with that of the building recently recovered, below the Cologne

[1] J. Szilágyi, *Aquincum*, 1956, pull-out 2, facing p. 24.

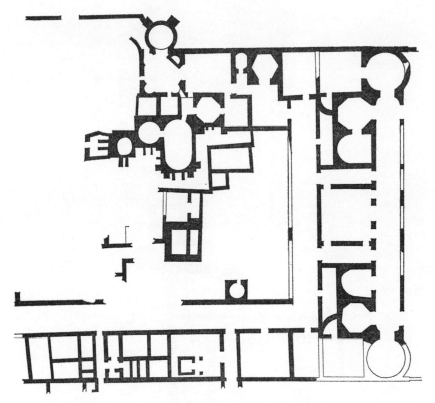

5. *Aquincum*: sketch-plan of the part of the governor's palace excavated down to 1955, after a perspective drawing by F. Fenesch and J. Schauschek (in J. Szilágyi, *Aquincum*, 1956, pull-out 2, facing p. 24). The right (east) wing is believed to have been the main façade.

Rathaus, on the west bank of the Rhine.[1] This highly complex building passed through two phases. The earlier stage (figure 6), of the third century,[2] is represented by a row of buttressed rooms

[1] O. Doppelfeld, *Germania*, xxxiv, 83 ff., especially pull-outs 1 and 2, facing pp. 92 and 94; (*Gymnasium*), *Germania Romana*, i, *Römerstädte in Deutschland*, 1960, 20 ff. K. Baedeker, *Cologne and Bonn with Environs*, 1961, pl. facing p. 67.

[2] v. Petrikovits, *op. cit.*, 89, fig. 30, dates the *third c.* A.D. 180: there were in fact *four* distinct Roman phases. The first lasted from *c.* A.D. 50 to 69.

[267]

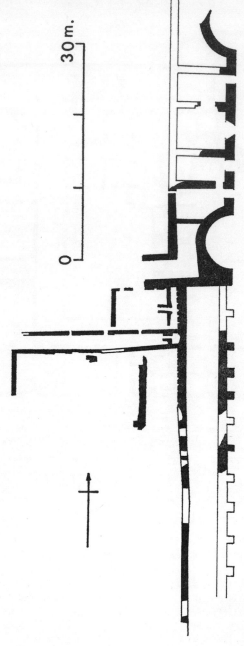

30 m.

6. Cologne: fragments of the first phase of the palace (first-century) (after O. Doppelfeld, *Germania*, xxxiv, pull-out I, facing p. 92).

which served as substructures for an elaborate and monumental river-bank front. They afford little clue to the arrangement of the suite which they carried. But to north of this the river-bank was dominated by a still more ambitious group of rooms, in which the central dining-room unit is again outstanding and is seen to be flanked by passage rooms and niched *exedrae*. The junction between the two riverside features is made at the point where a range of important rooms runs back at right-angles to divide a pair of courts. The general resemblance to the *Aquincum* plan, however great the divergence in detail, is clearly apparent. It is even more manifest in the later version of the building (figure 7),[1] in which a very large and ambitious river-façade takes the place of the southern end of the east front, projecting further forward on to the river-bank and developing, or more probably completely superseding, the earlier northern front. The superb new front had a large domed dining-room as its central feature, while the terminal niches of the previous arrangement are echoed by much larger niched pavilions at each end of a colonnaded or arcaded portico. The main front at *Aquincum* was indubitably more elegant, just as it was certainly more laboured: but it is quite surpassed by the scale and simplified grandeur of the Cologne planning. Here may be recognized first the seat of the *legatus* of Lower Germany, and of his later successor the *praeses* of *Germania Secunda*.

A useful comparison may next be made between the palaces of *Aquincum* and *Colonia Agrippinensis* and that of the third-century *dux ripae* at Dura on the Euphrates.[2] Whereas at the former places the planning, whatever its precise completed form, has manifestly been somewhat loose and sprawling, at Dura all is trim and tight[3] while the plan as recovered is very nearly complete

[1] Doppelfeld, *Römerstädte in Deutschland*, 21, fig. 4; *Germania*, xxxiv, pull-out 2; v. Petrikovits, *op. cit.*, 90, fig. 31: the construction-date of this phase is uncertain.

[2] M. I. Rostovtseff (ed.), *The Excavations at Dura-Europos, Preliminary Report of the Ninth Season of Work 1935–1936*, pt. iii, 1952, especially figs. 1, 2, 7.

[3] *cf.* Pfalzel, in the next century (see below, p. 279, n. 1).

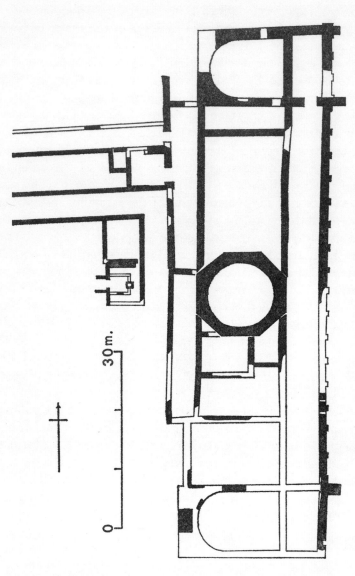

30 m.

0

7. Cologne: palace, fourth-century phase (after O. Doppelfeld, *Germania*, xxxiv, pull-out 2, facing p. 94).

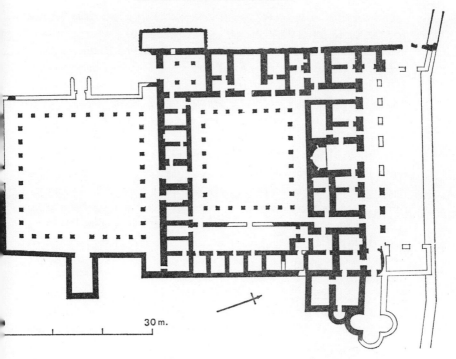

30 m.

8. Dura-Europos: palace of the *dux ripae* (after A. H. Detweiler, in M. I. Rostovtseff (ed.), *Dura-Europos, Ninth Season*, iii, 1952, fig. 7, facing p. 96).

(figure 8).[1] Only crosion of the river-front following the ruin of the embankment wall has removed wing pavilions and the most of a trefoil exedra. The identity of the palace is given by a *dipinto* in Greek, which within its ansate frame commemorates

[1] The excavators of the Dura palace argue for a Western architect – and the arrangement of the north wing in particular indicates at least a Western or Westernised patron – but the occurrence of three of the principal features of the palace (the open-fronted pillarless hall, the hall with four pillars and the use of a peristyle as an entrance court) also in the Parthian palace at Assur of the first and second centuries A.D. is remarkable (see M. A. R. Colledge, *The Parthians*, 1967, 122, fig. 29). The first two features almost certainly had different uses in the two palaces, but the possibility of a local architect using local solutions for new problems posed by Roman masters cannot be ruled out.

Elpidephorus, *alumnus* of Domitius Pompeianus, *dux ripae*.[1] A date
for the building is also offered by fragments of a fine large-scale
painted inscription from the entrance courtyard to the building
which refers to an Emperor as the son of Caracalla and which
must belong either to Elagabalus or Severus Alexander, probably
the former A.D. 218–22.[2] The arrangement of the Dura palace is
simple and logical. Once more a great dining-room is the
principal feature in the front or north wing; and the baths and
the principal rooms of the house were also concentrated in this
area. But the main court contains as well a much larger and more
public dining-room, presumably for state banquets. In the east
wing are principally servants' quarters, ranged round a narrow
court of their own, while the coach-house and stables for horses
and donkeys are ingeniously accommodated in the south-west
corner and are made accessible from outside by subtracting
something from the width of the front courts of the building
next to the city. This great quadrangle forms a sort of *yamen* or
open-air court of justice, with a covered hall on the east side
where the details of cases could be heard. As the excavators
remark,[3] the scene of the judgment of Christ before Pilate must
have had a rather similar setting with the judge in or on his
tribunal and the people, fierce, unruly and bitter, waiting in the
court before him. As for the aspect of the place, the architectural
remains of fallen ceilings and walls demand a restoration with
flat roofs and frontages of Eastern functional simplicity. The
materials available, sun-dried brick and plaster, would in any
case render nothing else practicable; and the weary brilliance of
light excluded other schemes. Variety would be supplied through
humans and their dress: and a fine gold brooch, with an exag-
geratedly proportioned intaglio, and jewels *en cabochon*, supplies
a sudden flash of almost barbaric brilliance and splendour.

[1] Rostovtseff, *op. cit.*, 30 f., no. 945.

[2] *Ibid.* 27, no. 944: [*Di*]*vi Mag(ni)* [*Antonini Bri*]*t. Ger. Ma*[*x*].

[3] *Ibid.* 89 ff.: in fact the excavators emphasize that Pontius Pilate's *tribunal* was
in front of the palace. Here there is a large entrance court in front of the palace,
but is is enclosed and not really a parallel. The entrance is narrow and can not
have encouraged the entrance of the populace.

VIII. Val d'Aosta: Roman bridge or aqueduct at Pondel.

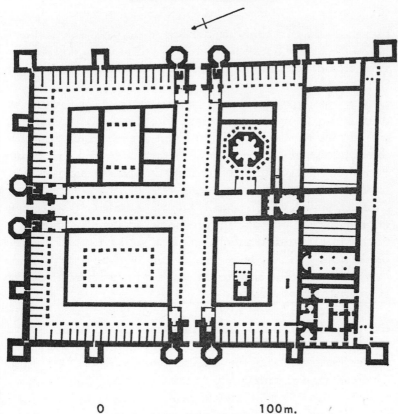

9. Split: Diocletian's palace (after H. Kähler, *Rome and her Empire*, 1963, 204, fig. 44 [Holle Bildarchiv]).

From the palace of the *dux ripae* on the Euphrates it is not a very difficult transition to that prepared for his retirement by the Eastern Emperor, Diocletian, near *Salonae*, at Spalato or Split. This remarkable palace, a fortress to landward and an inaccessible towered façade to seaward, notably combines military and civilian elements (figure 9). The plan[1] resembles in part a fort of the later third century, with garrison quarters or storehouses at

[1] See *e.g.* H. Kähler, *Rome and her Empire*, 1963, 204, fig. 44.

the back of its fortified wall and two courts for stables and the military in the two landward quarters of the plan. The next two halves are divided between a temple and mausoleum, towards the axial cross-street and the palace proper which, as at Dura, is concentrated upon the water front. We can recognize an audience-chamber or throne room, reminiscent of that at *Carnuntum*: but other details, except for an obvious suite of baths at the west end, are difficult to diagnose. The current French restoration[1] has thinned down all the elements in the tree-beclouded style of the Paris Beaux-Arts, shifting the emphasis and introducing misunderstanding where it would have been better to confess ignorance. A comparison with what is actually known of the front wing cannot fail to bring this out; and the one point of value that emerges is the residual fact that if a dining-room is to be fitted in anywhere on the front (and only failure makes this obligatory) the place for it would have to be close to the east end: nowhere else is there appropriate space available.

When Robert Adam[2] made his great study of Spalato in 1757 the palace front still towered in ancient magnificence above humble houses on the sea-shore. Today stone-built quays and higher houses built into the palace structure have spoilt the effect. The huge façade, with stately arcading enlivened and broken by special features at significant points, has nothing of the fortress about it: a glance at an African villa will be sufficient to confirm the point even to towers.[3] Even the main entrance on the landward side, the so-called '*Porta Aurea*', is so enriched that it recalls the monumental gateways of earlier centuries, although its exciting arcading springing from corbels translates their stage-setting into the idiom of later Rome.[4] Late in style also is the treatment of the actual door-frame as a tympanum above a flat

[1] Probably E. Hébrard & J. Zeiller, *Spalato: le palais de Dioclétien*, 1912 (the clue to this reference was provided by J.M.C.T.).

[2] R. Adam, *Ruins of the Palace of the Emperor Diocletian at Spalatro in Dalmatia*, 1764.

[3] A mosaic from Tabarka (R. Wood and Sir Mortimer Wheeler, *Roman Africa in Colour*, 1966, 115, pl. 37).

[4] Kähler, *op. cit.*, 205.

arch with joggled voussoirs looking the more odd now because its filling has been renewed.

Much more ornate, however, and purely civilian in feeling is the entrance to the vestibule of the palace,[1] a great arched doorway breaking into the lines of a pediment, which contrasts with the curved pediment of the corresponding feature on the east front. The rich and heavy corbelling of the close-spaced modillions combine with the thin treatment of its crowning mouldings to create depth amid welcome lightness which makes the baroque composition possible and translates into marble the effects which had long been obtained in brick and stucco. There is the sharpest contrast between the treatment of this vestibule door and that of the interior of the mausoleum, where the whole weight of the cornice lies in its mouldings and the function of the modillions, which hang like stalactites in a fashion that almost anticipates Moorish detail, is to anchor the sharply curving horizontal lines firmly in the field of vision. The total effect is like a rich casket, and what is now seen is only the frame for a still richer picture, in which human costume and perishable fabrics supplied the polychrome. But the architecture, made up of older classical forms, has not yet knitted them into a new idiom. It is the first tentative manifestation of a style which on the same Adriatic shores was to produce with sure and practical touch the glories of Ravenna.

The last example before us and the nearest to these islands is Trier, where, on the fringe of a town[2] containing the most remarkable Roman buildings north of the Alps, there lies the audience-chamber of an Imperial Palace which is now the principal Lutheran church.[3] Here, as at Rome, the walls plainly surround an area which includes parkland and large temple precincts as well as the great buildings for amusement like the two vast baths, the amphitheatre and a huge circus.

[1] Kähler, *op. cit.*, 207.

[2] O. Brogan, *Roman Gaul*, 1953, 112, fig. 18.

[3] The church was gutted during the Second World War. The '*Basilika*' has since been repaired and restored.

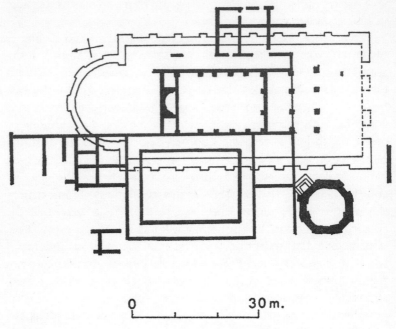

0   30 m.

10. Trier: remains of pre-Constantinian palace found under the '*Basilika*'
(after W. Reusch, *Basilika-Festschrift 1956*, 36, fig. 7).

The evolution of the palace is both interesting and peculiar.[1]
The area began as part of the regular street-system of the town,
with private houses of the second century bordering the northern
approach to a crossroads. Next came the appropriation of the
street and the erection over it of an audience chamber comparable
with those at *Carnuntum* and Spalato with its front level with
the main building-line, at the back of the colonnade bordering
the street, and a tetrastyle portico wider than the colonnade which
it replaced (figure 10). On the west, almost exactly blocking the
old east-to-west street-line, came an octagonal shrine, reminiscent

[1] For a new discussion of the identification, layout and history of the palace see
E. Wightman, *Roman Trier and the Treveri* (unpublished Oxford D.Phil. thesis),
43 f.; 169 ff.; 320 ff.: for the plan see W. Reusch (ed.), *Frühchristliche Zeugnisse im
Einzugsgebiet von Rhein und Mosel*, 1964, 146.

of the much more symmetrically placed octagonal mausoleum at Spalato, and similarly situated in relation to a main entrance. This building formed part of the palace of the period of the Tetrarchy, and will have been that used for example by Constantius both as Caesar and as the first Emperor of his name. Little can be said of the rest of the building except that it continued to incorporate parts of the older houses, the implication being that the palace was built into and round already existing houses that became Imperial property by sale or confiscation.[1] The large internal courtyard to west of the new audience-chamber is, however, a new element, indicating that the scale of the building was being altered everywhere even if it incorporated here and there more ancient structures. The small audience chamber so far described[2] is only about one third of the size of the huge *aula palatina* which succeeded it when Constantine made Trier the most important Imperial residence in the West (figure 11). The new building was an immense hall, over 170 feet long by 75 feet wide, and three storeys high, with a very large and slightly stilted apse occupying almost the whole of the north end. At each side were long narrow courtyards, not matching one another in width, with a passage or colonnade round two sides of them. The ground floor contained no windows, but each floor above them had large ones, inserted in very large-scale blind arcading on the external face of both side-walls and of the apse. In the apse internal niches correspond to the thickening or buttresses formed by the piers of the blind arcades. In the hall itself there are no niches, because the inner side of the wall was in fact heated from a vast hypocaust and the walls were jacketted with flue tiles to a point just below the windows, flues from the jacketting passing out at intervals through the arcading piers, avoiding the windows so that they did not become smoked.

[1] Wightman, *op. cit.*, 43 (citing P. Steiner, *Trier. Jber.* x/xii, 28 ff.; J. B. Keune, *Trier. Zeitschr.* x, 58) argues from the military tile-stamps that the building on this site was already official before A.D. 70.

[2] See Reusch, *Die Basilika im Trier, Festschrift zur Wiederherstellung, 9 Dezember 1956*, 35 ff. (cited by Wightman): this hall was built in the second century. The building was probably the residence of the *procurator* of *Gallia Belgica* and the two Germanies and later became an Imperial palace.

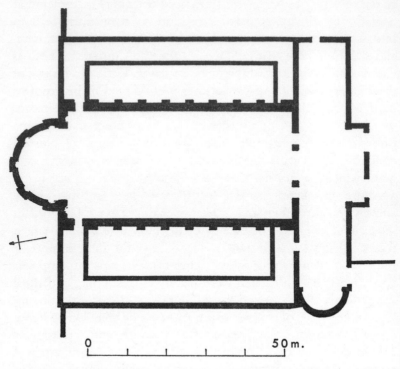

11. Trier: '*Basilika*' (after W. Reusch, *Frühchristliche Zeugnisse*, 1964, 146).

The height of the great hall is such that it would have been very difficult to clean or repair the windows and the means of doing this is afforded by external balconies to which access is gained by service newel staircases contained in the extra large piers at the north angles of the building, on either side of the apse. The balconies themselves do not survive but their existence is proved by external doors in the newel staircases at the appropriate points, and by an elaborate series of put-log holes for the horizontal beams and angular struts which supported the floor of the feature. As for the external aspect of the building, while it is the present fashion to admire the unrelieved and powerful lines of the tile-faced concrete of which the building is made, it may be regarded

[278]

as highly doubtful whether this accorded with either Roman taste or practice. The *Curia* and the Basilica of Maxentius in the Roman Forum or the Baths of Caracalla arrest the attention today by their seasoned tile facing and veritably monolithic grandeur. But scanty yet indubitable traces of a stucco facing moulded to imitate large ashlar masonry shows that ancient taste was different, and desired the buildings to gleam white in a dazzling splendour not indeed foreign to Italian taste – think of the Vittorio Emanuele Monument adjacent to the Forum – but difficult to stomach unprepared. No such traces appear to survive on the Trier hall, but the treatment of the window reveals with a strangely inappropriate decorative panel of plaster-work containing winged floral *genii* which are never seen in correct horizontal position carries with it the implication that the whole outer face was plastered, whatever the exact treatment may have been.[1]

Tastes will continue to differ profoundly from age to age, and Roman taste is out of tune with that at present in fashion. As soon as it seems to approach it, in starkness and in love of powerful mass-effects, so soon a closer scrutiny reveals an illusion destroyed by breaking up the mass into smaller patterned units. But the essentials of the planning and the skeleton or armature of the elevation reveal a power which we can appreciate and enjoy, and if the palace plans of the Roman world have any special virtue, it is to show that powerful planning can emerge even amid the most varied demands of a complex society and a strong rococo tendency in decoration.

[1] The discussion of Trier might also have included the supposed Imperial villas in the neighbouring countryside (Konz, Pfalzel): see Wightman, *op. cit.*, 210 ff. and pl. 34; Reusch, *Frühchristliche Zeugnisse*, 150 ff., and pl. 144, 145, 145a.

INDEX

The names of those who assisted the editor with comments or information on the text are included in the index with references to the appropriate footnotes. A list of those names abbreviated to initials in the notes appears above on p. 15. It was not practicable to show the comments received from particular informants to the others or to supply the whole text to any: it should not therefore be assumed that those named necessarily agree with statements in the text or the notes to which their names are not appended. One (J.C.M.) disapproved of the publication of the Ford Lectures but was generous with his comments on them.

In the index well-known Romans are indexed under the name in common use; other Romans will be found under their *nomina*.

[281]

Index

[283]

Index

Index

Index

Faustina the Younger, 264
Felicitas, 242
Fell, C., 174
Fenesch, F., 267 (fig. 5)
Fenland, 42, 50, 128
field-systems, 127, 144, 155
Finkley, 107
Fishbourne, 142 n., 264 n.
flamines, 213, 245
Flavia Caesariensis, 97, 116–32
Flavius Antigonus Papias, 72
Flavius Bellator, 63
flax, 132
Flixborough, 128
foederati, 93
Forden Gaer, 26, 27, 28, 93
Fortuna Redux, Temple of, 224, 242
Fortune, 242
Fox, Sir Cyril, 54, 135, 167
Fox, G., 147
Frampton, 105
Frankish mercenaries, 41, 57, 85
Frere, S. S., 15, 22 n., 43 n., 44 n., 46 n.,
    59 n., 68 n., 91 n., 102 n., 118 n.,
    161 n., 186 n.
Frilford, 107, 109, 170
Frontinus, Sex. Iulius, 194 n.
Fronto, M. Cornelius, 232 n.
Froxfield, 107
fulling, 147
Fyfield, 145

Gaius (son of Agrippa), 214
Gargrave, 75
Gathercole, P. W., 95 n.
Gayton Thorpe, 52
genii cucullati, 153
Genius Populi Romani, 209, 221, 224,
    226, 234
Genius Senatus, 221, 224, 226, 243, 246
Germania Inferior, *legatus Augusti* of, 269
Germania Secunda, *praeses* of, 269
Germanicus Iulius Caesar, 214, 262
Gildas, 91, 166, 179
Gillam, J. P., 19 n.
Giraldus Cambrensis, 98

glass-making, 162
Gnosticism, 112, 139
Gog Magog Hills, 179
gold-mining, 249
Gortyn, 260
Gosbecks Farm, 169, 174
Gracchus, Ti. Sempronius, 194
Grassington, 127, 145
Great Casterton, 53, 95, 123, 125, 127,
    163
Great Chesterford, 159
Greatchesters, 192 n.
Great Orme's Head, 27, 128
Greaves Ash, 150
Greenwich, 107
Greetland, 156
Greta Bridge, 39 n.
Grimes, W. F., 119, 166
Groag, E., 231 n.
groves, sacred, 167, 168
Gwennap, 113
gynaecium, 112

Habitancum, see Risingham
Hadrian, 229, 230, 232, 233, 236, 237,
    238
Hadrian's Wall, 19 n. (destruction A.D.
    197?), 20 (restoration 205–7?), 21
    (milecastles as sally-ports), 183–9,
    191 (cavalry); pl. II
Hadstock, 125
Halton, 81
Haltwhistle Burn, 184
Hamberg, P. G., 242
Hambleden, 139
Ham Hill, 102
Hanson, R. P. C., 110 n.
Hare Hill, 183
Harpham, 74
Harlow, 109, 171
Hartley, B. R., 19 n., 42 n.
Hartlip, 107
Hassel, K. J., 229 n., 231 n.
Haverfield, F., 67, 70, 76, 97, 132
Hawkes, C. F. C., 51, 53, 112, 141, 143,
    146

Index

Headington Wick, 107
headquarters building, legionary, 247
Hébrard, E., 274 n.
Heddernheim, 158
Helicon, Mt., 122
Helith, 178
Hen Drefor, 28
Hensington, 107
Hen Waliau, 82 n., 84, 91
Hercules, 178, 232, 234, 235, 247
Hestia, 123
High Rochester, 21, 23, 30, 33, 81, 86, 88, 122, 191
Hockwold-cum-Wilton, 51 n., 143 n., 173 n.
Holbury, 107
Holland, P., 183
Holyhead, 82, 91
Honos, 209, 219
Horace (Q. Horatius Flaccus), 203, 209
Horkstow, 131, 148
Horncastle, 123, 161, 164
horse-breeding, 131, 148
Hounslow Heath, 166
Housesteads, 32, 33, 39 n., 153, 156, 185
Hovingham, 126
Hucclecote, 107
Hunter Blair, P., 92

Ialonus, 156
Iazyges, 24
Iceni, 42 n., 45, 49, 51, 98, 116
Icklingham, 111, 126
Igel Column, 104
Ilkley, 20
Illyricum, 231
imperial estates, 51, 53
imperial family, 211
Inchtuthil, 264
iron-mining, 26, 77, 88, 115, 128, 130, 148, 258
iron-working, 26, 114, 131 n., 162
Isca Dumnoniorum, see Exeter
Isurium Brigantum, see Aldborough
Italia, 207, 209

L. Iulius Salassus, 258
Iulius and Aaron, martyrs, 179
Iuppiter, see also Jupiter
   Iuppiter Capitolinus, Temple of, 245
   Iuppiter Custos, Temple of, 245
   Iuppiter Optimus Maximus, 154, 234
Ivrea, 249
Iwerne, 54, 55, 141, 143

Jarrett, M. G., 15, 81 n., 82 n.
jet, 120
Jones, A. H. M., 203 n.
Josephus, 195, 202, 222, 228
Julia Major, 214
Julian, 129
Jupiter, 233, see also *Iuppiter*
Jupiter *Feretrius*, 232
Justinian, *Codex* of, 62
Justinian, *Digest* of, 35

Kähler, H., 273 (fig. 9), 273 n., 274 n., 275 n.
Kells, Book of, 106
Kenyon, K. M., 67
Keston, 107
Keynsham, 105, 106
Kirkby Thore, 71 n.
Kirmington, 128
Knag Burn, 87
Knighton Hill, 146
Knowles, W. H., 176
Konz, 279 n.

R. La Combe, 257
Lancaster, 31, 34, 39 n., 83, 156
Lanchester, 31, 33, 39 n., 156, 191, 192
land allotment, military, 35, 36, 64, 156, 164
Langton, 74, 126
Lansdown, 106
Lavinium, 209
lead-mining, 28, 29, 43, 114, 128, 129, 131
legio II Augusta, 85
legio VI Victrix, 62, 85
legio IX Hispana, 64

Index

Index

Index

Index

Stanegate, 184
Stapleford Down, 56
Statilius Taurus, T., 213
stationes, 39, 113
Stead, I. M., 131
Steer, K. A., 186 n.
Steiner, P., 277 n.
Stevens, C. E., 52, 72, 86, 88, 89, 94, 104, 113 n.
Stilicho, Flavius, 95
Stonesfield, 107
Stony Stratford, 174
Strabo, 68, 159, 167, 249, 250
Stratford-on-Avon, 106
Strathclyde, 92
Stretton, 163
Strong, D. E., 195 n., 220 n., 222 n., 224 n.
Strong, E., 219 n.
Stuart Jones, H., 239, 244
stucco, 279
Studniczka, F., 208
Styrrup, 77
Suebi, 232
Suebo-Sarmatian War (A.D. 92), 226
C. Suetonius Tranquillus, 225 n., 264 n.
Sulis Minerva, 175
Sutherland, C. H. V., 56
Swinnerton, H. H., 129
Swoboda, E., 264 n., 265 (fig. 4)
Swoboda, K., 137
Szilágyi, J., 266 n., 267 (fig. 5)

Tacitus, Cornelius (historian), 145, 201, 220 n, 227, 259 n., 262 n.
Tacitus (king of Manau), 92
Taranis, 170
Tarraco, see Tarragona
Tarragona, 65
Tellus, 207, 209, 210
Templeborough, 86, 128
temples, Romano-Celtic, 166
C. Tetius Veturius Micianus, 157
Teutates, 174
Thales, 139
Thealby, 128

Theodosian Code, see *Codex Theodosianus*
Theodosius, Count, 89, 124
Thompson, H., 216 n.
Thruxton, 107
Tiberius, 214, 215, 216
Tiddington, 106
Tigris, 231
tin-mining, 113
Tintagel, 113
Titsey, 105, 147
Titus, 202, 218, 219, 220
Titus, Arch of, 218-23, 228, 229, 230
Tomen-y-Mur, 27
tools, 195
town and country, 48
towns, 43, 48
town-walls, 43, 46, 123
Toynbee, J. M. C., 15, 121 n., 173 n., 205 n., 207 n., 208 n., 209, 211, 214, 223 n., 224 n., 226 n., 243 n., 258 n.
tractus Nervicanus, 88
Trajan, 229-38
Trajan, Arch of, at *Beneventum*, 229-238
Trajan's Column, 187, 195, 197, 237
Trajan's Forum, 237
Traprain Law, 26
Tredington, 106
Tre'r Ceiri, 28
Trethevey, 113
Trier, 275
Trimalchio, 201, 203
Trinovantes, 98, 116
Triptolemus, 139
turf, 196
Twyford, 107
Ty-mawr, 28

Uffington, 178
Ulceby, 126

Valentia, 93
Valeria, dux of, 266
Valerius Messalla Corvinus, 249

Index